Law Office Technology

A Theory-Based Approach

Ninth Edition

Law Office Technology

A Theory-Based Approach

Ninth Edition

Douglas E. Lusk, J.D.
National Society for Legal Technology

Cynthia Traina Donnes, M.A.
Tulane University

 CENGAGE

Australia • Brazil • Canada • Mexico • Singapore • United Kingdom • United States

Law Office Technology: A Theory-Based Approach, **Ninth Edition**
Douglas E. Lusk, J.D. and Cynthia Traina Donnes, M.A.

SVP, Higher Education Product Management:
Erin Joyner

VP, Product Management, Learning Experiences:
Thais Alencar

Product Director: Jason Fremder

Product Manager: Abbie Schultheis

Vendor Content Manager:
Arul Joseph Raj, Lumina Datamatics, Inc.

Product Assistant: Nick Perez

Creative Studios Designer: Erin Griffin

Digital Delivery Quality Partner: Mark Hopkinson

IP Project Manager:
Anjali Kambli, Lumina Datamatics, Inc.

IP Analyst: Ashley Maynard

VP, Product Marketing: Jason Sakos

Cover Image Source:
10'000 Hours/Getty Images – ID 878980536

For product information and technology assistance, contact us at
Cengage Customer & Sales Support, 1-800-354-9706 or support.cengage.com.

For permission to use material from this text or product, submit all requests online at **www.copyright.com.**

Library of Congress Control Number: 2021915918

Student Edition:
ISBN: 978-0-357-61925-4

Loose-leaf Edition:
ISBN: 978-0-357-61926-1

Cengage
200 Pier 4 Boulevard
Boston, MA 02210
USA

Cengage is a leading provider of customized learning solutions with employees residing in nearly 40 different countries and sales in more than 125 countries around the world. Find your local representative at: **www.cengage.com.**

To learn more about Cengage platforms and services, register or access your online learning solution, or purchase materials for your course, visit **www.cengage.com.**

Printed at CLDPC, USA, 09-21

Brief Contents

Contents

Chapter 4

Ethics and Professionalism

Chapter 5

Electronic Spreadsheet Uses in the Legal Profession

Chapter 6

Electronic Databases and Utility Programs in the Legal Profession (Blockchain Technology)

Chapter 7

Office Management and Case Management Systems Used in the Legal Profession

Chapter 8

Document Management Systems and Document Automation

Chapter 9

Electronic Filing Process in the Courts

Chapter 10

The Discovery Process and Litigation Technology

Chapter 11

eDiscovery and the Electronic Discovery Reference Model

Chapter 12

Using Technology to Make Legal Presentations

Chapter 13

Courtroom Technology in Action

Chapter 14

Legal Apps and the Access to Justice Movement

Preface

Our lives are constantly intertwined with technology. We do everything using computers, and there is a software or computer application for each task in our life. This trend holds true for the practice of law. Everything is digital! We communicate with our clients, opposing counsel, and even the courts through email or online messages. We store and sort documents digitally. We keep track of our time and expenses, and pay our bills electronically. Every task we perform in the law office will involve technology, so it is crucial that you understand the role that technology will play in your career.

Law Office Technology: A Theory-Based Approach (Ninth Edition) is designed to give students an understanding of the theory and application of technology in a legal setting. This textbook has been reimagined by the authors to address the "why" and "when" a software program is used, and we removed all the prior editions' content that addressed "how" a software program is used. This textbook is designed to be a companion guide to the National Society for Legal Technology (NSLT) Legal Technology Certificate (LegalTechSociety.org). The NSLT's revolutionary method for teaching software using Web-based software simulations means gone are the days of students needing to download and install limited trial versions of the software. It also means no more textbook full of software screen shots and difficult-to-follow instructions taking up most of the pages in the book. The NSLT's interactive tutorials teach the "how" of software functions in a way no textbook can. This textbook is a way to introduce the theory and application of when and why the software programs would be utilized in a law office. Together, the textbook and the NSLT lessons make the perfect pairing for teaching a law office technology course. It truly is the best of both worlds!

Although *Law Office Technology* and the NSLT Legal Technology Certificate program go nicely together, each is not exclusive, nor are they reliant on the other. You can use this book without utilizing the NSLT program and vice versa.

Organization of the Text

This text book consists of 14 chapters. The first chapter is an overview of why legal technology is an important part of your education and a look at how the COVID-19 pandemic and the work-from-home movement has affected the work cycle for legal professionals everywhere. We then dive into the heart of our book in the following 13 chapters, which cover every major category of legal technology. They cover videoconferencing software, word processing, data spreadsheets, document management, case management, document automation and collaboration, presentation software, eDiscovery, electronic court filing, litigation support, timekeeping and billing, and trial presentation. Each topic is presented in a clear and organized manner and discusses ethical issues that are presented by each type of software as well as how the software is used by legal professionals in a law firm. Inevitable change is the only consistency in this inconsistent area of law that is legal technology. While "how" a software functions is constantly changing with each new feature update, the "why" behind the software use remains steadily constant and unshaken. This constancy is the reason the authors have elected to shift the focus of this edition to strictly discuss the theory behind the technology.

Learning Features Included in This Edition

Chapter features include the following:

- Learning objectives open each chapter to focus the student's attention on the main learning outcome for the chapter.
- NSLT tasks to accomplish are associated with each chapter to reinforce the reasons why each software is being studied and to encourage students forward as they work to complete the NSLT Legal Technology Certificate.

- Glossary terms are boldfaced in the body of the text, and definitions appear in the margin for easy review and reference. A comprehensive glossary appears at the end of the book.
- *Stop and Think* sections are included with each chapter to encourage readers to contemplate key concepts or new ideas as they continue reading the chapter.
- A section titled *Tech This Out!* is in each chapter. This section highlights new emerging technology or points out software features that are associated with each chapter's topic.
- Discussion questions at the end of each chapter allow students the opportunity to reflect on what was learned and encourage independent thinking about each topic.
- Additional resources are listed at the conclusion of each chapter to promote learning beyond the information included in the book.

Cengage Instructor Center

Additional instructor resources for this product are available online. Instructor assets include an Instructor's Manual, PowerPoint® slides, and a test bank powered by Cognero®. Sign up or sign in at www.cengage.com to search for and access this product and its online resources.

The Cengage Instructor Center is an all-in-one resource for class preparation, presentation, and testing. The instructor resources available for download include:

- **Instructor's Manual.** Provides activities and assessments for each chapter (including business cases with corresponding assessment activities) and their correlation to specific learning objectives, an outline, key terms with definitions, a chapter summary, and several ideas for engaging with students with discussion questions, ice breakers, case studies, and social learning activities that may be conducted in an around, hybrid, or online modality.
- nk. A comprehensive test bank, offered rd, Moodle, Desire2Learn, and Can-tains learning objective-specific hoice, and essay questions the test bank into your ge questions and to cre-

- **PowerPoint Slides.** Presentations are closely tied to the Instructor's Manual, providing ample opportunities for generating classroom discussion and interaction. They offer ready-to-use, visual outlines of each chapter that may be easily customized for your lectures.
- **Transition Guide.** Highlights all of the changes in the text and in the digital offerings from the previous edition to this edition.

Cengage Testing Powered by Cognero

Cognero is a flexible online system that allows you to author, edit, and manage test bank content from multiple Cengage solutions; create multiple test versions in an instant; and deliver tests from your LMS, your classroom, or wherever you want.

ACKNOWLEDGMENTS

A special part of writing a book is acknowledging those invaluable people that worked on this project. The authors wish to express gratitude for all their assistance, guidance, and support.

A special thanks goes out to the wonderful people at Cengage Learning, including Abbie Schultheis and Erika Mugavin, Product Managers, Mara Vuillaume, Learning Designer, and Jennifer Ziegler, Senior Project Manager. They are a wonderful team to work with and their patience, help and support have been invaluable to the success of this textbook. Many people worked diligently to help keep this project moving, including Arul Joseph Raj, Project Manager at Lumina Datamatics, Ltd.

Additional Acknowledgments from Douglas E. Lusk

Foremost, I would like to thank the many colleges and universities that have been utilizing the NSLT program. I am honored to count you all as friends. It has been a joy working with you to bring my dream to life. Thank you for believing in me and including the NSLT in your students' educational journey. Your devotion to providing the best education to your students is what fuels my passion to do this every day.

Profound gratitude to my family and friends, especially my husband, Peter, and son, Jared, for supporting me through all the countless late-night hours and weekends spent working in my office to keep this dream alive. I couldn't do this without you! Thank you to my team at the NSLT for always providing a shoulder to lean on and keeping me on task.

Additional Acknowledgments from Cynthia Traina Donnes

I would like to thank the many colleagues that have provided invaluable input and suggestions, including the members of the School of Professional Advancement at Tulane University. It is a privilege to be affiliated with an organization that is open-minded and promotes creativity. I am especially grateful to Robyn Ice and Kathryn Beachy for providing tremendous support to me during this second project with Cengage.

I am deeply grateful to my family and lifelong friends for their love and encouragement in pursuing my second textbook. A global pandemic presented difficult and trying times for everyone, but in the end, their support was my salvation. And as always, my children (Dominic, Erin, Antonia, David, Louis and Sara) are my inspiration!

Chapter 1

Law and Technology Uses in the Legal Profession

Chapter Objectives

- Identify basic hardware and software to function effectively and efficiently in the legal profession.
- Explain the concept of technology competency and its importance to the practice of law.
- Recognize and evaluate technology issues affecting the practice of law.

NSLT Tasks Associated with This Chapter

- Complete all learning modules and knowledge checks in the NSLT learning portal in order to complete various exercises assigned and ultimately obtain a Legal Technology certificate through NSLT.

Introduction

It is inescapable: Computers and technology go hand and hand with the practice of law. Before the 1980s, the most sophisticated technology in a law office was likely an electric typewriter and a collating copy machine. Today, technology advances have expanded to include artificial intelligence (AI). Now we can use automated computer systems to enter data into word documents and spreadsheets and to conduct research and discovery during litigation. Given the rapid changes in technology and its integration into the legal profession, it is imperative that lawyers, paralegals, and their legal staff be familiar not only with electronic and computer **hardware** but also with application **software** programs used in the legal profession.

Along with having a good handle on the hardware and software used in the legal profession, lawyers, paralegals, and their staff must appreciate the importance of legal technology competency. Technology has no value in a law practice if it incorporates a lot of sophisticated computer systems and software programs that no one can operate efficiently. In fact, the lack of knowledge could turn out to be

Hardware (Computer)
The physical components of a computer system.

Software
A list of instructions for the computer to follow that is stored in the computer's memory.

an ethical nightmare for the law practice. Lawyers, paralegals, and their staff must understand how to use technology so that client information is protected and ensure that general information provided to the public does not violate ethical rules with unauthorized practice of law.

Technology in Today's Law Office

Technology has changed the appearance of every law office. Thirty years ago, no one could imagine seeing a computer on individual office desks. A typewriter, yes, but not a computer. Today, not only is a desktop computer common, but everything on that computer is now synced to a smart device that is portable and accessible at any time, day or night. So, lawyers and paralegals entering today's legal profession should have a working knowledge of computer technology and legal software. Information technology knowledge is essential in developing an efficient and productive law practice as well as giving lawyers and paralegals a competitive edge in the job market.

Electronic Hardware Used in the Legal Profession

First, it is important to distinguish between "computers" and "technology." The computer receives, processes, stores, and transmits data, while technology is the activity associated with designing, constructing, operating, and programming the computer. When we think of a computer, we most often visualize a desktop computer with a monitor to see the data or maybe a smaller version known as a laptop computer that is portable and fits in your lap. However, your phone, your car's media source, your fitness tracker, and even your electronic watches are likely functioning as computers. In fact, with today's technology, these smart devices are more powerful that the computers NASA had when it sent Apollo 11 to the moon and back. More important, the new devices are automated so that we can communicate with them.

In recent years, technology has most notably changed to include wireless networks and mobile technology, with the concurrent ability of these devices to receive data passively. For example, most smart devices or smartphones are enabled with various geolocation devices that allow for tracking without any input by the user. This constant data processing allows the device to retain information so that it can automatically develop additional resources. One popular use of this passive data is map directions that will include arrival estimates based on traffic conditions because the device is tracking in real time. Another commonly used feature is receiving text messages with time and date information that can be immediately transferred to a calendar with reminders. This data is then synced across all devices to ensure that a meeting or an appointment is consistently reflected. Although this textbook is not intended to provide technical and scientific information on how a computer operates, it is important to briefly cover some basic computer concepts.

As mentioned earlier, a computer is an electronic device that receives, processes, stores, and transmits data or information. The system contains a central processing unit (CPU) that organizes and processes the information: It is the "brain" of the computer. It performs logical operations—in accordance with the operating system

---

Computer
An electronic device that receives, processes, outputs, and stores data or information.

Information Technology
The technology details involved with the development, maintenance, and use of computer systems, software, and network uses for processing and distributing data.

Desktop (Computer)
A device designed for regular use at a single or stationary location, often with all components that fit on top or near a desk due to its size or power requirements.

Laptop (Computer)
A portable, personal computer, also known as a notebook. It carries out the same functions as a desktop.

Wireless Network
A network where users can access the Internet without the use of fixed cables.

Smart Device
An electronic gadget that can connect, share, and interact with its user; despite its size, it typically has enormous computing power (gigabytes).

Central Processing Unit (CPU)
Also known as the microprocessor; the brains of the computer.

Operating System
Software used to control the computer and its peripheral equipment.

Exhibit 1–1 Storage capacities

Kilobyte (K)	=	One thousand bytes	(1,000)
Megabyte (MB)	=	One million bytes	(1,000,000)
Gigabyte (GB)	=	One billion bytes	(1,000,000,000)
Terabyte (TB)	=	One trillion bytes	(1,000,000,000,000)
Petabyte (PB)	=	One quadrillion bytes	(1,000,000,000,000,000)

software. It also coordinates and communicates with auxiliary storage devices and input, output, and communication devices.

At the heart of the CPU is the processor chip. One or more processor chips perform the actual arithmetic computations and logic functions. The speed of the processor and thus of the computer is determined by how many bits or bytes of information the chip can process at a time and how fast it acts to process the information. The more bits that can be processed in one cycle, the faster the computer will be. For example, a processor that processes 64 bits at a time is considerably faster than one that processes only 32 bits. The number of bytes of information a computer can hold is measured in kilobytes (KB), megabytes (MB), gigabytes (GB), terabytes (TB), or petabytes (PB) (see Exhibit 1–1).

The computer hardware also includes peripheral devices: additional equipment connected to a computer that performs special functions. For example, auxiliary storage devices or external hard drives are used to permanently store information. This should not be confused with **RAM (random access memory)**, which is where information is temporarily stored on the computer and erased when the computer is shut down or turned off. Removable drives, commonly referred to as flash drives or thumb drives, are used to immediately access the computer through the computer's USB port and copy large files from one system to another.

The computer also operates with input devices and communication devices. Input devices include the mouse, keyboards, printers, copiers and scanners, and **voice recognition** devices. Communication devices allow the computer to exchange information and include Wi-Fi, modems, **Voice Over Internet Protocol (VoIP)** to make telephone calls, and **videoconference** programs to conduct face-to-face meeting using the Internet.

In most law offices, the computer will be connected through a **server** to network with other office computers. This is an efficient method for interoffice **online collaboration**. However, some small offices or solo practice lawyers may just have a **workstation**. In some shared offices, the computer operates as a **thin client**, allowing multiple individuals to use the same desktop and the Internet to access their own software programs and work remotely.

Software Uses in the Legal Profession

Computer hardware is useless without computer software to make it operate. Computer software (i.e., a computer program) is a set of step-by-step instructions that direct a computer on how to function and perform tasks. Three basic types of software are available: operating system software, utility software, and application software.

RAM (Random Access Memory)
The area on the computer's workspace that stores the information and data for processing by the computer's CPU.

Voice Over Internet Protocol (VoIP)
A technology that allows you to make voice calls using a broadband Internet connection instead of a regular (or analogue) phone line.

Voice Recognition
The use of software to convert spoken words to text.

Videoconference
A virtual meeting using a network or the Internet to connect two or more people in different geographic locations and share data by electronic means.

Server
A computer or computer program that manages access to a centralized resource or service in a network.

Online Collaboration
Using the Internet to conduct meetings and share documents.

Workstation
A computer that runs a desktop operating system and connects to a network.

Thin Client
A computer terminal that resembles a desktop but has limited capabilities and relies on a network for resources to operate programs.

Drivers

A group of files that enable one or more hardware devices to communicate with the computer's operating system. Drivers allow the computer to send and receive data correctly to the hardware devices.

End-User License Agreement

A license agreement between the software creator and the software user.

Backup

A copy of a user's hard disk or other storage device that can be restored if the hard disk is damaged or lost. Backup utility programs allow users to schedule times to ensure reoccurring backups to protect the data.

Uninterruptible Power Supply (UPS)

A device that provides backup power when the electrical power fails or drops to an unacceptable voltage level.

Virus

A destructive program that harms data, hard drives, operating systems, and computer programs.

The operating system software instructs the computer hardware that ties the hardware and software together. Application software instructs the computer to perform specific functions or tasks, such as word processing, spreadsheet, or presentation software. Today, especially since the COVID-19 pandemic, everyone over the age of one year likely has skills to use a computer. It goes without saying that most lawyers and paralegals are sufficiently prepared to handle computers in a modern law office. The computer will also use **drivers**, which, as the name implies, will direct the computer to communicate with the operating system to correctly send and receive data.

It is important to be familiar with use rights of software programs. Nearly all software programs are subject to an **end-user license agreement**. The license agreement provides terms for the uses permitted by either an individual or a group of people along with any restrictions, such as making copies of the software program. Some license agreements are based on the number of computers on which the software can be loaded, whereas others are based on the number of people who can use the software. Copyright infringement should be a concern of any lawyer or law firm because the software limitation, if violated, could result in lawsuits.

Utility software helps manage either the hardware or the software aspects of a computer. Some utility programs come as part of the operating system; others are separate programs. Utility programs include compression software like WinZip, designed to reduce the data space to transmit large files quicker over the Internet. Other utility programs include **backup** programs to create hard drive copies, something that is invaluable when the computer system has crashed or files are corrupted. As a side note on backups, make sure to always have backup power. An **uninterruptible power supply (UPS)** is extremely important when there is a power failure or voltage drop that could also cause the computer to shut down unexpectedly, and damage data.

There are also utility programs designed to protect the computer from **viruses** or other "malware" caused by some unfamiliar application software programs or other unknown files downloaded from websites.

Application software will be discussed throughout this text with specifics related to technology utilized within the legal profession. It is worth noting that there are thousands of application software programs (applications, or apps) developed and continuing to be developed. In the legal profession, the most common application software programs include word processing, PDF creation, spreadsheets, office and/or case management, timekeeping, and billing programs. Additionally, many lawyers and law offices use litigation support programs for discovery and computer-assisted legal research along with presentation software for trials. And many application software programs are now entirely cloud based or, if not, contain both downloaded software and Web-based access as well as cloud storage.

There is also document management software that organizes, controls, distributes, and allows for extensive searching of electronic documents, mostly found in a networked environment. As the legal community moves to the "paperless office," each legal organization will most likely have to use a document management program to manage electronic files. Document management software also provides extensive searching capabilities and allows users to add a profile of every document, which can be easily searched on later.

Tech This Out!

Zoom Court Is Here to Stay!

Online meetings have been available for several years. At first, the technology made conducting meetings over the Internet both difficult and unsecure. There were a limited number of programs that could be used, and real-time interaction was "spotty" at best. In recent years, the technological advances have made online communications common. When the recent pandemic locked down the world, working remotely was not an option, it was a necessity. Programs like Zoom became common software used to connect to the outside world without being together. It was next best thing to being in person. Zoom was used not only for education but also throughout the court system. The success of conducting meetings remotely expanded to include having court hearings online. Now that restrictions are lifting and society is going back to in-person meetings, you would think that remote meetings over the Internet would diminish significantly, but that is not the case. The time and cost savings associated with meeting online versus travel expenses with meeting in person have found that it is beneficial to continue with online hearings and meetings. Does this present more advantage than disadvantage? So far, the jury is still out, but most people can see the benefits of both sides.

Trends in the Legal Profession

Legal technology is continuing to move forward, and technology trends are significantly changing how legal professionals will be performing their jobs in the future. Legal professionals have dramatically changed the ways they communicate with the use of laptops, tablets, netbook, and smartphones. These smaller, portable devices are extremely powerful and operate with the same functions as the office desktop computer. With constant access to the Internet, you can send and receive emails, maintain appointments, review and edit files, and synchronize with a user's desktop system. Small laptops or tablet computers can store millions of pages of documents electronically, fully access online legal databases such as Westlaw and Lexis on the go, and remotely access files and records nearly globally. This kind of mobile and immediate access to information will continue to change and drive the way legal professionals practice law.

Another trend is the expansion of electronic filing and discovery. The Federal Rules of Civil Procedure and many state court rules now require electronic discovery, and all federal courts require case filings electronically. This fact is forcing legal organizations to develop internal systems that can produce, store, search, and handle the production of electronic information in a variety of formats and across multiple computing platforms (desktops, servers, laptops, etc.). Electronic filing may sound easy, but there are procedures that must be followed that can make filing electronically somewhat daunting. Issues concerning standardization, control, security, and the establishment of hardware and software systems to support electronic filing have all had to be overcome. Nevertheless, many states, courts, federal agencies, and other regulatory bodies have successfully implemented electronic filing, and many others are currently entering the implementation stage.

Cloud computing has also changed the legal profession. Although cloud computing is relatively new, the concept is as old as the Internet. For example,

Exhibit 1–2 Example of cloud-based law office technology

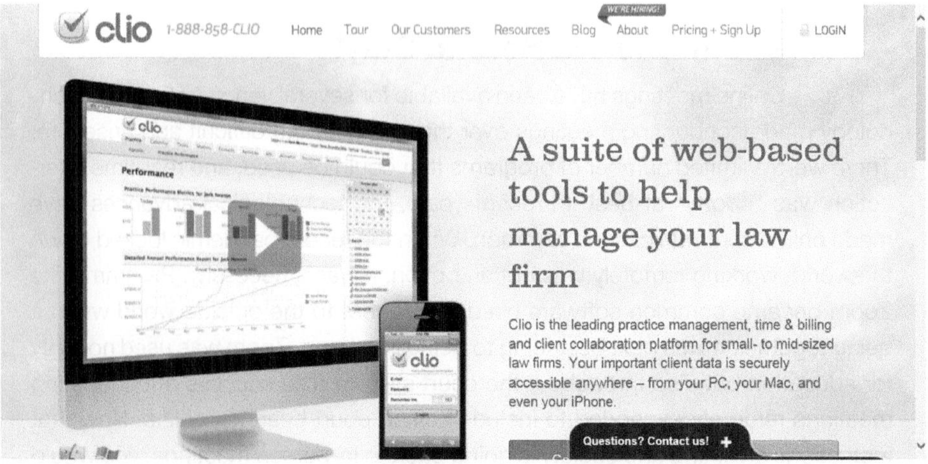

Themis Solutions Inc.

Westlaw is a form of cloud computing. So is Web-based email, such as Google's Gmail. Cloud computing has affected law offices in several ways. One is the use of hosted software applications. These are software applications that are not downloaded onto the user's computer; rather, users access the software via the Internet. This allows each user to store information on the host computers, ensuring that the user always has the latest version of the software, and eliminates the need to download and install applications. Another use of the cloud is as a place to store documents and other data. This raises ethical issues: How secure is the data stored with a third party, and what is the law firm's liability for any breaches of confidentiality? There are more questions than answers as the law struggles to keep up with emerging technologies. See Exhibit 1–2.

Remote Collaboration
A process in which two or more parties work together on common documents and other resources regardless of their location.

With the expansion of online and **remote collaboration**, we have also seen technology take over the courtroom. Many courts have installed sophisticated electronic systems that can display evidence via monitors to everyone simultaneously. The master controls are located at the judge's bench so that he or she can control all monitors, sound systems, and cameras in the courtroom. In some cases, the courtroom technology can offer out-of-state witnesses with the ability to testify at a trial without being present in the courtroom. Since the recent pandemic, many courts conducted hearings via Zoom and in many cases are continuing this method.

Of course, we cannot ignore the trend surrounding the legal profession and social media. Many law firms and lawyers have created websites that include components that allow people to communicate via the Internet. Some lawyers use sites like Facebook, Twitter, and LinkedIn to market and network. Some lawyers include blogs and resources on their websites. For legal professionals, social media is the new frontier, but they do face challenges, both practically and ethically.

Technology Competency

Using technology in the legal profession has tremendous benefits, but with it comes tremendous responsibilities to understand it. Attorneys along with paralegals and their staff must be aware of communications via electronic sources that could violate ethical duties. This could result in disqualifications and/or malpractice issues with client representation.

Ethical Duty Regarding Technology

Attorneys have a duty to perform legal services in a competent manner. Computers, though incredibly helpful, can also be a vehicle for incompetence and legal malpractice. If a user fails to understand how a computer or a piece of software works, they will likely fail to anticipate or discover an error. Computer-related errors resulting in legal malpractice and ethical breaches can take place in a variety of ways. For example, ethical issues could result from legal research inadequately or less than thoroughly performed. Or, when new documents are prepared using previously saved word processing documents that contain old information from previous clients. This is not only embarrassing but may present an ethical issue concerning confidentiality.

Malpractice issues could arise from using improper computerized forms or templates which result in improperly filed case records. And, using automated software with arithmetic and logic formulas for calculating settlements and compensation is great. But, a lack of oversight in proofreading/review by the attorney or legal professionals could causes a client major financial losses, resulting in a malpractice claim against the attorney.

Attorneys are responsible for their work product. It does not matter whether it was prepared by or with the assistance of a computer: If the end product has errors in it or is incompetently prepared, the attorney is still ultimately responsible. If the error or incompetent work product causes harm to the client, the attorney may be subject to attorney discipline charges and a legal malpractice claim.

The exercises performed with the NSLT programs will help develop the skills needed to ensure that you can efficiently perform word processing, spreadsheet, and accounting/billing software programs. Additionally, you will become familiar with features to develop safeguards to avoid common errors and mistakes that often result in technology incompetence and disciplinary actions.

Education and Certification

Today, most paralegal programs have a least one technology course that is required in their curriculum, especially if it is an American Bar Association (ABA) approved program. Several programs also have advanced technology training courses as well as courses dedicated to specialty software, such as litigation and discovery software training. Some programs are dedicated to subject areas that include specialty software utilized, such as bankruptcy practice and family law practice courses. Additionally, several law schools have an elective course for learning about technology uses in the law practice. With the National Society for Legal Technology (NSLT), you can obtain a certificate in legal technology that is extremely valuable when interviewing in the job market.

Keep in mind that almost every software program on the market, especially the ones that are used in the legal profession, offer tutorials and training videos. These can be found on the software programs' websites as well as thousands of YouTube video creations. The amount of help resources associated with application software can be overwhelming, so it is recommended to start with the help features within the program. This is usually connected to the program's website but may also be linked to video produced outside their resources. In most cases, the built-in help features will provide instructions to perform the task and operate the software efficiently. If you cannot find the answer within, simply do an Internet search.

Stop and Think!

If It's Not Broke, Don't Fix It: When Should You Update Equipment?

The truth is that as software developers create advanced features, it takes more RAM and faster processors to run the programs correctly. Today's software has numerous basic features, along with tremendous graphics and animation. Hardware manufacturers are constantly expanding the capacity to keep up with software updates. Most software updates take place automatically, being connected through Internet downloads. This includes operating systems as well as specific programs being used. However, some software advances may not work with older hardware equipment. The question becomes, do you need the updated software, which would then require new computers? Several factors should be considered when upgrading, including cost. But make sure not to compromise needs, which in the long run will be very costly.

Technology Issues Affecting the Legal Profession

Outdated Hardware and Software

At one point, updating computer hardware and software was a complicated task. During the 1980s, a desktop had a motherboard with 256K of RAM, which meant the computer could store about 5,000 words of text. Software programs were operated from floppy disks or hard disks, and data was saved on additional disks. By the 1990s, computer hardware equipment was developed with larger internal drives. This allowed software programs to be loaded within the computer system and the data created to be saved to the system. This also meant that software and hardware updates occurred frequently. This trend has remained the same.

Some businesses have a two-year upgrade policy, but depending on the office budget and software needs, your computer system and software could last a little longer. So, the rule of thumb is to consider upgrades somewhere between 18 months and three years. Depending on the office size and needs, this can be a tremendous expense. Make sure to review software updates for **compatibility** with minimum and recommended hardware requirements. Do not compromise minimum needs when it relates to critically utilized software. For example, an older word processing program may function perfectly for the law office's needs, but the litigation software updates can't run on the older system. You do not want to compromise this important software update because the computer is outdated.

Compatibility
In technology, the ability of the computer hardware to effectively operate the application software and communicate with software updates.

Security Issues

Considering the sensitive nature of client information. Protecting confidential information is not only critical but also ethically required. If confidential information is accessed, attorney–client privilege may be compromised, which could result in ineffective representation and malpractice lawsuits. In most cases, your Internet service provider offers security features, including at minimum a **firewall**.

Along with a good firewall, computers, as well as any mobile devices that sync with office equipment, should have anti-malware applications. An email attachment or download from websites may appear to be reputable but be disguised

Firewall
A computer security system (hardware and software) designed to block unauthorized access.

to infiltrate your computer to access personal client information. Clients may send records and material that come from sources that contain viruses to infect or destroy your computer systems. Symantec and Norton are two popular companies that offer protection software that can be installed on computers and run in the background to detect security breaches.

Another concern to address with security is cloud storage. Many lawyers and law firms back up client data with cloud services, such as Microsoft Office. They may also use private cloud services and/or outsource their record or document management. If outside cloud storage services are being used, encryption methods between the office computers and the cloud are a must. The law firm may also consider additional protection methods, such as Boxcryptor or similar encryption applications.

Outsourcing
A decision to have independent outside parties handle the business's workload and production responsibilities.

Networking Issues

Networking the law office is essential for communication. It is important to have a reliable network that includes a high-speed connection for accessing courts and clients. With the recent explosion of videoconferencing use, slower network connections have been quickly recognized. We have all experienced the talk lag time with spotty connections or large-group meetings where the video would not transmit. These issues are more noticeable when communicating over wireless networks. Small law offices may find networking issues difficult to handle because they lack the resources to hire the proper Internet technology staff. Today, many paralegals as well as lawyers have some training with technology that will be helpful in addressing network issues.

For the most part, the law office will be working with local area networks (LAN) and wide area networks (WAN). The networking within the office allows internal communication, while access outside the office will require routers and service providers to communicate outside the internal offices with other locations, even globally. As a rule, the wired network (Ethernet) tends to offer higher speeds, but today's wireless systems (Wi-Fi) are efficient and monitored regularly for security and updates, mostly by the Internet service provider. In some cases, it may be necessary to include dual-band Wi-Fi to provide the law office with both public and private networks. This will provide additional protection for the office's internal records while allowing clients to access the Internet from your office location. You may also consider a virtual private network (VPN) to create additional security with connecting remotely to the office computers. In any case, the network plan should include both a wired and a Wi-Fi setup with help support available continuously.

Local Area Network (LAN)
A computer network that interconnects computers within a limited area such as a residence, school, laboratory, university campus or office building.

Wide Area Network (WAN)
A network that covers a large geographic area and includes other networks; a "network of networks."

A network concern that many lawyers and paralegals face is working remotely on unsecure networks. Consider working at a coffee shop on an open network that has public access: a hot spot. Many security issues arise using these hot spot connections. It is important to make sure that data being worked on and transmitted remains secure, but remember that you have no guarantees and hackers are everywhere.

Hot Spot
A place where a wireless Internet connection is available.

Conclusion

Technology has become an integral part of the legal profession and in turn has created a more efficient method for handling the practice of law. Computers replaced typewriters, and in many cases, have replaced hard copies with electronic documents. This has resulted in federal courts becoming entirely electronic, and the trend is following in the state courts also. Along with the expanded use of computers, technology advances have grown to include text-to-talk transmissions and artificial intelligence (AI) to aid in legal research and litigation support.

To be successful and competitive in today's legal profession, lawyers, paralegals, and their staff must have a working knowledge of computer hardware and software. This includes understanding basic computer components and operating systems along with identifying specialty software programs used in the legal profession. As technology continues to evolve, it is important to stay up to date with advances to remain competitive in the legal market. Keeping up with technological changes often requires updating computer systems and programs. It is important to be familiar with program updates and the current hardware to ensure their compatibility to avoid operating problems with outdated hardware and software.

It is also important to keep up to date with security and networking issues. The trend in the legal profession is to work remotely and collaboratively across local and wide area networks using communication software. Client information and data must be protected. Using off-site cloud storage as well as transmitting data over wireless networks present major security risks. It is imperative that lawyers, paralegals, and their staff create safeguards that will ensure information and data on the computer are retrievable and secured from access by hackers and unauthorized users. Advanced knowledge with computer systems and technology will ensure a competitive edge in today's legal profession.

Key Terms

Backup
Central Processing Unit (CPU)
Compatibility
Computer
Desktop (Computer)
Drivers
End-User License Agreement
Firewall
Hardware
Hot Spot

Information Technology
Laptop (Computer)
Local Area Network (LAN)
Online Collaboration
Operating System
Outsourcing
RAM (Random Access Memory)
Remote Collaboration
Server
Smart Device

Software
Thin Client
Uninterruptible Power Supply (UPS)
Videoconference
Virus
Voice Over Internet Protocol (VoIP)
Voice Recognition
Wide Area Network (WAN)
Wireless Network
Workstation

Discussion Questions

1. What are the minimum computer hardware and software requirements for today's law office?

2. How has technology and technological competency impacted the legal profession? Make sure to provide examples.

3. Should all areas of technology be used in the legal profession (like voice recognition software and videoconferencing)? Explain why or why not. Make sure to provide examples.

4. What are technology issues that can affect the practice of law? Make sure to provide examples.

Additional Resources

Gabriel Teninbaum. " Law Firms Either Keep Up With Tech Or Get Left Behind, ABA Journal, Your Voice, The American Bar Association, February 14, 2019. Retrieved from: http://www.abajournal.com/voice/article/time-for-a-hard-reset-to-the-legal-industrys-approach-to-innovation-technology

Sally Kane. "Legal Technology and the Modern Law Firm." The Balance Careers, Legal Careers, Trends and Topics, Update July 28, 2019. Retrieved from: https://www.thebalancecareers.com/technology-and-the-law-2164328

Unknown author. "The Technology Checklist Every Law Firm Needs in 2018." CasePeer Website article, February 27, 2020. Retrieved from: https://www.casepeer.com/technology-checklist-every-law-firm-needs-2018

Chapter 2

Word Processing, Document Drafting, and Legal Formatting

Learning Objectives

- Explain the function and purpose of word processing.
- Recognize the common features used in document drafting.
- Identify and explain special features available in word processing software to efficiently prepare legal documents.
- Identify and explain security features to protect documents and confidential information.

NSLT Tasks Associated with This Chapter:

- Complete all the modules and knowledge checks in the Microsoft Word 2019 learning path in the NSLT's learning portal.

Understanding the Function and Purpose of Word Processing, Document Drafting, and Legal Formatting in the Law Office

Word processing software is used by lawyers to edit, manipulate, and revise text to create documents. Word processing involves the typing of correspondence, memorandums, pleadings, discovery, and briefs. It is perhaps the most widely used application software by lawyers and paralegals. Some examples of word processing programs used by lawyers and paralegals today are Microsoft Word and Corel WordPerfect, with Word being the program of choice today. The legal profession is built on the preparation of pleadings, letters, corporate documents, forms, and more.

Centralized and Decentralized Word Processing

Law firms use various approaches to word processing, including decentralized, centralized, or a combination of both. Law offices today typically have decentralized word processing, which relies heavily on the lawyers, paralegals, and secretaries to process documents at their desk. Medium-size to large law offices may have a combination of decentralized and centralized word processing. Centralized word processing is conducted in a specialized department, sometimes open 24 hours a day, for the purpose of typing documents. In this setting, the lawyers and paralegals will likely use a combination of both, performing some word processing tasks for themselves while sending overflow word processing projects to the centralized word processing department for completion. Due to the expense, small law offices will likely not have a centralized word processing department.

Features of Legal Document Formatting

Law offices use a variety of basic and advanced word processing features, including copying, pasting, deleting, inserting, formatting of text, printing, page numbers, footnotes, and **tables**, to name just a few. It is not uncommon for legal documents to number in the hundreds of pages, for footnotes to run across several pages in a document, or for a table to be extremely complex. Law offices also use more advanced word processing features, such as tables of authorities, macros, and merges.

One major waste of time is the need to repetitively retype the same information over and over for various documents. One of the fastest ways to get around repetitive typing of documents is to use macros, Revisions, and AutoText.

Table
A grid of cells arranged in rows and columns. A table is an office application feature used in Word to easily enter and present data.

Macro (Macroinstruction)
A sequence of input instructions or keystrokes performed by a command.

Macros: **Macros** are recorded keystrokes that play back in a document. Macros can add standard blocks of text to letters, pleadings, and forms. They are easily generated by simply turning on the keystroke recorder in Word, going through the keystrokes, and saving and naming the macro. For example, it may be useful to create a standard signature block for letters or pleadings that, with a simple macro, will insert the signature block that you use frequently. See Exhibit 2–1.

Exhibit 2–1
Macro in Word

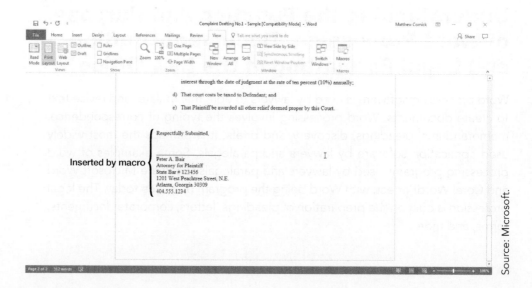

Source: Microsoft.

AutoText: AutoText enables users to reuse text and graphics by clicking a button or typing a few keystrokes. For example, if you wish to create an AutoText of the name and address for your client Samantha Stone, you simply record your keystrokes and name the AutoText "Stone address," and each time you type "Stone address," the client's name and address will be inserted into your document as:

> Samantha Stone
> 1111 E. Manhattan Blvd.
> New York, New York 10001

Formatting: Formatting allows the user to format paragraphs and entire documents to a predefined standard. After completing the document, you then apply an AutoFormat tool to apply, for example, a pleading format, a memo format, or an appellate brief format or apply other formatting of your choice. A document is like a roll of paper towels, where the pages freely flow and are connected one to another. The page separations are visualized by a dotted line on the document. The formatting and the words will flow from page to page. To force the words to start on a new page, you would insert a page break. To stop this flow of formatting from one page to another, you would create a section break. A section break would be like ripping the roll of paper towels and separating each page into independent sections.

Track Changes: Track Changes allows the recipient of the document to determine where text has been added, deleted, or moved. Fortunately, it is no longer necessary or efficient to print a hard-copy a document on paper in order to review it. Instead, when using Track Changes, you and others are able to simultaneously make changes to your document. Changes by various authors can be tracked to show who made the requested changes. The changes will show as *suggestions* that the person controlling the document can choose to either approve or reject instead of having them immediately take effect. This is important when various counsel are attempting to draft a settlement agreement or a joint motion, for example. Documents routed to other counsel can be protected from permanent change until final decisions are made.

Tracking changes saves significant time in eliminating the need to redraft copies and rechecking the entire document each time a new draft is prepared and routed to counsel. The reviewer can also accept or reject changes one by one throughout the documents or all at once. See Exhibit 2–2.

In addition to Word's widely used Track Changes, there is software called Comparite by Jurisoft that also tracks changes in documents.

Templates: A template is a blueprint of formatting and language used in your routine documents. A template is document you custom-made and drafted to fit your firm's specific requirements and needs. In contrast, a boiler-plate form utilizes generic wording and commonly used layouts. A template can contain the fonts, formatting, AutoText entries, AutoCorrect entries, styles, and macros for the specific document you are creating. It can also be linked to a database where the database automatically creates a document, such as a complaint, and fills in the templated formatting and language. In the legal field, boiler-plate language are generic in nature, and contain standard language commonly found in basic legal forms and documents.

Auto Text
Entries that are inserted automatically when you type a specific set of characters.

Page Break
A feature used to create a layout where a page ends, and a new page begins.

Section Break
A feature used to create layout or formatting changes in a portion of a document.

Track Changes
A feature that keeps a record of the modifications made to a document.

Hard-copy
a printed version on paper of data or documents that are also electronically held in a computer.

Template
A pre-designed document.

Boilerplate
A document using standard language and/or fill-in-the-blanks to create a form.

Exhibit 2–2 Track changes in Word

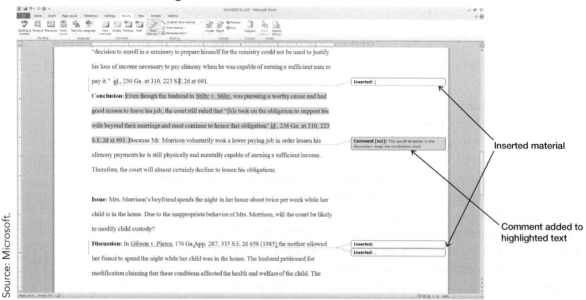

Inserted material

Comment added to highlighted text

Source: Microsoft.

Mail Merge

A feature that helps create a batch of documents personalized for each recipient, such as a form letter or notice sent to multiple recipients. A data source, like a list, spreadsheet, or database, is associated with the document.

***Mail Merge* (or Data Merge):** The Mail Merge features enable you to merge names and addresses as well as other data into any document of your choice. For example, you can set up a database to control a series of dates, times, and locations, and those data can be merged with a Notice of Deposition to produce notices to the parties involved. The Mail Merge feature can be used with client letters, complaints, answers, interrogatories, requests for production, and more.

Automatic Paragraph Numbering: Legal organizations extensively use a hierarchical numbering format, such as (A, B, C), (1, 2, 3), or (I, II, III), to mark paragraphs. When the Automatic Paragraph Numbering feature is used and a paragraph is deleted or one is added, all other paragraphs will be automatically renumbered. With the use of Automatic Paragraph Numbering, you are also able to indent paragraphs and position numbers and determine whether to continue a numbering sequence.

In addition to Microsoft Word's Automatic Paragraph Numbering, you may wish to use Payne Numbering Assistant (https://new.thepaynegroup.com/numbering-assistant). Payne enables you to insert Word paragraph numbering and tables of content; create, apply, and customize or delete client numbering schemes quickly; insert style separators, embedded headings, multiple number schemes, and complex features with just a few clicks; reset numbering and remove direct formatting to fix problematic documents with the click of a button; and work with existing paragraphs or start from scratch. If you find yourself often working on lengthy legal documents, Payne's Numbering Assistant is worth investigation.

Styles: Lengthy legal documents take significant time to put together, particularly when you also need to format the document. Fortunately, everything you do in Word has a style attached. Styles are formatting instructions that you can use repeatedly throughout the document. If you want each heading in your document to be in a larger font, uppercase letters, centered, and bold, you simply store the formatting commands in a style and apply the style to each heading in your document.

A user should also tag or identify parts of a document, such as a title, body of text, heading, footnote, or hyperlink, in order to apply certain styles. Word offers preformatted, standard styles that are ready for your use.

Footnotes and Endnotes: Footnotes and endnotes are frequently used in legal briefs. A footnote is a numbered reference that appears in the body of the text referring to material printed at the bottom of a page or multiple pages. An endnote also has a numbered reference in the body of the text but appears only at the end of a document. Word allows a user to easily insert footnotes and endnotes into the document.

Hypertext Briefs: In litigation, courts now prefer attorneys to use hyperlinks inside their briefs. One example is the linking of the citations to the brief. The judge need only click on the hypertext to immediately read the referenced case. This is a significant time-saver.

It is now possible to create hypertext HTML documents, which permit you to choose a word, phrase, or symbol that is linked to other information. After clicking on the word or other symbol, you are immediately taken to the other information, such as a cited case. It is also possible to link exhibits, deposition pages, video, and any other text for the reader's view. Hyperlinks are useful in a variety of legal documents.

Tables: Tables are created in rows and columns to display information. Tables can include text, numbers, and formulas. Word's Table command allows you to build a table by selecting the numbers of columns and rows you wish to use. Once you have done that, the table is displayed. A table is also useful if text in your layout needs to be positioned side by side or float at specific locations on the page. Tables are often used by law offices to separate the caption on a pleading, with the parties on the left and the case number on the right.

Headers and Footers: Headers and footers are usually where you will find the page numbers, document name, disclaimers, confidentiality designations, and other useful information. The footer is the area in the bottom margin of your document. The header is the area in the top margin of your document. Most legal documents require the page number and document name to be printed in the footer on each page of the document. Word allows you to add headers and footers with built-in, ready-made layouts or add your own custom headers and footers.

Table of Contents: A table of contents provides organization to a lawyer's brief. The table allows readers to easily navigate from the brief to find the section or information they are looking for, much like the index to a book. The table of contents includes a list of all the headings and subheadings used in the brief and the page number on which each appears. In Word, you simply need to click in your document where you wish to insert your table of contents, choose References and Automatic Table of Contents from the Style list. The table of contents will be automatically generated for you, assuming that you have pre-marked your headings.

Footnotes
Material that is printed at the bottom of a page; marked in text by a numbered referent.

Endnotes
Notes at the end of a document acknowledging sources and providing additional references or information.

Header
The area consisting of the top margin of the page.

Footer
The area consisting of the bottom margin of the page.

Table of Contents
A snapshot of the headings and page numbers in a document that can be updated as changes are made.

Exhibit 2–3

Table of authorities in Word

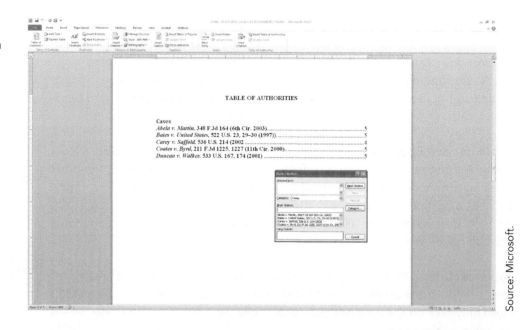

Source: Microsoft.

Table of Authorities

Used in legal documents and pleadings to index cases, statutes, and legal authorities contained within the material.

Table of Authorities: A **table of authorities** frequently accompanies an attorney's brief. The table includes a list of all cases, statutes, and other authorities referenced in the document or brief. The table of authorities is similar to the table of contents except that it lists cases and other reference materials, along with the page numbers on which they appear in the document. Creating a table of authorities can be very time consuming when done manually. However, with Word, you simply need to mark each citation, statute, and other authority in the document, and Word is then able to quickly generate the table. If changes are later made to the document, you can simply and quickly regenerate the table to include any additional authorities. See Exhibit 2–3.

Reveal Formatting: Word's Reveal Formatting feature allows a user to see hidden formatting codes, such as spacing, boldfacing, margin changes, font sizes, and more. Because these codes are hidden from the user, once Reveal Formatting is turned on, it is easier to then delete, edit, or change the formatting of your document by simply deleting the command in the Reveal Formatting screen.

Comments: Lawyers often collaborate on a document using Word's features, such as Comments, Compare Documents, and Track Changes. Word's Comments feature allows a user to annotate and make notes or comments on a document without actually changing it. Once a comment is inserted, the reviewer can respond, and the original user can then make changes, delete the comment, and/or respond to the reviewer. Many times, documents are reviewed by multiple people, including attorneys, cocounsel, and clients. In this instance, Word assigns a different color to each reviewer's comments so that it is easy to determine who made the changes.

Ribbon

A Microsoft user interface that consists of tabs, each with specific groups of related commands, providing quick access to commonly used commands needed to complete tasks.

Collaboration: If you wish to share your document, select Share from Word's top **ribbon** toolbar, enter the email addresses of the recipients, and select Send. The recipients then receive a document link that can be opened in their browser or on their desktop. Sharing can be done with people either inside or outside your firm. When the recipients open the link, they will be able to collaborate in real time, and you will be able to see who is working on the document along with the changes. To use the collaboration tools, you need to have an account with OneDrive (Microsoft's cloud-based storage tool).

Stop and Think!

Get on the Same Page

IT is typical for a law firm to have multiple people work on the same document. A paralegal might complete the first draft, then send it to the attorney to work on. The attorney then adds to the document and sends it to a partner to assist review. The partner adds to the document and sends it back. The cycles continue through many different people over and over again. Keeping track of what version is the most current draft of the document is crucial the efficiency and effectiveness of the office. This issue is exacerbated by employees working from home that rely solely upon email attachments to send the documents back and forth. Far too many opportunities for someone in the workflow to accidentally be working off of the wrong version of the document. It is crucial that a law firm find a way to manage the workflow of a document and ensure that everyone in the cycle know which file is the most current version of the document. What methods can a firm put in place to ensure everyone is working on the most current version of the document?

Comparing Documents: Word's Compare Documents feature enables you to compare two separate documents. Word is able to compare the two documents and produce a third document that shows the differences between the two versions. Law offices find the Compare Document feature to be useful in comparing joint motions and other pleadings, contracts, and agreements. Note that Word allows you to synchronize the documents so that they scroll side by side on your screen as you move through the documents.

Security Features: There are features in Microsoft Word that focus specifically on security and protection of the document. One of these ways, is **password protection**. Creating a password for the document is an easy way to ensure that only those with the password can access the document. When the restricted editing option is enabled, it will prevent readers from adding or deleting content, thus protecting the authenticity of your content. You can also enable formatting restrictions, which will allow the reader to edit the content but not alter the formatting of the document. Documents can also be set to **read only** mode, which prevents the user from making any alterations of any kind to the document and only allows them to view the document.

Password Protection
A security process that prevents access to information via computers and requires authorization codes for reveal.

Read Only
A setting that allows a file to be read or copied but not changed or saved.

Version Control: It is important that each team member is working on the same version of a particular document; otherwise, valuable time is lost. This is where version control becomes important. One way this can be accomplished is through Microsoft's SharePoint tool (as Microsoft Word lacks a version control built-in tool). With SharePoint, the team create sites on which to share documents and information with colleagues and partners. With SharePoint's "enable versioning" tool, you can see the history or prior versions or restore a prior version of the document in order to see the changes made.

Proofreading

An editing feature in Word that checks spelling and grammar as a document is typed.

Spell-Check, Grammar Check, and Proofreading: Word enables you to run what is called spell and grammar checks on your documents. You should use these features on every document you prepare. However, you should never rely on spell and grammar checks alone. There are many typographical errors that a spell checker will not catch and that can be picked up only with careful proofreading. For example, a complaint should demand a jury *trial* and not a jury *trail*. Every document should be carefully proofread for errors.

According to the Writing Center of the University of Wisconsin, Madison (https://writing.wisc.edu/handbook/grammarpunct/proofreading/), "proofreading means examining your text carefully to find and correct typographical errors and mistakes in grammar, style, and spelling." Here are some tips:

- Spotting mistakes requires concentration, which means getting rid of distractions and potential interruptions by switching off the cell phone, television, or radio and staying away from email.
- People read differently on-screen than on paper. Instead, work from a printout of your document instead of the computer screen.
- You may find it helpful to use a blank sheet of paper to cover up the lines below the one you are reading to prevent you from skipping ahead.
- Reading your document out loud is helpful in spotting run-on sentences. You will also hear other problems that you may not see when reading silently.
- Homonyms are words that share the same spelling or pronunciation but have different meanings. Switching *accept* with *except* or *complement* with *compliment* are errors that should be caught and corrected.
- People often mix the words *their* and *they're*, *its* and *it's*, *your* and *you're*, and so on. If there is something that can hurt the credibility of your text, it is a similar mistake.
- Stating that the value of an acquisition was *$10,000* instead of *$100,000* is definitely not the same thing. Check and double-check all numbers.
- Use the Search function of the computer to find mistakes you are likely to make. Search for "*it*" if you tend to confuse "*its*" and "*it's*." Search for opening parentheses or quote marks if you tend to leave out the closing parentheses or quote marks.
- End with a spelling/grammar check, keeping in mind that a spell-checker won't catch mistakes such as "*he*" for "*the*" or the misuse of words such as "*they're*," "*their*," and "*there*."
- It is important to validate cited cases in a document before using them to make sure they are still good law. Also, it is important to validate fact citations to make sure the fact is valid. Avoid the chance that the validity of the cited case or fact is inaccurate by always checking before citing.
- The most common error in legal word processing is leaving old information in a newly generated document.

Word Quick Reference Guide: Learning these keyboard shortcuts can save you time in document editing. See Exhibit 2–4.

Exhibit 2–4 Word Quick Reference Guide

Word Quick Reference Guide

HOME RIBBON

Dialog box launcher

Cut, Copy, Paste

Font format   Paragraph format   Styles   Find/Replace   Help

NAVIGATION

Up 1 Screen	[Page Up]	Beginning of Document	[Ctrl]+[Home]
Down 1 Screen	[Page Down]	End of Document	[Ctrl]+[End]
Beginning of a Line	[Home]	Go To	[F5]
End of a Line	[End]		

KEYBOARD SHORTCUTS

Copy Text	[Ctrl]+[C]	Undo a Command	[Ctrl]+[Z]
Paste Text	[Ctrl]+[V]	Redo / Repeat	[Ctrl]+[Y]
Cut Text	[Ctrl]+[X]	Print a Document	[Ctrl]+[P]
Bold Text	[Ctrl]+[B]	Save a Document	[Ctrl]+[S]
Underline Text	[Ctrl]+[U]	Select Everything	[Ctrl]+[A]
Italics Text	[Ctrl]+[I]	Open File	[Ctrl]+[O]
Find / Replace	[Ctrl]+[F]	New File	[Ctrl]+[N]
Go To	[Ctrl]+[G]	Reveal Formatting	[Shift]+[F1]
Spell, Grammar Check	[F7]	Hide Ribbon	[Ctrl]+[F1]

WORD FEATURE	COMMAND STRUCTURE
Attach Document to an Email	File Tab, Share, Email
Change Case of Text	Home, Font, Change Case
Clear all Formatting of Text	Home, Font, Clear Formatting
Clip Art from Internet (Inserting)	Insert, Illustrations, Online Pictures
Clip Art / Files / Charts, Shapes (Inserting)	Insert, Illustrations
Compare Documents	Review, Compare
Find / Replace	Home, Editing, Find / Replace
Font Control	Home, Font
Footnotes / Endnotes	References, Footnotes, Insert Footnote
Header / Footer	Insert, Header & Footer, Header or Footer
Indent text	Home, Paragraph, Dialog Box Launcher
Line Spacing Changes	Home, Paragraph, Line Spacing
Macros	View, Macros
Mail Merge	Mailings, Start Mail Merge
Margins, Paper Orientation	Page Layout, Page Setup, Margins
Shading	Home, Paragraph, Shading
Styles	Home, Styles
Tables (Inserting)	Insert, Tables
Tabs	Home, Paragraph Dialog Box Launcher, Indents and Spacing, Tabs
Track Changes	Review, Tracking, Track Changes
New Document	File Tab, New
Open (Existing) document	File Tab, Open
Save a document	File Tab, Save
Print and Print Preview	File Tab, Print
Table of Authorities	References, Table of Authorities

Source: Microsoft.

At the Touch of a Button

The LegalBoard (www.legalkeyboards.com) is a keyboard designed for legal professionals, which allows the user to access over 35 different legal-specific functions by switching the keyboard into legal mode. Once in legal mode, you can insert a section (§) or paragraph (¶) symbol in Word or Outlook with a single key, add a comment or a footnote and toggle back to the text afterwards, insert common terms like "id.", turn track changes on/off, and much more. The LegalBoard can be switched back to function as a standard keyboard with just the touch of a button.

Do you feel a legal specific keyboard would be worth the investment? Can the same thing be achieved by utilizing the special features that are contained in the software program already?

Merging and Document Assembly

Merging: Many letters, pleadings, and other documents used in law offices are essentially the same. The client names change from case to case, but the letters and documents produced are typically the same. Word's Merge feature allows you to save these forms so that you can simply retrieve them and quickly fill in the blanks. For example, if you want to send out the same letter to a list of clients but you want each letter to be personalized, you can use Word's Merge feature to quickly do this for you. The body of each letter remains the same, while the name, address of the client, and salutation change. This is accomplished by placing markers in the letter where the information is to be inserted and then creating a separate list of name/addresses/salutations and merging the two together.

There are also separate document assembly programs that work together with Word to create standardized templates, forms, correspondence, pleadings, contracts, and other legal documents in the fields of wills and trusts, domestic relations, corporate, immigration, criminal, and more. For example, if creating a template, users can respond to a series of questions and prompts to fill in the data. The document assembly program merges the template or form with the answers and builds a new document.

For firms that require a stand-alone document automation software, there are many software options, such as HotDocs, Documate, and Pathagoras. Small law practices that are not document intensive use document management features built into many *law practice management systems*, such as Clio, Smokeball, Rocket Matter, and MyCase. These programs will often be sufficient and more cost effective than using both law practice management software and document assembly software.

Helpful Add-Ins to Word: It is possible to install certain add-ins to improve your use of Word, such as the following:

Adobe Sign: Adobe Sign works inside of Word, allowing you to place an electronic (digital) signature on a document with a few keystrokes. After using Adobe Sign, you can send the document off from the app.

Grammarly: Microsoft Word has a built-in grammar/spell-checker, but it is by no means highly effective. Instead, with the use of software such as Grammarly, you can check grammar, punctuation, spelling, writing style, and tone.

Office Tab: Office Tab enables you to open, view, and edit multiple Word documents in a single window, like your browser. You can also open, save, and close all files at once and identify the files by marking each tab with a specific color. When working on multiple cases at once, Office Tab can be helpful.

Microsoft Word Meets Artificial Intelligence (AI)

Microsoft Word is now introducing Artificial Intelligence (AI) to its rich features. According to J. Brandon, "What This New A.I. Feature in Microsoft Word Teaches Us about Ourselves" (February 28, 2017),[1] "Word's newest feature, called Editor (offered in Office 365), can now look for weak language, passive voice, word choice problems, and many other writing problems on the fly while offering suggestions along the way. When the Editor flags something, you can choose to select from a suggested alternative (if one is available), or research the suggestion more and see explanations in the Editor window." Lawyers and paralegals will find Editor helpful in improving their legal writing. For more experienced lawyers and paralegals with extensive writing experience, it is a good reminder for creating exceptionally well-written documents. Look for more AI features in Word with each new version.

Artificial Intelligence (AI)
The capability of a machine or computer to imitate human behavior. Also known as machine learning.

Tech this Out!

Naturally Speaking

Dragon Naturally Speaking by Nuance Communications (www.nuance.com/dragon.html) is speech to text technology that allows users to dictate to the computer and it turns the dictation into typed text. This allows for hands-free working and legal professionals can now dictate their briefs and memos while commuting to work, or other multi-tasking moments. Many people can speak faster than they can type, and often have to slow down their thinking or repeat the phrase they just said, in order to get it typed out into the document. With Dragon Naturally Speaking, the brief can now be written at the speed you dictate it. Do you think there is a cause to be concerned about the program picking up background noises or conversations it should not be listening to?

---

[1]https://www.computerworld.com/article/3175788/what-this-new-ai-feature-in-microsoft-word-teaches-us-about-ourselves.html.

Conclusion

When preparing legal documents, it is important for users to carefully review their work to ensure that metadata is deleted, old information is not left in documents, research is updated and current, and there are no typographical errors.

Key Terms

Artificial Intelligence (AI)	Header	Ribbon
Auto Text	Macro (Macroinstruction)	Section Break
Boilerplate	Mail Merge	Table
Endnotes	Page Break	Table of Authorities
Footer	Password Protection	Table of Contents
Footnotes	Proofreading	Template
Hard-copy	Read Only	Track Changes

Discussion Questions

1. Have word processing programs had an overall negative or positive impact on the legal profession? What has created the positive effects? In which way have they had negative effects?

2. What are some basic and special features of the Microsoft Word interface ribbon?

3. How are special features (including security features) used for creating common legal documents? Provide an example to support your viewpoint.

4. Why or why not is it important to adapt to software changes/updates as well as to work with different word processing applications (Microsoft Word, GoogleDocs, Corel WordPerfect, Pages, etc.) and know where to locate "Help" resources? Provide examples to support your viewpoint.

Additional Resources

For your ease of reference, here are several links to free Microsoft Custom Word Guides (basic, intermediate, and advanced). Cut and paste the links into your browser:

www.customguide.com/cheat-sheet/word-2019-basic-quick-reference.pdf

www.customguide.com/cheat-sheet/word-2019-intermediate-quick-reference.pdf

www.customguide.com/cheat-sheet/word-2019-advanced-quick-reference.pdf

Chapter 3

Email Communication in the Law Office

Learning Objectives

- Identify and explain how to manage Address Books and Contacts to send Outlook items, create messages, and maximize the efficiency of the message using Quick Parts.
- Identify and explain organizational tools in Outlook, including creating folders, using Quick Steps, sorting, searching, and correctly using Categories.
- Identify and explain the Calendar options in Outlook to create calendars and schedules, share calendars, and send calendar information.
- Identify and explain how to efficiently use Outlook to work with others by delegating access to files and sharing folders.

NSLT Tasks Associated with This Chapter:

- Complete all learning modules and knowledge checks in the NSLT learning portal under Outlook 2019 and submit your completion certificate and software review.

Understanding the Function and Purpose of Outlook

Microsoft Outlook is one of many popular programs used for communications and personal information management (or PIM) by lawyers.

Outlook's email (electronic mail) capabilities provide lawyers, clients, associates, paralegals, and secretaries with the ability to send electronic messages and computer files to each other and then to save them into electronic file cabinets for later retrieval.

Outlook's PIM provides lawyers with capabilities such as calendaring, billing and docket control (**docketing** is a legal-specific term referring to entering,

Docketing
Entries that track a list of court proceedings and hearings that must be attended.

organizing, tracking, and controlling appointments, deadlines, and due dates for a particular case), and more.

Outlook and Email Communication in the Law Office

Outlook is the application most users have open on their computers more than any other program in the suite. **Email** has replaced the **fax** as the preferred method for sending documents. As the use of email has increased, fax volume has declined. Email is convenient, effective, inexpensive, and accessible.

Email has the advantage of the written word, which can be edited before sending. It is easy to save messages for future reference or share them with colleagues and coworkers for collaboration.

Today, email can contain more than just plain text due to **HTML (hypertext markup language)** which allows for the addition of many kinds of rich content such as images, tables, charts and more.

Typically, a file folder is created in Outlook for each client by name. Inside the client's folder are additional folders that divide up the documents for ease in locating, such as the following:

- Correspondence
- Emails
- Pleadings
- Contracts
- Workgroup ideas or discussions
- Billing

Email Retention

Email boxes are not intended to be a place for storage of client information. In the past, lawyers would send a client a letter by mail and keep a copy for his or her file. Today, law firms have record management software to store electronic case information in a central networked environment that permits searching and other access. Many states require lawyers to not only keep a record of email communications but actually store a copy of the email and any attachments in the firm's record retention system.

Record retention policies are in place so that email (and case records), subject to the firm's record retention rules, are destroyed at the proper time.

Record retention rules help firms manage the amount of storage the email system must continually use, help the email system retain speed of operation, and reduce liability for retaining records that are not needed but may contain information harmful to the legal organization or its clients.

Email Encryption and Digital Signatures

Clients often demand email access to their lawyers and paralegals. However, the security of email has long been a concern for lawyers. Many legal organizations indicate that they send confidential or privileged communication or documents to clients via email. The issue of security is managed by (1) requiring clients to provide oral or written consent to having confidential information sent via email, (2) adding a

Email
Messages distributed by electronic means from one computer user to one or more recipients via a network.

Facsimile (Fax)
Technology that transfers images electronically using telephone lines.

HTML (Hypertext Markup Language)
The predominant language used to create web pages.

Record Retention Policies
General principles determining the length of time that records, in which data is stored, must be maintained in accordance with policies and law.

confidentiality statement at the end of an email message, (3) using encryption software, or (4) simply not using email at all to send confidential information.

Because email passes through many **network servers** before it reaches its destination, it is subject to being read by **system administrators**, hackers, and others. Email is more like a postcard than a sealed letter, so some legal organizations use encryption software to protect confidential email sent to others. **Encryption** software locks email so that it can be opened only by the intended recipient.

When the sender runs the email through the encryption program, an **encryption key** is created that scrambles the file. The sender then sends the encrypted email to the recipient and separately transmits the **decoding key**, which is usually a password or a data file. While running the same encryption program, the recipient uses the decoding key to unscramble the message.

Secure Client Portals

According to the American Bar Association (ABA) ethics opinion, Opinion 477 (ABA 14-006, May 4, 2017, Securing Communication of Protected Client Information) establishes a new standard for secure client communication. In an ABA article, lawyer Nicole Black states that "using unencrypted e-mail may be appropriate for routine or low sensitivity communications, due to cyber-threats." However, "the proliferation of electronic communications devices changed the landscape [therefore] it is not always reasonable to rely on the use of unencrypted e-mail. One way around the problem with encrypted e-mails is to set up an encrypted online portal for each client. These are often built into other software programs such as legal practice management software. All communications occur within the portal, so once you log into the portal, your activities occurring therein, along with your communications, are encrypted from prying eyes."

Black further states that "as with all encrypted communications, client portals require a buy in from your clients. However, in light of the new ABA e-mail guidelines, the time saved by avoiding the case-by-case communications analysis and the security gained by using client portals will likely outweigh any push back from clients. Also, the ABA opinion gives new teeth to requirement that communications be secure, making it easier for you to explain to clients why such measures are needed" (N. Black, "Check Out Some Secure Communications and Collaboration Tools for Lawyers," *ABA Journal*, October 26, 2018).

Email Etiquette and Tips

The following tips will help you write your email messages to your intended readers in an effective manner:

- Be succinct and clear.
- Be sure to mention the topic in the subject area.
- Mark messages as urgent or ASAP only when absolutely necessary.
- Signature files included at the end of each email should reflect your name, firm name, address, phone number, fax number, and email address.
- Use spell-check and review your email for errors.
- Double-check the spelling of all names in the email.
- Be careful to treat email as business correspondence. These are formal documents requiring formal language (for example, do not use the letter "u" as a substitute for the word "you").

Network Server
A powerful, central computer with special software and equipment that enable it to function as the primary computer in the network.

System Administrator
A person in charge of managing and maintaining computer systems within a business or institution.

Encryption
A process of encoding messages to keep them secret, so only "authorized" parties can read it.

Encryption Key
A binary input to the encryption algorithm—typically a long string of bits used to scramble the file or message to render it unreadable.

Decoding Key
A password or a data file that allows a message or document to decrypted.

- Do not address a recipient by his or her first name unless you are sure it is appropriate to do so.
- Do not use ALL CAPS, which is the equivalent to shouting.
- Be careful not use "Reply All" unless you intended to do so.
- Check email twice daily if not more often as time permits.
- Do not use email to communicate with clients regarding sensitive information. For sensitive communications, it is better not to use email at all.
- Double-check the email address(es) of the intended recipient(s) before sending.
- When possible, limit each email to one specific topic (this is done for filing purposes).
- Password protect any word processing documents you are attaching.
- When attaching a Microsoft Word document, make sure to first scrub your document of any metadata.

Special Email Features of Outlook

- **Choose the Number of Lines in the Subject Area**
Outlook displays a preview of each message showing you a limited number of lines, including the sender, subject line, and one line from the body of the message. You can easily change the number of lines, giving yourself a better view of the topic involved.
- **Choose Which Folder Displays First on Outlook's Launch**
If you have multiple Outlook email accounts, you can select which email account inbox you want displayed first when you open Outlook.
- **Create an Outlook Search Folder**
It is helpful to set up a virtual Search Folder for words or phrases commonly used. You can create your own Search Folder, or Outlook provides some templates for your use. For example, Outlook's template Unread Mail Search Folder shows you your unread mail in one folder, even if they are physically located in different folders in your email account. The messages are not "moved" to the Search Folder. The original messages remain in their original folders.
- **Clean Up an Outlook Folder**
To clean your inbox and improve space, it is helpful to use Outlook's Clean Up Folder command, which removes redundant messages in a thread or folder by sending them to the Deleted Folder by default.

Stop and Think!

Dangers of "Reply All"

Replying to all on an email is not always the wrong choice, but it should not be the default thing that you do. It is more than just for etiquette reasons that we do not reply all (especially for nonsubstantive messages like "thanks") as it can possibly transmit confidential information to people who should not have it. On average, people receive three times more email than they send. The majority of which are messages they are carbon copied (CC'd) on. Also, consider all the junk email this causes when an autoreply "out of office" email from one of your addressees now goes out to all on the list. This can result in an avalanche of new messages in the inbox and leaves the reader to determine which messages are junk replies and which messages are important to read and reply. What features in Outlook can you employ to prevent this catastrophe from happening?

- **Flag Outgoing Emails**

    You may wish to flag an outgoing email, which is useful when the response you need is time sensitive. Rather than count on the recipient to respond in a timely manner, attach a flag and reminder for yourself to follow up with the recipient.

- **Pin Emails to Your Inbox**

    You pin an email by clicking the Pin icon at the top of a message to keep it at the top of your inbox. If there is a message you know you need to handle ASAP, pin it to the top of your inbox so that when you come back to your Inbox later, you won't lose track of it among all the other email that has trickled into your inbox.

- **Automate Repetitive Emails with Quick Parts**

    If you find yourself responding repeatedly to often-asked questions, do not waste time by typing the text each time. Instead, use Quick Parts to save the text, and the next time you need to respond to the same question, just click on Quick Part and select the text you wish to use.

- **Drag and Drop Emails to Create a Calendar Entry**

    When an email contains a deadline or appointment, rather than create a new calendar entry and copy that information to it, drag and drop the email onto your calendar. That action will turn the email directly into a calendar entry, and the contents of the email will appear in the notes field of the calendar entry.

- **Send an Email at a Future Date**

    Outlook's Delayed Delivery feature allows you to write an email and send it at a later time. After writing an email or replying to one, you can click Delay Delivery and select the "Do Not Deliver Before" box to select a date and time for delivery. You might also use Delay Delivery to schedule an email reminder to clients the day before they are due in court. If you change your mind, you can easily turn the feature off.

- **Use of Quick Steps**

    On the Home tab of Outlook is a Quick Steps section, which provides one-click access to common actions. You can also create your own Quick Steps, such as marking selected email messages as read and having them automatically moved to a certain folder.

- **Open Multiple Outlook Windows**

    Multiple Outlook windows are helpful for emailing, scheduling, and tasks. Multiple windows allow you to see your email, calendar, and tasks at the same time instead of using the continually switching views.

- **Create and Manage Rules**

    Outlook Rules are useful in allowing you to set specific events to occur automatically based certain actions. For example, you can create a rule that will move messages with specific words in the subject line in the body of the email, or from a specific person to a particular folder and mark the messages as read at the same time.

- **Change Your Outlook Account Name**

    The default name for your Outlook account is your email address. If you have a number of Outlook email accounts, you can change the account name to a more descriptive one, such as a client's name or case name, making it faster to locate the account you are looking for.

- **Focused Inbox**

    Outlook offers a Focused Inbox, which automatically sorts messages. The Focused Inbox is designed to keep email clutter at a minimum and to organize your inbox into two categories: "Focused and Other." Outlook then categorizes important messages into the Focused tab and the not-so-important messages, such as marketing messages, into the "Other" tab. Outlook prioritizes messages sent from people you have previously interacted with.

Quick Part
Building block you create from frequently used text, such as a name, address, or slogan, and then save so that you can easily access them.

- **Read Aloud**

  Outlooks Read Aloud feature reads text from a message out loud. This feature enables better accessibility for users and allows you to multitask.

- **@Mentions**

  The @Mentions feature in Outlook allows you to tag people into your messages. Simply type the "@" symbol, and a drop-down list of contact names will appear for you to choose from. All recipients mentioned will also receive a copy of the message.

- **Time Zone Scheduling**

  Outlook has the ability to schedule meetings in multiple time zones. This is helpful for anyone who often has meetings with colleagues or clients in different time zones. This feature allows you to add a second and third time zone that you can label with a client name or branch name instead of the actual time zone name.

- **Add Groups**

  Outlook allows you to create and collaborate in Office 365 Groups. You simply invite people to join a group by sharing a URL through email. Groups offer a platform where you can discuss and collaborate on various topics.

- **Create a Signature**

  Digital Signature
  A means of electronically signing a document with data that cannot be forged.

  Outlook allows you to create a **digital signature** that will appear in the footer of every email you send. Signatures are fully customizable. You can control the font, color, size, and justification of your signature, and you can also create different kinds of signatures for different kinds of messages. You can decide whether you want to include a signature on replies and forwards, and you can include your law firm logo on each signature.

- **Payment Reminders**

  The Outlook Payment Reminders feature retrieves details from bills you receive in email. Outlook shows you a summary of the bill and adds a calendar event by due date. You can also set up a reminder before the due date to ensure that you make payments on time.

- **Use Keyboard Shortcuts**

  There are many keyboard shortcuts associated with Outlook. Use can use Windows keyboard shortcuts for your most frequent Outlook actions, such as the following:

  - *Compose new email*: Ctrl + N
  - *Send*: Ctrl + Enter
  - *Reply to sender*: Ctrl + R
  - *Delete*: Ctrl + D
  - *Flag for follow-up*: Ctrl + Shift + G
  - *Switch to mail*: Ctrl + 1
  - *Switch to calendar*: Ctrl + 2
  - *Switch to contacts*: Ctrl + 3
  - *Switch to Tasks*: Ctrl + 4
  - *Make a new appointment*: Ctrl + Shift + A
  - *Create a new contact*: Ctrl + Shift + C
  - *Start a new message*: Ctrl + Shift + M
  - *Send message*: Alt + S
  - *Reply to a message*: Ctrl + R

Email Issues and Tips

- Do not assume that because an email was sent, it has been read. Email relies on computer technology that occasionally fails or is delayed.
- Be careful what you say in emails, as they can be forwarded to others.
- Remember that email is not necessarily confidential. Email security can be breached in many ways, such as leaving confidential email open on your computer screen for others to read, leaving your office for lunch or break while logged into your email program, printing email that others can find at a network printer, or using a password such as "password" or names of family members that would be easy for others to guess.
- Phishing is a user's hope of gaining personal information from a user, such as a Social Security number, passwords, bank account information, and more. Phishers send fraudulent emails impersonating legitimate senders and may ask you to confirm or reenter personal or confidential information because attempts have been made to access your account. They may also pose as a government agency alerting you to security issues. Often, phishers create exact replicas of real websites that look legitimate; however, anyone who follows links in such an email will end up at a false site where your information may be stolen and used for fraudulent purposes.
- Email and Internet users should always be suspicious of any message that ask for personal information. It is important to simply delete the email without clicking on any of the associated links inside the email. If you have genuine concerns, go to the actual website and sign in to see if you have fraud alerts. If you do not, you can ignore the phishing email you received.
- Spam is another concern for law firms. Due to the proliferation of spam, many law firms have spam filters in place that limit the amount of spam that gets through to your inbox.

Phishing
An attack that sends an email or displays a Web announcement that falsely claims to be from a legitimate enterprise in an attempt to trick the user into surrendering private information.

Spam
Unsolicited email.

Tech this Out!

Are you a Slacker?

Slack is a communication application that allows businesses or law firms to communicate with their employees. Slack brings team communication and collaboration into one place. The application allows users to do group chats, chat rooms, or private messages. The instant method of communicating has become a popular method for reducing the number of emails being sent internally and eliminating inbox clutter. The user-interface is very sleek and easy to understand. The intuit design of the interface eliminates the need to train employees on how to use the system, thus speeding up its adoption in the workplace. One of Slack's most prominent features was that private channels and direct messages could not be read by admins without either the open consent of the members or a message being sent to all the users saying that an export of messages had happened. This provides a sense of privacy and security to users that other products (especially email) do not offer. What ethical issues are raised by utilizing this type of platform for inter-office communication?

Outlook and Personal Information Management

Personal Information Management
A system and software program utilized to acquire, organize, maintain, retrieve, and use information.

Calendaring
The software that helps you manage email, calendars, and tasks.

Outlook is just one kind of **personal information management (PIM)** tool used by law offices today. Outlook is a generic PIM, but attorneys also have access to legal-specific PIMs, such as Amicus Attorney, Time Matters, Lotus Organizer, LawBase, and more. Each PIM varies, but all PIMs are generally designed to manage case or transaction information, calendaring, docketing, managing client information, tracking time and billing, email, and more.

Outlook consolidates many different tasks into one computer program, including calendaring; things to do; a contact database that tracks names and addresses of clients, counsel, and judges; note taking; email; and other tasks. Outlook often comes bundled with the Microsoft Office suite of products, which is one reason it is commonly used.

Outlook can sync with mobile devices so that paralegals and attorneys can manage their appointments, scheduling, and to-do lists wherever they are located. For example, if during a court hearing the judge gives the attorneys the next hearing date, the attorneys can easily enter the date into Outlook on their phones, eliminating the need to write down the date and enter it once back at the office.

Most PIMs now have network-based group scheduling capabilities that enable users to share information (attorney to paralegal or paralegal to attorney or among cocounsel) related to scheduling and case management.

The firm's PIM should have the ability to share information easily with the firm's word processing program in order to eliminate the reentering of common case data for pleadings (such as captions or case numbers), correspondence (such as an inside address), and other legal materials.

Scheduling of Appointments

Legal professionals will have a number of important appointments, such as client meetings, meetings with cocounsel, witness interviews, interoffice meetings, and more. See Exhibit 3–1.

Calendaring of Deadlines and Reminders

There are case deadlines throughout any particular case matter. For example, one of the most important deadlines is the statute of limitation, which sets a limit on the length of time a party has to file a lawsuit. Statutes of limitation force parties to bring their lawsuits in an efficient and timely manner. If the suit is not brought in a timely fashion, the defendant could be prejudiced by the loss of evidence, the inability to find witnesses, or the inability of witnesses to recall relevant information.

If an attorney allows a statute of limitation to expire without filing a case, he or she will likely be liable for legal malpractice. Each state's statutes of limitation vary depending on the particular matter, such as personal injury, breach of contract, and so on. It is vital to know and understand your particular state's statues so that the deadline date can be added to your calendar. Many firms take out additional firm malpractice insurance to cover calendaring mistakes should they be sued for missing a deadline.

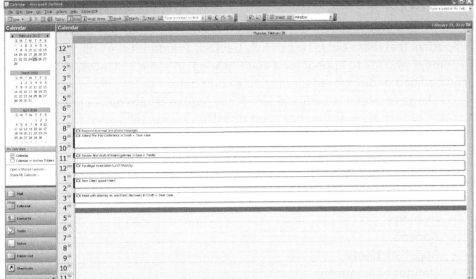

Exhibit 3–1

Calendaring/PIM program:
Microsoft Outlook

Source: Microsoft.

Many court dates and deadlines are set after a case has been filed. In many courts, the judge and the attorneys on both sides meet and schedule the deadlines for the case. These deadlines must be tracked carefully and followed. An attorney who does not adhere to the deadlines may cause the case to be dismissed by the court or may be sanctioned. Courts are generally reluctant to extend the case deadlines once they are established. Below is an example of some typical court deadlines:

- Motion to dismiss = February 1
- Response to motion to dismiss = April 10
- Reply to motion to dismiss = May 15
- Propound interrogatories = June 30
- Response to interrogatories = July 15
- Summary judgment motion = August 10
- Pretrial order = October 1

Because attorneys and paralegals are usually busy working on more than one case at a time, the firm must have a system for tracking upcoming deadlines. This is done not only by calendaring the deadlines but also by creating reminder notes or ticklers in the calendar in advance of the deadline so that the deadline is not inadvertently missed.

It is important to understand that you will be calendaring not only the deadlines that must be met by your attorney(s) but also the deadlines to be met by opposing counsel. For example, if opposing counsel files a motion to dismiss with the court, it is important that you calculate your attorney's deadline date to "respond" to the motion and defense counsel's deadline to "reply" to the motion. If opposing counsel fails to "reply" to your attorney's "response," your attorney can then move to have the motion dismissed if done by the due date. Each of these actions is controlled by a due date. Calendaring can seem challenging at first, but with some practice, you will become accustomed to accomplishing it.

Hearings, Court Due Dates, and Court Deadlines

Court dates and hearings are formal proceedings before the court. It is very important that these dates be carefully tracked, as judges have little tolerance for attorneys who fail to appear for a court hearing. In some instances, the attorney can be fined or disciplined for missing a court date.

A large case that is being litigated may require hundreds of entries into the docket system, such as the dates and deadlines for the following:

- Complaint
- Answer
- Motions
- Discovery
- Hearings
- Appeals
- Appellate briefs
- Statutes of limitation
- Trial court appearances
- Trial court briefs
- Judgment renewal

Client Billing

Outlook can simplify and automate the law firm's billing process when used in association with a professional billing system, such as Clio, My Case, TimeSolv, Smokeball, LawPay, Zola Suite, Abacus Law, and Practice Panther, to name just a few. These billing software programs can be integrated with Outlook in order to obtain the stored PIM information for each client, such as the client billing number, client address, phone number, email, invoices, time sheets, expense reporting and more. Different features are included in different software billing programs and may include the following:

- Outlook forms for time sheets and expense reports are easy to use, improving the accuracy of customer billing. These forms are linked to projects and tasks. Users can quickly and easily charge time against their assigned tasks or expenses against travel/lodging and other business expense categories. This simplifies reporting and minimizes the error potential inherent in paper or spreadsheet processes that require manual entry.
- Review and approval **workflows** are automated, allowing the law firm to generate invoices for customers in a timely and consistent manner.
- Reminders are automatically sent to ensure that employees report their billable hours consistently.
- Automated approval routing delivers time sheets and expense reports directly to designated approvers via Outlook.
- Audit trails and electronic signatures are stored for every time sheet, expense report, and invoice, creating a trail of responsibility for every item.
- Reports are provided on the firm's billable activities, simplifying the generation of invoices for managing partners of the firm.
- Invoices are stored in a client's folder, establishing an accessible invoice history.

Workflow
Includes the tasks, activities, and responsibilities required to execute each step in a business process.

Conclusion

When preparing legal documents, it is important for users to carefully review their work to ensure that metadata is deleted, old information is not left in documents, research is updated and current, and there are no typographical errors.

Key Terms

Calendaring
Decoding Key
Digital Signature
Docketing
Email
Encryption

Encryption Key
Facsimile (Fax)
HTML (Hypertext Markup Language)
Network Server
Personal Information Management
Phishing

Quick Part
Record Retention Policies
Spam
System Administrator
Workflow

Discussion Questions

1. What benefits are there to a firm using Microsoft Outlook? Provide an example to support your viewpoint.

2. Why should a firm use Outlook instead of just having a Gmail or Yahoo! account that they check in their browsers? Provide examples to support your viewpoint.

3. Take a moment and read the article "GMail Messages Read by Human Third Parties."[1] Identify the possible ethic violations if a law firm were to use Gmail.

Additional Resources

For your ease of reference, attached are two references to free Microsoft Custom Outlook Guides (basic and intermediate). Cut and paste the links into your browser:
    www.customguide.com/cheat-sheet/outlook-2019-basic-quick-reference.pdf
    www.customguide.com/cheat-sheet/outlook-2019-intermediate-quick-reference.pdf

---

[1]https://www.bbc.com/news/technology-44699263#:~:text=Google%20has%20confirmed%20that%20private%20emails%20sent%20and,given%20human%20staff%20permission%20to%20read%20their%20messages.

Chapter 4

Ethics and Professionalism

Learning Objectives

- Identify and explain the difference between legal ethics and professionalism.
- Become familiar with the American Bar Association's *Model Rules of Professional Conduct* along with the professional rules promulgated by NALA and NFPA.
- Explain the unauthorized practice of law and the attorney's supervisory responsibilities with paralegals and other legal team members.
- Identify ethical issues associated with technology and Internet communications.

NSLT Tasks Associated with This Chapter:

- Complete all learning modules and knowledge checks in the NSLT learning portal under OneNote and submit your completion certificate and software review.

Introduction

Today's law practice is filled with technological advances that allow attorneys and paralegals to collaborate and to work remotely on various tasks. First, it became almost impossible to practice law without a computer. Then it became necessary to have email, which in turn required Internet service. Then, as courts began to encourage and in some cases to require electronic filings (federal courts), computers and the Internet were essential. After that, it was all but malpractice not to use computerized citation checking. Electronic data production, storage, and communication broke the floodgates long ago. Today, many lawyers own their domain names, publish a Web page, participate in online forums or chat rooms, use online referral services, and transmit and store all documents electronically. Handling technological issues would seem to be outside the scope of practicing law, but it is not.

Technological skills are not lawyering skills, and it is not uncommon to hire paralegals with technology training and/or technology staff to assist with integrating technological advances within the law practice. Although the attorney must oversee the work to ensure that no ethical violations occur, delegation of this type of work would be appropriate. However, there are times when attorneys delegate duties that clearly must be performed by a licensed practitioner, and this can result in ethical violations. At other times, a lawyer's behavior may be not unethical but unprofessional. Lawyers are also responsible for every team member, including paralegals and legal assistants. Technology and Internet communications create additional ethical issues for the legal profession. This chapter provides a quick review of the code of professional conduct that attorneys must follow, focusing on rules that are commonly violated, including the unauthorized practice of law. Additionally, this chapter explores technology's impact on practicing law and client relations along with developing legal documents (templates) to protect client information.

Distinguishing Between Ethics and Professionalism

When evaluating ethics and professionalism in the law, these two concepts may at times overlap, but they are distinctly different. First, ethics or legal ethics addresses the standards of conduct (the duty) that lawyers shall maintain to ensure proper representation of their clients and the legal profession. This duty extends to the legal team, including paralegals, law clerks, and staff. The duties to protect the lawyer–client relationship, advocate for the client, and maintain professional conduct is set forth in rules that, if not followed, may result in disciplinary actions ranging from reprimands to disbarments. These rules, which set forth standards or guidelines, were promulgated by the *Model Rules of Professional Conduct* of the American Bar Association (ABA). All states have adopted these rules in some form, but it is each state, through its rules or laws, not the ABA, that will govern ethical violations by attorneys.

Ethics or Legal Ethics
The minimum standards of conduct required by an attorney in practicing law.

Professionalism or legal professionalism, on the other hand, focuses on how a lawyer should treat the profession and those involved with it. An immediate response about legal professionalism may be that the client should come first or even emphasize the importance of being an officer of the court. However, focusing on professionalism through the client does not consider the entire profession. Legal professionalism considers not only the lawyer's conduct but also the moral character and fitness of the lawyer within the legal profession. This will include everything from the lawyer's appearance to one's behavior, temperament, and demeanor.

Professionalism or Legal Professionalism
The proper morals and behavior one should exhibit in the representation of clients and the law profession.

Although legal ethics and professionalism are distinguishable, it is easy to see how the concepts overlap. If a lawyer acts unprofessionally, this will likely affect one's reputation and ability to grow a practice, but it does not mean that the lawyer has violated any ethical rules. In contrast, a lawyer who violates ethical rules will likely be seen as acting unprofessionally as well and be sanctioned for one's overall conduct.

Model Rules of Professional Conduct

The ABA was developed in the late 1800s with the goal of creating a national organization to unify the law profession. One of the most important purposes for the ABA was to create a set of rules and guidelines for lawyers to follow that would ensure the integrity of the profession and protect the public from any unscrupulous

Model Rules of Professional Conduct
The rules developed by the American Bar Association to govern the conduct of lawyers in practicing law.

behavior on the part of lawyers. The ABA initially developed the *Canons of Ethics* in the early 1900s, which over time and modifications became the *Model Rules of Professional Conduct*. Although membership in the ABA is voluntary and the ABA's *Model Rules* are suggested guidelines, over time, all states have adopted the ABA's *Model Rules*, almost verbatim. In doing so, the states enforce the rules through laws to discipline lawyers for unethical and unprofessional behavior.

The rules in general address the lawyer's responsibility to the profession and the public. They are written in such a way that certain rules are imperative, using the terms "shall" and "shall not" to impose disciplinary actions against a lawyer. Other rules use the term "may," indicating permissive requirements that a lawyer should consider in order to maintain professionalism with the practice of law. The rules are categorized with a focus on the various relationships that may exist between the lawyer and the public whom they will represent or interact with while practicing law.

Rule 1.1: Competence

Competence
Rule 1.1: A lawyer shall provide competent representation to a client. Competent representation requires the legal knowledge, skill, thoroughness, and preparation reasonably necessary for the representation.

Among those relationships with a lawyer is with that with the client. The first section of the model rules deals with the lawyer–client relationship. A lawyer must be competent to properly represent a client. **Competence** does not mean that a lawyer is required to have special training or prior experience to handle a legal matter for clients, but it does require the lawyer obtain the necessary knowledge about the law of a particular area. This can be done through research and study. In 2012, the ABA added comments to Rule 1.1 (Competence) as well as Rule 1.6 (Confidentiality) to include that lawyers must be responsible for maintaining technological competency.

Technological competency covers a wide spectrum of work performed in a law practice. Consider, for example, maintaining paper documents. If your documents are on a computer (entirely electronic), will there be any requirement to keep backup hard copies? Communications are no longer just phone calls and letters mailed to clients and other parties. They include emails and attachments in electronic form. Attorneys and their staff, including paralegals, must ensure that client communications are confidential and preserve attorney–client privilege. Something as simple as an "auto-reply to all" by a staff member responding to emails could destroy privilege and expose confidential information, which in turn may lead to a malpractice claim against the attorney.

Rule 1.6: Confidentiality

Confidentiality
Rule 1.6: A lawyer shall not reveal information relating to the representation of a client unless the client gives informed consent, or the disclosure is impliedly authorized in order to carry out the representation or otherwise permitted by rules.

Not only are electronic communications at issue, but access to online client files within the firm creates problems with **confidentiality** as well as potential conflicts. It is invaluable for the attorney and the staff to be familiar with methods to encrypt or protect access to avoid conflicts that could cause the attorney to be disqualified from client representation. Also, communications and information provided through a law firm's website have been the focus of much controversy, particularly in the area of unauthorized practice of law.

Rules 1.7—1.10: Conflict of Interest

Conflict of Interest
In law, representing one client that will directly and/or adversely affect the client's interest, the attorney, or another third party that is not a client.

Another area of ethical concern involves **conflicts of interest**. Although most if not all conflicts involve the lawyer's previous or ongoing client representations, paralegals may create conflicts since they often work with different law firms and/or lawyers. The new law firm or lawyer may find that after hiring the paralegal, that a current or potential new client has litigation matters that the paralegal worked on at their previous employer. At this point, the new employer must determine if they can avoid a conflict by preventing the paralegal from working on the case file. If not, the new employer may be prevented from continued or future representation with the client. If the paralegal fails to disclose working on a case file that is adverse to a current or new client, the law firm or lawyer may be disqualified from representation.

This can be problematic with freelance paralegals who work with multiple attorneys from different firms at the same time. The ABA's *Model Rules* address this problem, recognizing that conflicts are not cut and dry (meaning that if you represent or did represent a client, you can never represent a client that is an adverse party to them). There are options that includes client waivers and conflict checks within the firm to avoid interactions by another lawyer or paralegal with previous client relationships. Conflict checks or law firm screening are critical to avoid ethical issues that result in disqualifying not only the lawyer but also, in some cases, the entire law firm. If conflicts arise, prompt notice and immediate removal of the attorney and/or paralegal from the case could avoid disqualification under ethical rules.

What is the Unauthorized Practice of Law?

There are many areas in which paralegals and nonlawyer staff members assist attorneys in their law practice. Some of those areas include conducting legal research or drafting pleading. Paralegals are trained through education and internships to properly research and prepare legal documents. However, there are times when lawyers delegate duties to nonlawyers or give legal advice outside a jurisdiction where they are not authorized to practice law. This would be considered the unauthorized practice of law (UPL).

It is imperative that not only attorneys but also paralegals and other staff members understand what constitutes UPL. This means that members of the legal team, including paralegals, must be familiar with the rules so that they not only avoid performing tasks that would constitute UPL but also be able to support the attorney to ensure that client representation is properly handled and that attorney–client privilege is protected. UPL can occur not only when nonlawyers give legal advice but also when attorneys provide legal services in a jurisdiction where they have not been authorized to practice.

It is also the attorney's responsibility to supervise nonlawyer team members to ensure that their conduct would not result in UPL. This nonlawyer assistance responsibility is specifically set forth in the in the ABA's *Model Rules*. The ABA has noted that paralegals are responsible in their profession to be aware of what constitutes UPL and to make efforts to avoid it. There are times when workloads are overwhelming, and time crunches unavoidable. This is not the time to compromise ethics, but this is likely when such will occur. Having a paralegal run over to court to stand in for a hearing or to sign papers to file in court are examples of prohibited activities. Additionally, when clients are speaking with paralegals, they should not leave clients with the impression that they can advise or consult. This could happen when the lawyer has come to rely on an experienced paralegal. But this should never happen because it is UPL.

Unauthorized Practice of Law (UPL)

Rule 5.5: The practice of law by a person, typically a nonlawyer, not licensed or admitted to practice law in a given jurisdiction. This also applies to lawyers not admitted to practice in a particular jurisdiction as well as a disbarred or suspended lawyer.

Attorney–Client Privilege

A rule of evidence requiring that communications between a client and his or her attorney be kept confidential unless the client consents to disclosure.

Nonlawyer Assistant Responsibility

Rule 5.3: A requirement that lawyers having direct supervisory authority over nonlawyers make reasonable efforts to ensure that the person's conduct is compatible with the professional obligations of the lawyer.

Are Law Firm Website Chats UPL?

Law firm websites are often set up for live chats. When that operator icon appears with the comment "Can we help?" that open dialogue might be language constituting UPL. It is important to create responses that distinguish gathering information for the attorney to meet with a potential client to avoid any miscommunication that would establish the attorney–client relationship. Something that may create an attorney–client relationship and cross the line with UPL would be directly answering questions. Even though some questions may not necessarily be legal in nature, the context of asking questions within a potential representation inquiry could blur those lines.

Another issue that arises with website information is publishing newsletters about legal issues or blogs on legal topics. Lawyers must think about how the Internet will access clients outside of their jurisdiction and be careful when they do answers questions with clients, especially using online portals and the type of material they publish. Professor Lanctot's 1999 *Duke Law Review* article discussed the attorney–client relationship and cyberspace, noting that much of the live chat activities between attorneys and clients would be sufficient to form an attorney–client relationship. He pointed out that relationships arise when an individual believes the attorney will provide legal services they are requesting and the attorney either establishes an intent or fails to clarify that they do not intend to represent the individual. If the individual reasonably believes the services will be provided and the attorney failed to clearly establish otherwise, then a client relationship would be established. In short, when is a client a client? When the client believes the attorney represents them. Attorneys should make sure that websites and online chats are designed to avoid attorney–client relationships or UPL where they are not authorized or admitted to practice law. Additionally, they provide disclaimers with published material that it does not contain legal advice.

Tech this Out!

Chatbots and the UPL

With the onset of artificial intelligence, up pops the "chatbot!" So what exactly is a chatbot? The advances in technology have now expanded to preprogramed software that acts as a conversation piece to answer questions without a human involved. This should immediately raise a few eyebrows. First, how does this affect the legal profession and the unauthorized practice of law? Imagine that the computer is programmed with an if/then logic sequence (this should make lawyers shutter in fear recalling the LSAT). So, if a potential client accesses the law firm website and the automated chatbot" appears and then the potential client asks whether you handle bankruptcy cases" and the program responds with your programmed answer, "Yes," that seems generic. But then the potential client asks about the rates and how soon they can file their case. What now? Chatbots can be developed to answer many rule-based conversations that may seem generic and nonbinding, but has an attorney–client relationship been established? Is UPL being performed? And who is responsible?

Ethical Issues Involving Technology and the Law

Every advance in technology that impacts the practice of law will also impact competency and diligence required by the attorney in representing clients. Lawyers today must be able to perform basic online research activities and perform routine email and attachment functions with security features. Given the ABA's modification of competency and confidential rules regarding technology, lawyers now have a duty to gain technology experience in their law practice. Since documentation, advertising, communications, and court filings all have some aspect of technology tied to them, improper handling of matters in any of these areas could lead to ethics issues.

Cloud-Based Storage Issues

Since nearly every piece of documentation can be or is in electronic form these days, electronic storage of this information is a concern. Considering client confidentiality and privilege concerns, third-party storage services must be carefully evaluated to ensure that they understand how to protect data to avoid any breach in access to private client information. Security issues (cybersecurity) present additional concerns for attorneys and the law practice. The federal courts have been addressing this issue since the early 2000s when bankruptcy courts transitioned to the electronic court filing system. By 2006, the entire federal court system had incorporated the electronic filing system. Many security features have been implemented to protect data, including PDF (Portable Document Format) files used for submitted pleadings online and password-protected access. When considering third-party cloud storage services, many factors should be reviewed, including protected access, potential breach issues, licensing and user agreements, and cost.

Artificial Intelligence Issues

Legal research and discovery are essential parts of any law practice. Over the past 25 years, electronic databases have been developed by case law textbook companies to have all reported cases that lawyers use for research online and accessible from the Internet. Law libraries still exist, but it has not gone unnoticed that the stacks and shelves are absent of people. Computer terminals are constantly occupied, not necessarily in the library but anywhere the Internet is accessible. The technological advances of key words and connectors, along with voice-prompted inquiries, can perform research requests expeditiously. Artificial intelligence has also assisted with the efficiency of discovery in litigation, particularly eDiscovery. Using these tools has many benefits but must be handled with tremendous care and oversight. Recently, research and discovery have been compromised by an overreliance of systems to provide responses without proper review and oversight. In the end, attorneys, as well as their staff, must check the information to ensure proper details to avoid costly mistakes and disciplinary complaints.

Cell Phone and Videoconferencing Communications

With the technological advances of videoconferencing (Zoom and the like), court hearings, some trials, and status conferencing are routinely conducted remotely. Imagine that the office is shut down (not hard to do these days) and everyone is working remotely. The client has a few questions to ask the attorney, but the call is forwarded to a paralegal, maybe through FaceTime or Zoom. The paralegal tries to help the client with a few questions the client has. Think about how you would answer those questions. Some information, such as conveying information that the attorney directed, is fine. This is usually where attorneys cross the line and put paralegals who are not well trained into precarious situations. For example, telling a client a fixed-fee amount that has already been established by the attorney is simply conveying information. But when the attorney says, "You know, my general, rates; just see what they can afford!" you get the picture. Beyond communicating lawyer-specific information over a cell phone or by FaceTime or Zoom, we are faced with security issues over unsecure networks (outside the office), allowing the interception of a call from a third party. Or, better yet, you happen to take the call remotely—in a coffee shop! Attorney–client privilege is destroyed when a third party is privy to the confidential information.

Stop and Think!

Reflection on Social Situations

Another common occurrence takes place in social gatherings. There you are, partaking of a few spirits, and everyone's guard comes down. Suddenly, a very close friend introduces you to one of his close friends. They know you work for a prominent attorney who specializes in an area of law they need help with. They tell you about their problems and inform you that they do not know what to do. You immediately blurt out, "You should . . . (you tell them what to do). Then you tell them, "I'll just text my boss," which you proceed to do, with all the details. The boss responds, "Sure, no problem." And you communicate that to your close friend's friend. What have you done? People talk to each other like this every day. But, as a paralegal, you can't do that, You work in the legal community, and you are a professional. You must be aware of every word spoken to avoid misrepresentations or crossing the line to UPL. So how would you handle this situation?

Limited Licensed Professionals

Limited Licensed Professional

Legal permission to engage in a regulated activity on a limited basis.

Finally, it is worth discussing the emerging field of limited licensed professionals and how their services are delivered using the Internet. Paralegals in general are not licensed and therefore have no legal liability for their actions. The attorney is responsible for all members of the legal team and is the person subject to ethical violations that may result in sanctions against them. However, several states have limited licensing or commissioned positions that give nonattorneys authority to perform legal services in limited areas. As such, they are personally liable for their own actions. Many other states are exploring the idea of limited licensed professional to represent underserved communities in family law, landlord–tenant and contract agreements, and administrative law areas. For now, Washington State has limited Licensed Legal Technicians, Utah has Limited Paralegal Practitioners, and Arizona has Certified Legal Document Preparers. Most of these practitioners advertise on the Internet and offer document preparation and forms to help underrepresented groups with legal matters. As such, these individuals should be careful to review their state and local laws to avoid litigation and crossing the line to be found guilty of UPL.

Although all states have Notary Publics, most of whom sign documents acknowledging signatures only, Louisiana has bestowed on commissioned individuals a unique legal authority. Louisiana notaries, both lawyers and nonlawyers have the same legal authority which involved most aspect of civil law, outside of litigation practice in court. Louisiana Notaries can receive will, make protest, take depositions, and prepare contracts and all forms of writing. (RS 35.1, et. seq.). If you have ever attended an act of sale for a house or transferred title to a car in Louisiana, a Notary Public is required to pass those acts. Without a notary commission, an attorney is not authorized to perform those acts in Louisiana. Nonattorney notaries in Louisiana must sit and pass a very difficult examination to qualify and then must be bonded to ensure that the public is protected from any acts performed that may be improper or incorrect. Louisiana notaries are independently responsible for their own acts, and there are several notaries throughout the state who are also paralegals who work under attorneys. Attorneys must ensure that their acts, if conducted in the attorney's office, are insured and that there are clear lines distinguishing any of their notarial acts that are outside the scope of the law practice.

Conclusion

Understanding legal ethics and professionalism is essential to proper client representation and the practice of law. The *Model Rules of Professional Conduct*, developed by the ABA and adopted by the states, provide guidelines for attorneys and their legal teams to follow. The guidelines help to ensure that the public is safe from improper conduct by attorneys. Using of technology in the legal profession created additional ethical concerns that were addressed with amendments to the model rules (Rule 1.1). The amendments included technological competency requirements for lawyers and their legal teams to avoid ethical issues involving computer use and Internet communications. Creating templates with electronic software and restricting access are good solutions to avoid ethical problems with technology. Supervision is key to the effective employment of paralegals.

Key Terms

Attorney–Client Privilege
Competence
Conflict of Interest
Confidentiality

Ethics or Legal Ethics
Limited Licensed Professional
Model Rules of Professional Conduct
Nonlawyer Assistant Responsibility

Professionalism or Legal
   Professionalism
Unauthorized Practice of Law (UPL)

Discussion Questions

1. How has technology impacted the legal profession's ethical responsibilities to its clients and the practice of law?

2. What are some mistakes that lawyers and their legal teams make regarding social media? Make sure to provide examples.

3. How were the *Model Rules of Professional Conduct* impacted by technology issues with client communications? Make sure to provide examples.

4. Should attorneys develop strict guidelines for social media uses for themselves and their staff? Why or why not? Make sure to provide examples.

Additional Resources

American Bar Association - Model Rules of Professional Conduct
    https://www.americanbar.org/groups/professional_responsibility/publications/
    model_rules_of_professional_conduct/model_rules_of_professional_conduct_table_of_contents/
NALA - The Paralegal Association
    https://www.nala.org/certification/nala-code-ethics-and-professional-responsibility
National Federation of Paralegal Associations NFPA
    https://www.paralegals.org/files/Model_Code_of_Ethics_09_06.pdf

Chapter 5

Electronic Spreadsheet Uses in the Legal Profession

Learning Objectives

- Explain the function and purpose of electronic spreadsheets in the legal profession.
- Identify common and special features used in preparing electronic spreadsheets.
- Explain the benefits of properly preparing electronic spreadsheets to efficiently handle the data used for settlements and negotiations.

NSLT Tasks Associated with This Chapter:

- Complete all the modules and knowledge checks in the Microsoft Excel 2019 learning path in the NSLT's learning path.

Introduction

Electronic spreadsheet
A program used to perform numeric calculations as well as to analyze and present numeric data using formulas created within the program.

Most law offices fail to use **electronic spreadsheet** programs to their full potential. Electronic spreadsheets can be used to organize large amounts of data, but this only scratches the surface of the powerful features available with these programs. Electronic spreadsheets can be used to create calendar layouts with appointment and automated task features. Mostly, though, electronic spreadsheets are used to produce formulas that automatically calculate settlements and other financial documentation. A law practice can utilize electronic spreadsheets for budgets as well as calculations and data organization within the cases. Lawyers use electronic spreadsheets to calculate child support and alimony payments in domestic relations cases; to prepare amortization schedules, truth-in-lending statements, and loan calculations in real estate matters; and to estimate taxes and help prepare tax returns for tax matters.

Some examples of electronic spreadsheet programs used by lawyers and paralegals today are Microsoft Excel, Corel Quattro, and Google Sheets, with Excel being the preferred program. This chapter will explore the benefits of using spreadsheets and other features, such as tables and graphs for reporting and presentations for court and the law practice, in the legal profession.

Understanding the Function and Purpose of Electronic Spreadsheets, Precalculated Formulas, and Computations in the Law Office

Electronic spreadsheets have valuable functions in a law practice, but most lawyers do not take the time to learn how to use them. Ask most lawyers their thoughts about spreadsheets, and you will likely hear horror stories or fear about using them. It seems easier and quicker to manually calculate a list of expenses and figure out a percentage and then create a document and enter formulas that will automate the tasks. But these functions are routinely necessary for settlements and negotiations in litigation, requiring repetitive work that takes additional hours to complete. Electronic spreadsheets offer a solution to avoid re-creating the same document over and over as well as mistakes in calculations from manually entering data into a document. This will not only save time but also create a more efficient method to handle calculation tasks involving the practice of law.

Characteristics of Spreadsheets

A spreadsheet is a computerized version of an accountant's worksheet or ledger page. Spreadsheet software is used to create a spreadsheet, sometimes called a **worksheet**. In the past, worksheets were commonly referred to as ledgers, which was a sheet with lines that made up rows and columns. Each row that included figures and numbers would be manually added up for totals. This was extremely time consuming, especially if records needed to be added or calculation errors occurred.

Spreadsheets manipulate and process numbers, much like word processors manipulate and process words. With most application software programs, there are overlapping features that include copying, pasting, deleting, printing, and so on. When it comes to spreadsheets, the most notable characteristic that identifies it would be the **column** and **row** layout. The rows, which extend horizontally, and the columns, extending down the page vertically, are designed with the same features as paper versions. However, the electronic spreadsheet's rows and columns will continue indefinitely on the worksheet. That is just one of the many features unique to electronic spreadsheets.

The intersection of a row and a column in electronic spreadsheets is known as a **cell**. On a paper worksheet, this is the location where a specific item or number would be written down. With electronic spreadsheets, the information entered in the cell is identified by a **cell address**, usually represented by a row number and a column letter (e.g., "A1"). This is useful for locating specific information on a worksheet, especially when it contains large amounts of data. It is also helpful with finding a point on the worksheet that needs to be corrected. See Exhibit 5–1.

Worksheet
A "page" within an Excel workbook that contains columns, rows, and cells.

Column
A vertical series of cells in a table.

Row
The horizontal placement of cells in a table or worksheet.

Cell
A box formed by the intersection of a row and column in a worksheet or a table in which you enter information.

Cell address
The row and column location of a cell, usually expressed with column identifier first and row identifier second.

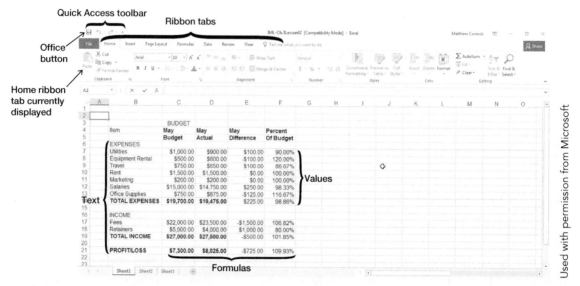

Exhibit 5–1 A simple spreadsheet using Microsoft Excel

Electronic spreadsheets offer easy and flexible methods to correct errors because entries can be edited, moved, or copied to other places or cells in the spreadsheet. If a record needs to be added, it is easy to insert additional rows and columns to accommodate the new information or delete unnecessary records. Once the details are entered, a cell can be formulated to perform functions such as adding, subtracting, divided, and averaging, to name just a few. When a formula is added to the cell, deleting, or including additional records with the column or row will automatically update to reflect the changes. After that, the numerical information can be presented using graphs and charts.

In the legal profession, gathering information is a critical part of properly handling clients and practicing law. Clients will have a volume of records and documents that must be reviewed. Before the advent of computers, lawyers would review documents and handwrite a list for maintaining records. But all that documentation needs to be organized and specific details extracted from the material. You could organize it using Microsoft Word and create a table. You can even add calculations in some fashion. Better yet, if the office has a sophisticated case management program, much of the documentation can be scanned and uploaded into the system, which is then populated into appropriate sections and calculation automatically performed where needed. However, most offices are equipped with application software that includes electronic spreadsheets, which lawyers or their staff can use to create a worksheet to list all the documents reviewed. Now, when clients bring additional records (because they never have everything you need), listing the new information will be quick and easy.

Stop and Think!

Are Google Sheets Sufficient for the Legal Profession?

Depending on the amount of data being entered or evaluated, Google Sheets could very well offer a small law practice or solo practitioner an economic alternative to proprietary software. Let's face it: Google Sheets are free, and that sounds great. For much of the work done in the legal profession, this is probably sufficient. And now that we are so Internet connected, it seems that being completely Web based is no longer a disadvantage. However, if you do not have access to the Internet, you have no access to the electronic spreadsheets. Imagine needing to meet a deadline to enter the data and create a settlement document and a severe weather storm knocks out Internet service. This is a problem to consider because a proprietary software program will also be on your local system and accessible without the Internet. But what about document security? Is your Google Sheets document as secure as using a document in Excel that is housed on your computer's hard drive? Can employee's at Google see your Google Sheets documents? This is an important thing to consider when selecting software since confidentiality is very important in the legal profession.

Electronic Spreadsheet Programs

There are several office suite programs that provide electronic spreadsheets. Along with Excel, there is Corel Quattro and Google Sheets to name a few. When working with electronic spreadsheets, it is important to establish some type of layout in the beginning so that you can develop a strategy for extracting relevant client information. Obviously, the layout will change depending on the litigation type, but at the very least, you will create column labels so that anyone entering data will know what information to use. Similar to boilerplate forms developed in Microsoft Word, creating templates in Excel is very useful. For example, having the calculation percentages for child support guidelines that are dictated by state law already set up in an Excel template allows the lawyer to simply open that Excel file and quickly plug in the income and percentages for the specific client. The information is immediately calculated, and then a new client file is saved, keeping the template for later use with a similar type of client case. In fact, Excel has volumes of prebuilt templates that can be easily modified so to fit your exact need. See Exhibit 5–2.

Label(s)
Refers to text that is typed into the cells of a spreadsheet; it has no numeric value and cannot be used in a formula or function.

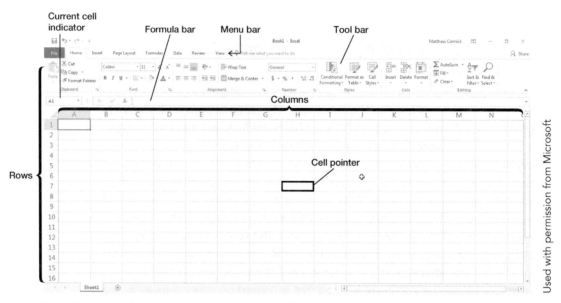

Exhibit 5–2 A simple spreadsheet using Microsoft Excel

Identify the Common and Special Features Used in Preparing Electronic Spreadsheets

One reason that lawyers avoid electronic spreadsheets and waste hours of time manually organizing documents is that they do not know where to start. It is not hard—it just takes a little organization and some familiarity with the office programs' functions. Once you have gathered the documentation, access the Excel program to start with a new spreadsheet document that will open a "blank" worksheet containing rows and columns with **gridlines**. Depending on the volume of records, you may want to add multiple sheets for different record types, such as a worksheet for phone records, one for medical records and expenses, one for witnesses, one for evidence, and so on. The additional worksheets added to the file are referred to as a **workbook**. At this point, familiarize yourself with the program's layout, starting with Excel's ribbon.

Microsoft Excel Ribbon

Microsoft Office Suite developed a ribbon interface designed with a similar look for all the products but distinguished by colors. On the Home menu in Microsoft Word, there are the common features associated with documents (font, paragraph styles, and so on). In Excel, the Home tab reflects common features associated with organizing (numbers, cells, alignment, editing, and so on). One tab that is on the Excel ribbon but not in Word is Formulas.

A **formula** is a sequence of values in Excel that allows the document to have automated features, such as addition and subtraction. Formulas in Excel and other electronic spreadsheet programs are expansive, and it requires advanced training to understand them all. But if you know what you need, locating it and entering a formula in a cell for functioning can be accomplished relatively quickly and easily. Formulas are automated in a cell by using the "=" symbol followed by a descriptive word, such as "SUM" (i.e., =SUM). The formula may also be entered using the **Formulas bar** located just below the ribbon. In fact, you can enter any data intended for the cell using the Formulas bar including **text**, **values**, and formulas.

Gridlines
The lines in a table that form the rows and columns.

Workbook
An Excel file with one or more worksheets.

Formula
A sequence of values, cell references, names, functions, or operators in a cell that together produce a new value. A formula always begins with an equal sign (=).

Formulas Bar
A bar located between the ribbon and the worksheet in which users can edit the contents of a cell.

Text
Descriptive data, such as headings and titles, used for reference purposes in a spreadsheet; cannot be used in making calculations.

Values
Numbers that are entered into a spreadsheet program for the purpose of making calculations.

Excel Quick Reference Guide

HOME RIBBON

NAVIGATION

Up One Screen	[Page Up]		To Cell A1	[Ctrl]+[Home]
Down One Screen	[Page Down]		To Last Cell with Data	[Ctrl]+[End]
Beginning of a Row	[Home]		Go To	[F5]
Cell Below Current Cell	[Enter]			

KEYBOARD SHORTCUTS

Copy Text	[Ctrl]+[C]		Undo a Command	[Ctrl]+[Z]
Paste Text	[Ctrl]+[V]		Redo/Repeat	[Ctrl]+[Y]
Cut Text	[Ctrl]+[X]		Print a Workbook	[Ctrl]+[P]
Bold Text	[Ctrl]+[B]		Save a Workbook	[Ctrl]+[S]
Underline Text	[Ctrl]+[U]		Open a Workbook	[Ctrl]+[O]
Italics Text	[Ctrl]+[I]		Find/Replace	[Ctrl]+[F]
Edit a Cell	[F2]		Absolute Cell Reference	[F4]

EXCEL FEATURES	COMMAND STRUCTURE
Absolute Cell Reference	(=B10*a1); $ signs represent an absolute cell reference, the F4 key will insert the $ signs in a formula.
Adjusting Column Width or Row Height	Drag the right border of the column header or the bottom border of the row header. Double-click to Auto Fit the column/row. Or **Home>Cells>Format>Cell Size**
Autofill	Point to the fill handle of the bottom corner of the cell(s), then drag to the destination cells(s).
Chart	**Insert>Charts>**
Clear Cell Contents	DEL key or **Home>Editing** group>**Clear, Clear Contents**
Clear Format	**Home>Editing>Clear>Clear Formats**
Delete Row/Column	**Home>Cells>Delete**
Edit a Cell	Select the cell and click the Formula bar to edit the contents or press [F2].
Find and Replace	**Home>Editing>Find & Select>Find or Replace**
Fit to One Page	**Page Layout>Scale to Fit Dialog Box Launcher>Fit To**
Format Cells	**Home>Font>Font Dialog Box Launcher>** or Right-click **Format Cells**
Formula	Select the cell where you want the formula, press = (equal), enter the formula, and press [ENTER] when done (e.g., =a1+a2; =a1*10). Excel performs operations in this order: ( ), :, %, ^, * and /, + and −.
Freeze Pane	**View>Window>Freeze Panes**
Functions	Click **Insert Function** icon next to the Formula bar; or **Formulas>Function Library>Insert function**
Hide/Unhide a Column	Right-click **Column Header>Hide**; right-click **Header>Unhide**; or **View>Window>Hide**
Insert Row/Column	**Home>Cells>insert**
Macro	**View>Macros>Macros**
Page Breaks for Printing	**Page Layout>Page Setup>Breaks** or **View>Workbook Views> Page Break Preview;** Drag page break indicator line to where you want the page break to occur.
Password Protect	**File tab, Save>Tools>General Options>Password to Open**
Total a Cell Range	Click the cell where you want the total inserted, click the AutoSum icon (**Home, Editing, Sum** icon), verify the range, and press [ENTER].
Worksheet Tab Name	Click Sheet1 name and type over it to rename.
Wrap Text	**Format>Cells>Alignment>Wrap Text**

Used with permission from Microsoft

Features of Excel Computation Formatting

When you are working with calculations, you can enter a formula using arithmetic calculations or the **function commands** in Excel. Electronic spreadsheets offer the ability to work with cells in groups or within a range. Although most formulas used in the legal profession are basic (addition, subtractions, averages, and so on), some are complicated, and manual entry of the arithmetic

Function Commands
A predefined calculation used in a spreadsheet program to speed up the process of entering complex formulas.

method may result in errors. Also, lengthy cell ranges would be unnecessarily repetitive and time consuming. Using the function commands simplifies the calculation activities. Some of the more common functions include the following:

- MAX, which computes the largest value within a range of values
- AVERAGE, which computes the average of a range of values
- SUM, which adds numbers in a range and computes the total
- COUNT, which counts the number of cells that contain numbers within a range

Features of Electronic Spreadsheet Formatting

After including the data and formulas, it may be desirable to add formatting to the columns and/or rows. For example, a column that reflects monetary values, such as bank balances, would be formatted to include the currency symbol, "$," for all the entries. This a common feature for Excel and appears on the ribbon's Home tab under Numbers.

Sometimes, it is necessary to rearrange the material because the layout is not working well. For example, you may want to shift all the data in Column B and have it displayed in Column C. With a paper form, this would be impossible—you would have to create an entirely new ledger spreadsheet. With electronic spreadsheets, this is easily done by selecting the entire column and performing a "cut," then "insert cut cells," to move everything. Then this little bit of information can be quickly converted into a visual representation by creating a chart.

One of the powerful features of Excel is its ability to predict information and display with a few clicks. By selecting (highlighting) a group of cells and then choosing an option (e.g., a chart), Excel offers a variety of styles to visually display those dates and numbers (e.g., bank statement dates and bank balances) over a specific period. Including a basic chart within an Excel spreadsheet is actually a simple process. It begins with highlighting the rows and columns of the information to use in the chart. Once the material is highlighted, the Excel menu will populate a dialog box that will offer various chart methods. You can display the material in graphs, pie charts, lines, and so on.

The chart and graph choices are flexible, but Excel offers suggestions based on the information being shown. For example, a line chart may be used to show an increase and/or decrease in numbers. A unique feature with lines includes sparklines that will embed the graphic display within the cell instead of a chart visually shown on the Excel document. Additionally, using a PivotTable will allow you to select a limited set of information to include in the graph or chart so that unnecessary material is not displayed.

Another prediction feature found in electronic spreadsheet software is the ability to determine sequential activities. For example, if you begin typing "January, February . . .," you can highlight those two months and extend the copy feature across or down, and Excel with automatically begin with March, continuing with April through December, and then start the process over across the highlighted cells chosen. This can be done with number and date sequences as well.

Sparkline
A tiny chart embedded in a cell that provides a visual representation of data.

PivotTable
An interactive, cross-tabulated Excel report that summarizes and analyzes data, such as database records, from various sources, including ones external to Excel.

Tech this Out!

Excel Practice Tips

Advanced preparation is key to a useful Excel spreadsheet. There are several practice tips to consider that will make creating a spreadsheet quick and easy. For starters, *leave room in the upper left corner*. Do not start your spreadsheet at the top corner (i.e., A1). Always leave room to add labels and notes. Remember that if you do start in the corner, you can always "insert" a row above and move the previously entered material down on the spreadsheet.

Consider another tip: adjusting formulas after inserting rows and columns. Inserting additional rows and columns after the spreadsheet is designed may interfere with formulas that are already part of the spreadsheet. Make sure to adjust formulas already entered so that the new additions are included. If not, you may find a lawsuit resulting from improper calculations.

There are useful tips with copy and paste features. Using features under the Paste Special menu option will give the user the option to cut, move, and/or copy material and include the formulas contained in the group or range of cells. This can be done between worksheets in the workbook. You can copy with formulas and then include the same formula on another sheet.

Cell widths should be used wisely so that you can print more columns on the document. When the heading or title description is too long, take advantage of the wrap text feature found on the Microsoft ribbon.

Additional tips to consider: filtering to only show only a portion of records in a large file. PivotTables are another method to organize and group a limited portion of records to evaluate or review.

Wrap text
A feature that allows text to be included with pictures, shapes, or tables without covering or hiding under the image, giving the user control over how the text is positioned.

Understand the Benefits of Properly Preparing Electronic Spreadsheets to Efficiently Handle the Data Used for Settlements and Negotiations

Manually preparing list and calculations from data that will then be entered on a document to present the information results in excessive hours of work that is likely not billable hours for attorneys, or clients will not want to pay for it, especially when they realize that a technology competency is required. A well-trained attorney or paralegal with skills preparing electronic spreadsheets can complete tasks using large amounts of data efficiently, saving time and money for the law firm. However, it does take planning.

Spreadsheet Preparation

Planning is important to create a spreadsheet that will reflect the intended purpose of the documentation. Drafting a layout for the spreadsheet in advance will be helpful to begin the process of entering the data. Keep in mind that the document will be used and reviewed by many parties, so it is better to keep it simple. Use headings and titles that are easy to understand and formulas that are specific for the tasks being used in the electronic spreadsheet.

Some basic methods for properly preparing a spreadsheet start with knowing what you want to do. For example, the spreadsheet might include data to calculate totals, or maybe there will be a need to average numbers or statistics, use date ranges or monthly reviews including calendar references, and perform tasks on specific dates. At this point, you should have an idea on the column labels, column formatting ($, text, dates, and so on), and how many columns are needed. The data will be entered on each row, which can go on indefinitely.

After determining what to do, consider what the input will be to include the proper formulas. Evaluate the source of information being used, such as numbers, receipts, income, monthly or yearly figures, database sources, and so on. Ultimately, you should understand what result will be accomplished with the data entered into the spreadsheet. The final results will likely be individual totals, grand totals or totals by ranges, averages, or specific categories. These results will determine what formulas are used in the spreadsheet (=SUM, =AVERAGE, =COUNT) cell configuration. See Exhibit 5–3.

Once the initial document is created, it should be saved as a template for future use. This will avoid having to rebuild the same spreadsheet. The labels and formulas can be added in the template and saved without any values. When the template is used by others for a specific client, the values are added, and then a new file is saved for the specific client. Remember that Microsoft Excel, as well as other application software programs, include predefined templates so creating a document from scratch is unnecessary. Make sure to include notes within the spreadsheet, using comment features, to explain any details about formulas and/or titles so that others understand the document. Notes are also helpful for the document creator when the form is not used on a regular basis.

It is important to make sure that the spreadsheet is functioning as intended. If there is a mistake with the formula, it may be difficult to recognize. Always test the formulas by entering data and use a calculator to confirm that formulas are accurate and that calculations are correctly performed. Most spreadsheets allow you to see the formulas entered instead of the calculations, which is helpful in

Exhibit 5–3

Entering arithmetic operator formula

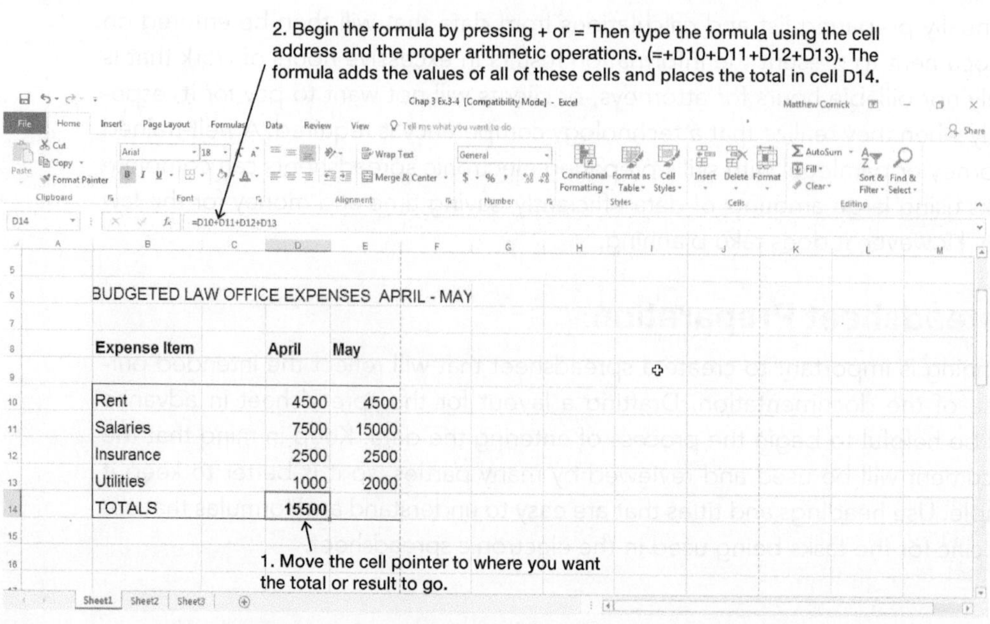

2. Begin the formula by pressing + or = Then type the formula using the cell address and the proper arithmetic operations. (=+D10+D11+D12+D13). The formula adds the values of all of these cells and places the total in cell D14.

1. Move the cell pointer to where you want the total or result to go.

checking the logic and formulas of your spreadsheet. If it necessary to audit formulas, it can be done through the Formula tab on the ribbon by clicking on Show Formula in the Formula Audit group.

Collaborate Work on Spreadsheets

Now consider that the data to enter include thousands of pages and cannot be accomplished by one person over the next few days to meet a deadline. The Excel document can be placed in the share drive (OneDrive or Google Drive), and everyone can work on the same file at the same time. It does not matter how the information is entered because after everything in listed, it can be rearranged (sorted or **filtered**) using whatever any method that produces the desired result. When the worksheet is finished, only one document is saved.

Concerns with Spreadsheet Preparation

Some concerns regarding spreadsheets are accuracy and competence. Errors not only cause issues with improper information being provided that may result in monetary settlements but also may create ethical problems. Unfortunately, often when paralegals work with spreadsheets, they are not working only with raw numbers, mathematics, and research—they are working with spreadsheets that relate to actual money and financial projections that have a dollar impact.

Most spreadsheet users fail to understand the likelihood of spreadsheet errors or the absolute importance of careful quality control of every spreadsheet, no matter how small. Surprisingly, spreadsheet errors are relatively high: about 5 percent, or one error for every 20 cells. Every study that has been conducted on spreadsheet errors has found that error rates would be unacceptable in most organizations.

To avoid potential errors, it is important to double-check all numbers that are entered into a spreadsheet for accuracy and to triple-check every single formula in a spreadsheet, including using the Formula Auditing mode to print out all formulas. Additional proofing actions would include making comments in specific cells regarding assumptions and creating notes at either the top or the bottom of the spreadsheet for readers and users to review. Finally, be extremely careful when adding rows or columns to a spreadsheet in which formulas already exist. It is also recommended to have someone else review the spreadsheet and formulas for proper function.

Security features are also prudent functions to include with electronic spreadsheets. Use the Protect feature to protect cells, particularly formulas, from being changed accidentally. If working with a spreadsheet is outside your knowledge base or comfort zone, ask your supervising attorney to get an expert, such as an accountant or a financial analyst, to prepare and/or review the calculations. In the end, it is far cheaper to do this than to discover an error later.

Passwords are an easy way to increase the security of your documents. Password protecting spreadsheets is easy to do and should always be done if the spreadsheet is going outside of the firm. You can also protect specific cells and even portions of the spreadsheet when multiple people work on it. This will avoid formulas from accidentally being deleted or changed. In Excel, for example, to protect all or part of a spreadsheet, you simply turn on the protection feature under Review on the ribbon.

Filter
To display only the rows in a list that satisfy the conditions you specify. You use the AutoFilter command to display rows that match one or more specific values, calculated values, or conditions.

Conclusion

Attorneys and paralegals can use spreadsheets to perform and track a huge variety of information, including damages calculations, budget plans and problems, and tax plans and tax return calculations. Spreadsheets also include graphs and charts so that large amounts of data can be visually demonstrated for a clearer understanding of the information.

Most people use only a small portion of the commands, formulas, and functions that are available with electronic spreadsheets. However, as you become more proficient with the software, many of the more advanced features will become recognizable. It is beneficial to take time viewing instructional videos and reading the Help features to develop additional skills that in turn create efficiency in the law profession. It is important for end users to adapt to software changes and updates. It is also important to evaluate the equipment to determine compatibility with software updates.

Key Terms

Cell	Formulas Bar	Sparkline
Cell address	Function Command	Text
Column	Gridlines	Values
Electronic spreadsheet	Label(s)	Workbook
Filter	PivotTable	Worksheet
Formula	Row	Wrap text

Discussion Questions

1. How do electronic spreadsheets benefit the law practice?

2. What are the parts of a spreadsheet and the steps required to create it, including information that should be conveyed?

3. How much of the spreadsheet can be set up ahead of time? What data fields will be left open? Explain with examples.

4. Should attorneys use spreadsheets in a settlement negotiation, and will this be helpful in managing the negotiations? Explain why or why not. Make sure to provide examples.

Additional Resources

Using Excel in the Legal Profession
   https://youtu.be/TDWhZlfY3T0

Finding and Reviewing Comment boxes in Excel Files
   Blog posted on January 25, 2018 by excelesquire (Ben Kusmin)
   https://excelesquire.wordpress.com/2018/01/25/finding-and-reviewing-comment-boxes-in-excel-files/

Highlight Every Other Row of a Privilege Log (or other spreadsheet)
   Blog posted on January 10, 2017 by excelesquire (Ben Kusmin)
   https://excelesquire.wordpress.com/2017/01/10/highlight-every-other-row-of-a-privilege-log-or-other-spreadsheet/

Chapter 6

Electronic Databases and Utility Programs in the Legal Profession (Blockchain Technology)

Learning Objectives

- Explain the benefits of using database programs in the legal profession.
- Identify various utility programs used within computer systems and software programs.
- Recognize the importance of utility programs used in the legal profession.

NSLT Tasks Associated with This Chapter:

- Complete all learning modules and knowledge checks in the NSLT learning portal under Workshare and submit your completion certificate and software review.

Introduction

Gathering and organizing client information is tedious. This is also true when conducting legal research and preparing for trials. Although lawyers and law firms still maintain physical files and records, most if not all of this documentation is additionally maintained on computers. The use of computer technology in the legal profession relies heavily on **database** programs to efficiently maintain client records. Database programs are invaluable for running an efficient law practice with today's technological advances. So, it is important to understand them and their uses. Along with understanding databases, it is also important to identify and recognize the value of utility program in the legal profession. Data are sent, received, and shared over the Internet, creating the need to protect and preserve confidential client information. Utility programs offer solutions to accomplish this task.

Database
A collection of organized data, generally collected in tables, that allows access, retrieval, and use of data.

Understanding Electronic Database Programs

Technology is rapidly expanding before our eyes. Much like the uncharted depths of the ocean, technology remains vastly undiscovered. However, as we start to learn more, we quickly see how technology can be used to our advantage (rather than being a detriment), such as using database programs to organize daily workloads and the massive amounts of records to review. These systems have transformed the way legal teams keep track of their clients' information. They offer a solution to old-school physical spreadsheets and ensure that sensitive client information is protected. Databases are the future of legal aid, so start learning about them and using them to your advantage today.

Benefits of Electronic Databases

Databases can be infinitely helpful in the legal field. They make it easier to analyze, configure, optimize, and maintain information on your clients within your computer. You can think of databases in terms of paper copies as well. For example, a phone book lays out every number and name following a certain structure. Also, the library follows a database for keeping track of what cards are checked in and out to know what is in stock. In this way, a database is like a spreadsheet, with some variations regarding terminology of its parts. For example, a **table** consists of data arranged in horizontal rows and vertical columns. A **field** is a single characteristic of data that appears in a table as a column, and a **record** is a collection of fields that appear in a row in a database or table. Digital databases help you not only organize client information but also automate, search, and use other important functions.

A **Database Management System** help lawyers and law firms keep track of client data and synthesize information. A database management system allows the administration of databases. This can include defining the database, creating it, querying it, and updating it along the way. Database management systems can also validate, convert, and expand data from existing databases to encompass additional information entered, maintaining and updating client information that previously existed. A few examples of database management systems that you may want to evaluate are Microsoft SQL Server, Microsoft Access, Oracle, SAP, and others. These are just some of the functions of a database management system and how you can help your database work to its best ability for you.

Components of Databases

Now that we know what a database is, let's look further into what makes up the database software. We can start with software as an important component for databases. There are various programs that help your database operate more efficiently, such as the database management software mentioned earlier. Also, the database operating system itself, along with the network used to share and communicate the database with others in your office, is an important component of databases. However, the database components really start with the software.

Next, there is the hardware that runs the database that we can operate from. These are the physical electronic devices, such as computers, input-output devices, and storage devices. Any physical electronic equipment used in conjunction with the database can be considered hardware. Not surprisingly, the

---

Table

An arrangement of data made up of horizontal rows and vertical columns.

Field

A single characteristic of data that appears in a table as a column.

Record

A collection of fields that appear as a row in a database or table.

Database Management System (DBMS)

A software program that handle the storage, retrieval, and updating of data in a computer system.

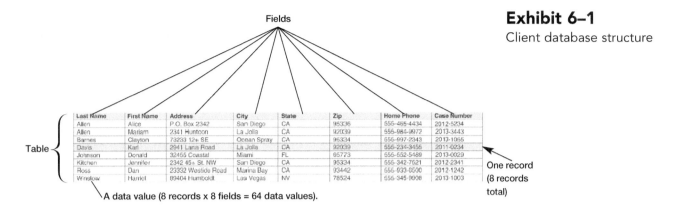

Exhibit 6–1
Client database structure

next component is data. Already in the first part of database's name, data are what are stored in your database. See Exhibit 6–1.

We then have procedures, which are the instructions and rules that come alongside of the database, for the user's convenience. The user will also have database access language to use for adding, changing, and updating data. These are commands that turn the database into a readable format that was formerly coded for safety purposes. When there is talk of coding, you may often see references to Extensible Markup Language (XML). Along with reading the data, data must be in a format that is transmissible. XML is the markup language designed to carry the data. If this sounds a bit confusing and you have a question, that is where the query processor comes in. This tool can help you find the information you need with step-by-step plans.

The runtime database manager is the central control of the database and where the user can control how the information in the database is stored and protected from outside forces. Then the data manager makes sure all the information is backed up on the server in case of an emergency. The database engine controls processing, storing, and securing data. The data dictionary is similar to the physical spreadsheet of the database. This logs all the information in the database into rows and columns. However, it is more for the database itself to keep track of information, not the user. Finally, the report generator is a component of the database that lawyers find extremely important because it can take information from various files and convert it to be used in a specified format. There are many components and functions of a database, each working in harmony to keep your database running optimally.

Data

As it relates to computers, these are facts, figures, or information that may be in the form of text documents, images, audio, software programs, and so on that are stored in or used by a computer.

Extensible Markup Language (XML)

A way of writing data in a document for tagging and creating formats to identify and describe information.

How to Set Up and Use a Database

There are a ton of database sites you can use to get started with your clients and your overall firm's progress toward a better-run electronic spreadsheet system. Picking your program, downloading, and getting started are the main steps you have to take for a database system. Here are some tips when setting one up.

Learning Databases

You can also use databases for learning. This can come in handy when you are in law school or if you need to refresh on a certain concept. Databases can give you all the information you are looking for in one concise place. To start, try a free legal database before you try a paid subscription. Many universities have free legal databases. This is a great way to start your research, figure out the system, and decide | whether you like it prior to paying fees for a paid subscription. Also, local law libraries have a variety of legal materials, such as legal encyclopedias, practitioner guides, and continuing legal education resources. This is going back to the physical copy but can be good to start with to compare your ease of experience from using hardcover books to using online databases.

Regarding free databases, you do not have to create an account or sign in for most free databases. Many come with effective but basic search engines. This leads us to the advantage of paid legal databases. For the paid experience, you will get access to legal forms, more historical cases, and more secondary sources with explanations, such as law journals and treatises. The advantage of a paid database is the ability to find a broad range of topics as well as being able to plug in your own findings. Also, learning databases can provide annotated versions of the U.S. Code. This way, you can search for your topic and read directly from the primary source U.S. Code. The annotations help you out even further by giving you an explanation and guide to the more complex legal language in the code. Many other primary sources also have hyperlinks to follow on materials. Here, you can learn more in depth about the topic you are looking for versus what you would find using a standard search engine.

Also, paid sites have more sophisticated search engines. Many also have citation generators that will pull the most up-to-date sources as materials that are updated regularly. With a free site, you would have to search for updated materials and not rely on the first source that arises. Databases update frequently, so make sure a provider still offers what you are looking for before paying for a subscription, especially for an ongoing commitment. These are learning databases and can help you alongside the traditionally discussed databases.

Marketing and Management Databases

There are several ways that law firms can grow their practice. Law firms should have an online presence on reputable social media sites as well as create their own website. The online presence for a law firm should be recognizable with a clear and professional branding and logo, be easy to navigate, and reflect the services specialized in. However, once you have achieved that status, the focus should be on maintaining your current client base and attracting new clients. Building a client database is an important step in this process.

First, add to your database the clients and contacts you already have in your Outlook contacts. These contacts may not have a legal need currently but reminding them of your services will increase the likelihood that they will reach out to you should the need arise; they may also pass your information on to their own contacts for their legal needs. As you gather more contacts in the normal course of your workday, remember to add them to Outlook and to your client database.

Send out a firm newsletter on a regular basis and have a link on your website to sign up for distribution of that letter. Add all interest clicks to your database as well. Have a call to action on your social media accounts that will link to your newsletter sign-up. Any interest, no matter how immaterial, may lead to a paid client in the future.

Tech this Out!

Seeing Double? Digital Twin Technology

Much of the work with data entry is done collaboratively, with those responsible for supplying the data often located in multiple areas, throughout the office, or even around the world. These parties are developing workloads and products that should be reviewed or tested prior to the material being released. Digital twin technology is a virtual model of the process service or product. A "digital twin" is a connection between the physical material and the digital material. When data are being reviewed or created for demonstrative or analytical purposes, the twin component can be used from gathering real-time information and then transmitting after review to the physical component. Ultimately, creating a "digital twin" of data, it can be analyzed for accuracy in the virtual world before it is released to others. This will allow the parties to evaluate their existing product or service to perform better and create new business. In the legal profession, this will help build and develop a law practice that has more benefit and profitability for continued success. Imagine being able to correctly evaluate what areas of law to focus on or even how many lawyers to employ for each area (as well as support staff) and having the information evaluated before it becomes incorporated with the actual data so that it can be tweaked to reflect the best light for growing the law practice. Digital twin technology offers that option. To better understand the full benefits of digital twin technology, check out the March 2017 Forbes article "What Is Digital Twin Technology—And Why Is It So Important?"

Types of Client Database Software

Before technology, law firms kept their client databases in a Rolodex, handwriting the potential client's information on individual cards and risking human error in transposing numbers. Next came the Excel spreadsheets that many firms still use. However, there are many client database software systems that may save the law firm time and accuracy. These software systems will help you track contact information and the history of transactions with your firm. You can also use this software to compile thank-you acknowledgments for generating leads.

Find a database tool that works for you. You will want to consider a few key factors. Is the user interface clean and modern? A good database management system will look easy to use, and clean and clear instructions will be available. Is the system easy to manipulate, or will there be extensive training involved? Databases will have a slight learning curve like all technology, but overall, you want it to serve you without being too complex. Will the client database be secure in the cloud so that you can access it anywhere? Can you access the database through an app? How is the database backed up? Does the search function allow for a wide array of capabilities? These are a few questions you'll need to ask about the functionality of the system as a whole and the different capabilities. Next, will the database easily integrate with your other software? Finally, how expensive is the software on initial purchase as well as through regular subscription fees? Good database management software will be sold at a fair price. An initial purchase will typically be less expensive than subscription because it's a one-time payment rather than reoccurring.

Overall, the system that matches your needs will be up to you, but here are a few client database software systems worth looking into for your firm:

- Monday.com: 14-day free trial and $17 per month thereafter for two users
- Zoho CRM: 15-day free trial and $14 per month thereafter for a single user
- Kintone: 30-day free trial and $24 per month thereafter per user with a five-user minimum
- Keap CRM: 14-day free trial and $79 per month thereafter for a single user
- Streak CRM: 14-day free trial and $15 per month thereafter for a single user
- Tray.io: 14-day free trial and $595 per month thereafter
- NoCRM.io: 15-day free trial and $12 per month thereafter for a single user
- Airtable: $10 per month for a single user
- All Clients: 14-day free trial and $29 per month thereafter for a single user
- Pipeline Deals: 14-day free trial and $25 per month thereafter for a single user

As you can see, the pricing will vary, sometimes greatly, for these client database software systems. Do thorough research to see what the benefits of the increased costs are and whether those benefits are necessary for your firm at this time.

How Databases Protect Client Information

Law firms are not immune and can become a victim to cyber-attacks. Because of this, its important firms are aware of the various ways they can become a victim to cyber-attacks, how to arm their databases against cyber-attacks, and how databases can actually help keep the client's information protected. When you think about it, an encrypted database is far safer than a physical spreadsheet of sensitive information, so do not be afraid to incorporate it into your practice.

This can start with malware that affects the integrity of the system the firm is using. Malware (short for "malicious software") does harm to a system or its data on the system. This can consist of viruses, ransomware, bots, spyware, and more. These can then block access to your hard drive or copy important client information to another hard drive. When malware has affected your computer, some signs will be shown. A virus can cause your computer or technology to run slower, send emails without your permission or creation, randomly reboot your system, and start unknown processes. It is important to be aware that these are signs that your information may be at risk and that you should act now to protect your clients.

The next way that your system may be hacked into is through phishing. This is less likely to affect your firm if everyone on your team is technically competent. Phishing is when a person steals your information by pretending to be a trusted person or legitimate website link. This typically will not be a huge problem for your firm itself but can be a problem for your clients. Unknowingly, clients may supply information over email if a hacker is impersonating your firm. To avoid this from happening, tell your clients from the start that all the information they supply will be done so through confidential means and will be stored in protected databases. This way, the client knows that if they get a suspicious message, they should ignore it.

Another way a hacker can steal sensitive information is through an eaves-dropping tactic. This can happen by someone hacking into a call between you and your client. This is why information that's private to the client, such as Social Security numbers, should not be given over the phone. Letting your client know this also allows them to stay safe from phishing phone calls from hackers pretending to be your firm. Make sure your clients are aware of the protection that comes with working with your firm and are aware of how to not get roped into a situation that could be dangerous for both them and you.

Knowing the ways that hackers operate can allow you to better prepare both you and your client for what a cyber-attack looks like and how to operate around it in the most efficient fashion. Now that you know what to expect from hackers, it's time to make your database difficult to get into. Databases already have some protection built in, but you can ensure that yours is fully protected by following these steps.

Making Your Database Bulletproof

This starts with your passwords to get into the database. Make sure your passwords are strong. This means using multiple numbers, characters, and letters. Store the password in a secure location. This will help make sure that no one can hack into your database. Also, enable two-factor authentication. This allows you to gain access to a site only when you pass through these two forms of authentication. This is an extra wall that hackers must break through and keeps your client's information safe. According to Microsoft, 99.9 percent of all cyber-attacks can be stopped by simply installing two-factor authentication.

Next, make an email policy across your firm that mandates using strong passwords and other security up front so that hackers cannot find information about your firm through an employee or phish clients through your firm's email address. The same can be applied for having a personal device policy. Whether it is a laptop, phone, or otherwise, all electronic equipment should adhere to the same policies to protect the database and email. Also, make sure to enable firewalls and antivirus protection on all the computers in your firm, personal or otherwise.

Security policies are put in place to serve as a first line of defense before the hacker even has the chance to get into the database. This includes training on awareness of social engineering threats. Malware protection policies should also be in place across the board. Also, software installation and removal processes should be customary for onboarding and offboarding new employees and when new software is added to your firm.

These policies will outline a clear standard across your firm. However, you will need to back it up with security awareness training. If your firm is unaware of security risks, they are more likely to not stick completely to the security policies, so make them aware. The best way to do this is right from the start of hiring a new employee. Here, you can have a baseline test that can assess whether they are likely to fail a phishing test. Like we said earlier, technically competent lawyers will have no problem passing a phishing simulation. However, if they fail, there is work that still needs to be taught.

From here, train your employees through interactive modules, games, videos, posters, and other interactive and inviting learning tools to help educate them on the latest cyber-attacks and how to stay safe from them. Then test to see how well the employees perform on a simulated phishing attack. Finally, look over the results and continue to work on different goals in protecting against cyber-crimes. The up-front cost you will spend on training will be leveled out by the amount you save by not having to pay for cyber-attacks.

Consider performing assessments about vulnerability in your computers to make sure everything is running at top speed. This can be done through various online programs with a simple search.

Database Security

When it comes to the database itself, you want to make sure your database protects many things. Your database software should be protected through two-factor authentication, strong passwords, antivirus software, and more. You can use database management systems, like we talked about earlier, to make sure your information is stored correctly. It is important that the data within the database is protected all the same. Associated applications on the computer are also important to be protected, as is the actual physical device itself, as discussed above.

It is important to keep all these systems up to date and protected, but, overall, databases are one of the safest ways to store your data on your clients. Here are a few more ways you can make sure your database is secure as can be.

Make Separate Database and Web Servers

This can mean keeping your database server in a secure and locked environment, but, even better, you should have your database on a separate physical electronic device from where your Web queries and searches happen. A Web server is more likely to be attacked compared to a traditional server, so prepare for it to happen and keep your database completely separate.

Update and Monitor

Regular updates to your system can help make sure that your database and computer attached will not be hacked into. This means also regularly updating the antivirus software and other protection patches you have available. Do not forget about third-party applications. They may require updates separate from your computer and entire database.

Also, make sure to monitor the activity that happens in your database. With consistent surveillance of your database, you can spot suspicious activity from the start and stop it right away. This allows you to get a head start on protecting the system if it has been compromised. It is important to watch out for suspicious activity coming from your employees as well. This sometimes can happen by accident but still should be dealt with immediately.

Encrypt Data and Backup Data

Encryption
A process of encoding messages to keep them secret, so only "authorized" parties can read it.

You should make sure that your firm is encrypting not only the stored data in the database but also data that are in transit. As well as encryption, you should back up data on a separate secure hard drive. Following all these steps will ensure that your database is nearly impossible to break into. This way, you can rest easy knowing that your client's information is safe and that your firm will not be liable to any acts of misconduct.

Electronic Databases and the Legal Profession

Electronic databases have transformed the way that lawyers manage data in their profession. For all professions, databases can be helpful in some form to secure and store information in a safe, reliable, and trustworthy manner. This is true for the legal profession as well. Specific to the legal profession, databases have allowed for multiple automation practices that have allowed lawyers to operate more seamlessly.

Lawyers can use databases to document current or recent laws and historic laws. Some databases cover British laws, something that is helpful for researching the origins of many U.S. laws. For lawyers, it is important to understand the processes and rationales for making the laws originally. The database can house all this information for an entire firm to look over and have on hand.

Databases are also used to manage case law for attorneys to quickly access. For example, lawyers as well as the public can access U.S. Supreme Court cases free of charge. This database covers each case taken up by the Supreme Court in detail, including parties to the case, the lower-court location information, and the votes of the justices and the dissenting opinions. Like the Supreme Court database system, even small legal firms can keep track of their cases in a similar fashion with the help of databases.

Along with case law, databases can also be helpful for legal treatises. Legal treatises are not primary legal sources, nor are they intended for any direct reliance on them. However, they can be used to help understand laws and provide an explanation in simpler terms. Databases are special in how they can extract information for use in report generation, as seen through legal treatises. Also, for federal, state, and provincial legislative journals, a database can provide an in-depth analysis and critique of legal topics. The lawyer can then find primary sources through the references used in journals.

The databases can also be used to store client information. Since the client's information is sensitive and of the upmost importance, databases keep it safe from hackers. Also, if a client uses your services again, you already have their information safely on hand. This reduces the amount of copying, pasting, and regurgitating of information that someone must perform. These are just some of the ways databases are transforming how lawyers manage and keep track of data. No longer are physical copies necessary for lawyers. Everything now can be automated online with the help of databases.

A great database and utility software that lawyers should try out in their firm is FileMaker Pro. This system allows you to manage all your client's contact information from one place, track your assets, and organize your cases from the past and upcoming cases for your clients. Most important, it allows you to create reports. Databases are great tools for generating reports. Traditionally, the legal team would have to enter all the information themselves. However, databases do the busywork for you by formatting and creating the report with the information you already plugged into the database.

When using databases such as FileMaker Pro, it is best to input that data from the start. When you come across important information that relates to the case, plug it into the database. You will find that if you do this at the beginning of the case with all your information, toward the middle and the end, the data will become infinitely useful in analyzing, organizing, and creating reports from the

Stop and Think!

When You Redact Material, Is It Really Gone?

Sensitive and confidential information can be found in many records, such as Social Security and bank account numbers or medical histories and diagnoses. In the legal profession, documentation is transmitted between the parties in litigation, particularly during the discovery stage. But not everything contained in the document or record must be disclosed. Redacting the privilege or confidential information is the method used to protect the information within a record that should not be shared. But is the material truly hidden and unavailable to be seen? That will depend on the procedures used to perform the redaction. Just because the protected information is "blacked out" does not necessarily mean it is gone. In many cases, the blacked-out area is just a cover over the confidential material and can be removed to reveal to protected information. This is because the blacked-out area is just covered and not really deleted. Proper redaction is usually done in multiple steps, which include covering the material, applying redaction to the area for permanent removal, and then, in most cases, cleaning or sanitizing the document to remove the metadata associated with the redacted information. So, when you look at some documents where redactions were performed, is the material really gone?

Redaction
The removal of confidential information from a "protected" document.

data. This way, all the information on your clients is stored in one place, and you can automatically make documents and records from the pre-logged data. All of this can help you better represent your client every step of the way.

Since you can hold sensitive data, such as Social Security numbers, in the database, client information your client's information is safe from the risk of a breach by hackers. You can store your client's name, address, Social Security number, and more. Then, when it is time to make a report, you can use a database, such as FileMaker Pro, to effortlessly complete forms and save a bunch of time and mindless copying and pasting on your end. In this way, technology helps us rather than replaces us.

Traditionally, you would have to search for the information, copy and paste it, and format the report exactly how you would like it. This could take up to an hour for a single form. Rather than go through all of this, lawyers can complete a form in mere minutes with database software. Also, since a computer is creating the document, human errors are avoided. This means that you will have not only documents that are ready faster but also documents that are of better quality and data available for future products and use.

It is important when making these additions to your database that you automate them into the database as soon as they arrive. That way, if you need it in the future, it is right there. Automating information into the database may be annoying at first because it takes time at the start. However, you will save countless hours of busywork if you get it out of the way from the start. Overall, databases are a key tool for lawyers to use. Not only do they make the processes involved day to day easier, but they also allow for time-saving practices that allow you to focus on work that really matters. Technology is here to aid you in your job, not take away from the great work you are doing. Use it to your best advantage.

Identifying Utility Programs and Their Benefits

Databases are a form of utility software. Utility software helps your computer run at top capacity. This consists of a variety of tools that help your computer run better than before and help you keep track of your information better. These tools are called **utility software** because they perform services for the computer. Just like your lights, water, sewer, and other utilities in your house that provide services to keep your life running smoothly, utility software does the same for your computer. Utility software performs computer maintenance, including, among other functions, data compression, disk defragmentation, data recovery, and system diagnosis. Other types of utility software, outside of databases, are also available. For example, disk cleaners are used to find and delete unnecessary or unwanted files, and antivirus protection utility software helps fight against malware that could otherwise infect your computer. Archive systems put various files together and into one archive. This tool is great for transportation of files and storage under one place. Another utility software that lawyers find helpful is File Manager. This tool can save you a ton of time by managing the files and folders you have. This software can create, open, rename, move, copy, delete, and search for any item you need at any time. The list of utility software available is expansive. However, we are focusing here on databases as a key utility software used with the practice of law.

A large part of practicing law is document preparation, which occurs with multiple people and on multiple computers. Many application software programs have built-in features that provide utility functions, such as "document comparison" in word processing software. This feature will cross-check a document's newer version against previous ones for various changes. These changes could include the inadvertent omission of a word or the inclusion of new words, sentences, clauses, or paragraphs; grammatical changes; and font or spacing changes. This process is often referred to by lawyers as "redlining." Lawyers are particularly interested in seeing specific differences between documents, such as contracts, in order to protect their clients. Other built-in utility features within application software include "search" and "find" options.

Document preparation also includes making sure that files are in a readable or accessible format for a recipient who does not have the program used to create the file. When a file is created in a specific program, the file's format is connected, or in **native format**, to that program's system. If the recipient does not have the program on their computer, one cannot access the file to view or edit. To resolve this program, Adobe created a format program known as called **Portable Document Format (PDF)**. Adobe's PDF program converts a document created in other programs from its native format to an accessible format that all recipients can view and/or edit, depending on the Adobe version. Adobe has a reader version that anyone can access for free. For more advanced features that allow edits and conversion features, there is a cost for the software. Nuance is another PDF program available to use for converting files from native formats for viewing.

In many cases, you still may have a document in hard copy that needs to be sent to other parties. **Scanning** is process that allows you to copy the file in a format that will be saved to the computer, most often either in a picture format

Utility Software
Programs that help analyze, configure, optimize, or maintain computer systems and their performance. The programs usually focus the computer's infrastructure (hardware, operating system, data storage, and application software).

Native Format
A file structure created in a specified application.

Portable Document Format (PDF)
A format that allows a document to be read and viewed from any computer regardless of the original program that created the document.

Scanning
Paper documents converted to electronic format.

(JPEG) or in a PDF. Once the file is saved on the computer, it can be sent to the recipient through email or saved to a flash drive or in the cloud on a shared drive.

When the recipient is viewing a file that has been scanned with images, they will not be able to search the file electronically because it will not recognize the images when the file is being searched. Searching the file is a common process in litigation discovery. Adobe's technology known as **Optical Character Recognition (OCR)** includes features that translate the images so that they can be read and edited. The recipient can use OCR to scan the electronic document that contains text and images. After the OCR scan is completed, the system will recognize the image in a readable format to locate specific information within the file that otherwise would require a manual document review. This is a time-saving feature with the discovery process, especially when handling large volumes of electronic records.

Blockchain Technology

Encrypting and protecting data are critical to every aspect of our daily lives and crucial to protecting client confidentiality in the legal profession. In seems that hackers are constantly breaching security features from financial institutions to industry operating systems and even high-level government operations. Each time hackers interfere or infiltrate security systems, there is an immediate focus to create additional security layers to prevent a reoccurrence of those breaches. **Blockchain Technology** is the latest development of cybersecurity protection.

When anyone hears the term "blockchain," the first thing that probably comes to mind is "bitcoin." That is because blockchain encryption was developed to handle ledger transactions of cryptocurrency, or digital currency. Digital currency provides a method to transmit payments between parties with different currencies without relying on government authorities to regulate the currency values. However, blockchain technology has valuable uses not only in currency transmission but also in data transmission in general.

A blockchain, as the two words originally used separately would suggest, is a digital ledger of records or "blocks" that creates an audit trail for the recipient to verify through time stamping. The blockchain is managed using a peer-to-peer review, and each time-stamped block or record is received and verified by the peer users in the chain. The blocks are recorded over several computers so that a block transmission cannot be altered. Participants in the blockchain can verify the transmission independently, reducing the costs of monitoring system data and security features. The blocks hold batches of transactions that are encoded for security.

When data are stored across network through multiple parties in the chain, the data become decentralized, which in turn avoids many risks associated with centralized systems being hacked. In the legal practice, this is extremely valuable to secure confidential records stored not only on the law firm's main system but also in the cloud for backup.

Optical Character Recognition (OCR)
Technology that can translate a scanned document image into text that can be edited and formatted.

Blockchain Technology
A type of database (collection of information) that is structured into chunks of information that are "chained" together, creating an irreversible timeline of data that are added to the database.

Conclusion

Database software is here to stay. Say good-bye to faulty spreadsheets and logs and files of information. Technology has allowed us to do much with the information we have and the tools that are given to us, and databases are no exception. They can be a great tool to store all your client's important information in a safe and secure manner. Client confidentiality is important, and through databases and the protective measures you take part in to protect your computer, you can safely keep all your client's information protected and secure from hackers. The more you become accustomed to how technology can benefit you, the more you will learn that, overall, it is here to help you grow stronger in your work by doing the busywork for you.

Key Terms

Blockchain Technology	Extensive Markup Language (XML)	Record
Data	Field	Redaction
Database	Native Format	Scanning
Database Management System	Optical Character Recognition (OCR)	Table
Encryption	Portable Document Format (PDF)	Utility Software

Discussion Questions

1. How have electronic databases impacted data management in the legal profession?

2. What are the database functions and components?

3. How would the legal team use a database (i.e., how would plan and set up a database)?

4. How have database security features benefited the protection of client information in a law practice?

5. Do electronic databases help to prevent conflicts in client representation? Explain why or why not. Make sure to provide examples.

Additional Resources

Types of utility software and their usage

RJ Frometa November 5, 2019
   https://ventsmagazine.com/2019/11/05/types-of-utility-software-and-their-usage

Utility Software (You Tube Video)
   https://www.youtube.com/watch?v=w8E7t7a6-mA&t=3s

What is utility software? (You Tube Video)
   https://www.youtube.com/watch?v=m6acF6MfYwA&t=1s

Chapter 7

Office Management and Case Management Systems Used in the Legal Profession

Learning Objectives

- Recognize office and case management programs used in the legal profession.
- Identify collaborative activities performed with case management systems.

NSLT Tasks Associated with This Chapter:

- Complete all learning modules and knowledge checks in the NSLT learning portal under CLIO and submit your completion certificate and software review.

Introduction

One of the worst feelings is finishing up a job, only for your coworker to tell you that he or she did the same job 10 times faster and far more efficiently than you. While we cannot take back time and do the project smarter, we can learn how to work more efficiently in the future. This all starts with office and case management systems that prioritize doing the annoying work for you. Legal professionals can find great help in these systems that are designed for an efficient work flow. These management systems can help you not only with your work flow but also with your firm's overall flow. Scheduling, billing, and other business logistics can be automated and completed smoother now more than ever. Technology is seeping into the legal world for the better.

What Are Office and Case Management Systems?

There are both office and case management systems that can help you with any **matters** you are dealing with. In simple terms, a case management system helps you and the firm out with all legal matters in terms of storage and organization. The office management system helps you from the business side of things, organizing your calendars, time sheets, and more. Both serve different roles in the legal world.

Case Management Systems

Your **Case Management System (CMS)** is the central repository that will help you manage all case and client documents maintained by your law firm. All matters, such as items, cases, files, or projects for the firm, can be found in the case management system. Your case management system will be created through a **Database Management System (DBMS)**. The DBMS creates, reads, updates, and deletes data in a database while controlling access and security.

A DBMS is central to a great law firm. Virtualizing your practice is essential in the modern world. There are tons of forms, information, and other vital papers you must keep track of in your practice. A DBMS helps you easily track and handle any old papers, forms, and matters you have. It also can create new documents while managing and organizing the old with the new. As your firm and client list grows, you will need to manage it accordingly. DBMS helps you keep this organization and management central to your practice, even as it grows. The DBMS helps store documents and manage and organize those documents. Rather than throwing it all into one bin, you can sort it into categories and manage it.

Components of a Database Management System

At the core of the DBMS is organization. When the legal world was all paper, stacks of documents would be organized based on various criteria. The same thing is achieved with DBMS, but it is automatic and more streamlined than traditional methods of organizing work. Legal-centric DBMS are great at creating lists of documents based on client or a matter of your choosing.

Also, instead of thumbing through a ton of files trying to find the paper you are searching for, with DBMS systems you can use the index and search functions. Through this, you can perform searches across all your files to easily find the documents you need. Version management is another benefit of the DBMS. This gives you the ability to see previous versions and notes on new versions. Rather than keeping a ton of drafts and staying up to date with the newest version in multiple places, you can keep everything on the same file.

These files can also be shared with anyone you give access to. However, there is also the lock document feature for when you are working on a document and do not want the rest of your legal team to try working on the document at the same time you are. Once you are done, you can turn off the lock function and let your coworkers access the document as well. Also, you can share documents off the platform easily with transfer tools. Microsoft Office allows you to directly save to your computer, and Outlook transfer allows you to directly email the content you have been working on. The formatting does not change, so it is a swift conversion.

Matters
Any item, case, file, or project that you need to track.

Case Management System (CMS)
Central repository to manage all client documents maintained by the lawyer or law firm.

Database Management System (DBMS)
A software program that handles the storage, retrieval, and updating of data in a computer system.

Source: PMS software

Optical Character Recognition (OCR)

A technology that allows the text of documents to be read or scanned into a computer so the text of the document can be searched or brought into a word processor to be edited.

You can also tag documents to find them easier. You can add classifications to documents stating the document types, statuses, and other classifications. This can help you quickly locate documents that are similar to the tag you searched for in the database. Also, **Optical Character Recognition (OCR)** is a tool that most DBMS have and is extremely helpful for the legal field. The OCR system allows you to convert scanned documents into text-enabled and searchable documents. This is just one of the many ways that DBMS systems do the tedious work for you. They allow you to focus on the work that matters while they optimize the files. Rather than typing in and formatting a previously physical document, the OCR scans it in for you.

Practice Management Systems

A case management system helps you organize your work and legal matters, such as cases. These are extremely helpful in making work more efficient and optimized for you. Another tool that lawyers have at their disposal are office management systems, also known as **Practice Management System (PMS)**. While a CMS organizes cases and client information, PMS manages the business side of the firm. This is a great additional system for your firm to use alone or alongside the case management system. Not only is it important to optimize your individual work and your coworker's work, but it is also important to optimize how your firm runs. The more efficient the entire firm is, the smoother your casework can be handled. See Exhibit 7–1.

Practice Management System (PMS)

Central repository to manage case files and the business side of the law practice.

Components of and Practice Management Software

PMS software helps you with various tools to run your firm. For example, you can keep a database of your clients' information here. You can store both client information and contact forms for each client you have in your practice. This can be helpful for referencing in the future. Also, you can store a collection of all your firm's cases in this software. A case database contains unique details of various

Exhibit 7–1 Law Firm Activities

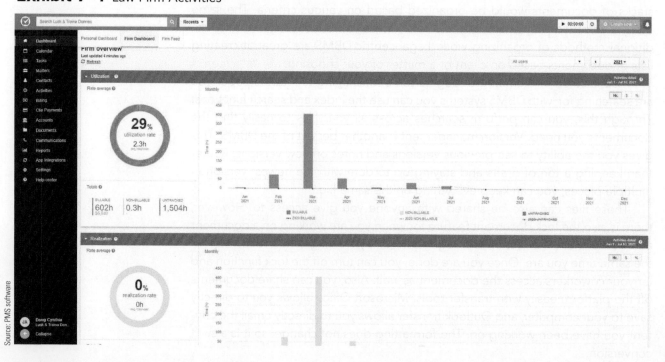

areas of law and types of cases. This can give you the entire record of what your firm has done. You will never know when you will need to reference either of these items, so having them on hand is a must in your practice.

Another side to the PMS is more firm-centric. There are many ways to ensure that everyone in your firm is on the same page and has coexisting schedules and such throughout the year. The PMS has tools like a virtual calendar on it. Rather than an old-school paper calendar, this calendar can go with you anywhere. It can act as a firm-wide calendar and a deadline management calendar. This way, your firm can be on the same page about what is happening and when. It is easier to schedule this way and can help you avoid common scheduling blunders.

PMS software also has time-tracking components that can be especially helpful for the business of the firm. These time-tracking tools help you keep a record of billable and nonbillable hours among all your employees. This allows you to easily bill clients by making invoices online. With PMS software, you can form and assemble new documents. Even better, this is an automatic process. You will not have to manually enter and formulate every document and contract because there are basic templates out there for you to use.

This expedites the process and makes your firm run a bit smoother. Both systems have their unique qualities that help you run your legal practice in a way that works for you, not against you. There are pros to both, so it is up to you to decide whether you want one or both of each system.

Which System Do I Need?

Both the case management system and the office management system can help you streamline your business to make everything function far more efficiently for you and everyone in your firm. You need them only to enhance your practice, not reinvent the wheel. If you have a system that works better than these automated digital systems, then stick with it. However, once you get past the learning curve and can use these management systems flawlessly, you will find that they are far better at helping you finish your work in comparison to the old system you had.

As mentioned previously, there are a few things that distinguish office management software from the case management software. You may need to invest in office management software if your firm needs a bit more help in terms of tracking time, creating invoices, managing the business side of your practice, managing cases and calendars, and overall organizing the business side of your operation.

You need a **Document Management System (DMS)** to store and organize docs and emails, manage document versions, OCR docs, and index and search documents. Basically, the DMS lets you work efficiently. With these two varying functions in mind, both are equally important to creating a successful practice. However, if you already have a system like this that works for you, you may need to implement only one of these. Office needs vary firm to firm, so decide what your office can improve on.

What you get with these systems are simple **e-repositories**. In today's world, we have many examples of e-repository systems. These are basically Web- or cloud-based services that store electronic information. This electronic information can be brought with you anywhere. Rather than being locked to a desk and chair in your office, you can now go remote with your work. In our changing world, this is more important than ever.

Document Management System (DMS)
A system used to receive, track, manage, and store digital documents. Most are capable of keeping a record of the various versions created by different users.

e-repositories
Web- or cloud-based services that store electronic information.

Integrated Database Systems
The sharing of different functions within multiple databases.

Having multiple databases is important to keeping all your information bundled up neatly and set aside according to different matters that describe the case or matter. These **Integrated Database Systems** allow the sharing of different functions within multiple databases. These systems will easily take your work to the next level through having this system entirely online. It is worth it in the end to invest in these systems if you do not have them. The key word is "investing" because you will end up getting a good bit of your money back from improving your work flow and showing your clients that you are armed with the latest legal technology to help them with their cases.

Many times, firms are hesitant about whether they should incorporate new technology into their law practice or just stick with "what works." Often, people are afraid of this change because they have gotten complacent with the system that they have. It is the old phrase, "If it isn't broke, don't fix it." However, your outdated system is broken. It is old and breaking down as the world speeds up around it. The truth is that office and case management software has become vital in running a law practice and your firm will wholly benefit from its addition into your office.

Who Practice and Case Management Systems Can Help

These systems can be used by any law firm, big or small. No matter what your situation is, these systems can help. If you are inherently not organized, these systems are for you. You may find that the main problems that arise in your firm are about missing items, arguments over information your coworker was supposed to keep memorized, and where that one contract is. By opening one system, you can convert over all your files easily and start having one database to check back on when you cannot find that one paper. Rather than searching for it manually, all you must do now is type the key word into the search engine, and poof! There it is.

Also, if your firm does not have a lead tracker, these systems can help. The more people reach out about your firm, the more successful it is. You can keep track of how well you are doing through these legal software systems. When you have all your leads in one place, you can easily track, organize them, and work to make the leads official clients. With using a manual system, human error may stop you from catching all the leads. Leave the checking and double-checking up to the management system.

This is the same for the expense tracker. Particularly with practice management systems, one of the key features is the ability to track where your money is going and what is coming back in return. Often, marketing efforts end up wasting money rather than bringing money in. You want to make sure you are getting a good return on every investment you make. With practice management systems, you can track your expenses, growth, and overall performance of your campaigns and expenses. This will lead you toward growth rather than loss.

Also, if you want to go remote but have not yet found a way to do so, management systems are your solution. Almost any office you ask says that they have gone at least partially remote. Do not fall behind with your firm. When you have digital files stored in the cloud, you can access your work at any time. Whether this be while you are traveling, are at home and are reminded of something late at night, or just need to pull up a document when not at work, you can do so with these new systems.

Simplified Client Communication

Clients today want to communicate with their legal team the same way they communicate with others in their life: through text messages and phone apps. The law firm helps an app designer to design a custom app branded with their firm's logo and information. The law firm's app is synchronized with their respective practice management platform, such as Clio. Clients will then be able to message with their attorney within the app. Clients view their matter calendar for scheduled events created by the firm and upload documents to their case file using their phone's camera and the app's document upload technology. Clients can view and complete tasks created by their attorney and view and pay their outstanding bills securely within the app. This means that anyone, anywhere, can have access to their case information when and where they need it most without even contacting their attorney. This application is changing the way clients communicate with lawyers. What is your preferred method of communication? When you need something, are you more prone to picking up the phone and making a call, or do you prefer to send a text message?

How Have Practice and Case Management Software Impacted the Practice of Law?

Practice and case management software have fully reinvented the way that lawyers work. However, this is a welcomed change that could not come soon enough. With practice and case management software, the daily struggles of the workplace are eased. This is not to say that all problems are expelled. The same problems exist now, but management systems help us solve them more efficiently. They have made daily tasks easier and how the firm runs much smoother. This is great in our digital age of constant change and collaboration through technology.

When clients know that your firm is organized and using the latest technology to your advantage, more trust is built between you and your clients. They will know they are in good hands and can relax and let you do what you do best. This client satisfaction can also turn into repeat clientele or new clients who find out about your firm through word of mouth and great reviews.

The reason these systems can help you manage your work more efficiently is through the automated work flow they provide. Less time is wasted on punching in numbers, searching through paper files, and overall engaging in busywork. These systems now make the process of formatting contracts and other files easier than ever. The search function also allows you to waste no time scrambling for that one document. Instead, you can easily locate it through the database along with all your other files.

This access to everything from one place is helpful when it comes to organizing your firm and making sure all employees are on the same page. Since everything is in one place, you can send and collaborate on projects much easier. The back and forth is all done online, so you do not even have to be in the same office to work on a case. See Exhibit 7–2.

Exhibit 7-2 Sample Case File

Source: PMS software

This can also expedite communication between the client and lawyer. Rather than having to commute to the office and meet with your client, you can now do much of this work virtually. This allows your schedule to be more flexible with your client's schedule since you do not have to take into consideration commute times between the two of you.

You are also able to work on the case from anywhere. This allows lawyers to do some of the work at home or while traveling. Since the database is secure, it is now an option to take work outside of the office. We know from this past year with COVID-19 that remote work has become far more popular and essential. There is no reason that lawyers should have to sit this change out anymore. This still allows your firm to operate out of the office if you choose to, but it also gives that second option of remote work to your staff that needs it. More flexibility is a great perk that comes with this change.

You ultimately end up saving time by optimizing your time. You are still doing the same amount of work that you were before. There are still the same hurdles you previously came across. However, now you can automate some parts of the process, find information more quickly, and have your mind put at ease by the organization that the systems offer. It is less about the amount of work and more about the steps you take to complete it. Office and case management software allow you to get the same amount of work done in far less time, saving you hours in the day.

This allows you to provide a better service to your clients that will increase your visibility in the world. For your firm to keep growing, it must continue to use the latest technology to keep up with the competition. We all want to be the best, get the work done well, and avoid problems. Managing software is your solution to these daily struggles that may arise. You can even have documents such as intake forms at the ready to send to your client. Then you can easily store them with all the additional information on your client moving forward.

This software focuses on the details of your job so that you can focus on running your law firm. Busywork can take more out of us than we realize. When we spend a good part of our day dealing with details rather than the big picture, we can quickly lose steam. Software enables you to focus on the human element of your law practice rather than details that can be picked up and completed just as well by a system as by the human mind. These systems are not a replacement to lawyers. We fully need human minds in legal practice for the system to stay afloat. What this managing software allows is an alternative to work that is mindless and that does not serve your end goal.

Since you can share case files easily and securely, you can also see who did what work and when rather than relying on memory alone. It is unreliable to expect humans in your firm to remember random numbers and dates you throw at them on top of the information they already must hold in their brains. Now, these systems allow you to keep everything in a place that you know is secure and well maintained.

You can easily search files throughout the system as well. For example, a **conflict report generator** is a great feature built into most case management software. This feature allows you to sort names of parties and clients to identify similar names or cases. This can be a good way to cross-reference cases, train employees, and look back on cases that are similar to the one you might be working on now. The benefits to practice and case management software are endless for legal practitioners. As technology evolves, we are sure to see changes in how we handle our work. It is important that we move with these changes rather than against them. It will only end up benefiting you and your practice in the end, so get to using these systems today to better your firm overall.

Conflict Report Generator
A program for sorting names of parties and clients to identify similar names or cases.

How Vital Are Time Records and Calendaring in the Practice of Law?

No matter how small or large your firm is, you can benefit from the help of **calendaring** systems and time record keeping online. This is vital in almost every job environment, and that includes in the practice of law. These services can help you level up your entire office. When your staff is on the same page and able to get into a pattern that works for the benefit of both the employee individually and the entire firm, great things can happen.

If you want to increase your revenue, you will have to update the way you do business. You cannot expect change to just happen and customers to fly in through the door. However, when you start managing your time better with online time records and calendaring services, you can efficiently bring in new customers and help increase your revenue by promoting your use of these services. Soon, your time management will allow you to spend more time on your customers' needs rather than your booking mishaps and scheduling blunders.

Also, having an online calendar makes collaboration for your team easier. When you have the option to schedule yourself at a time that works for you, it allows your employees to work more often because it is at times that work for them. Online calendars allow you to easily create appointments that work for both you and your coworkers. Since everyone will have their schedules set, it is easier to see who is available and when. Also, if something comes up, appointments can easily be changed to a new time.

Calendaring
A term used to describe the function of recording appointments for any type of business.

You can also avoid double bookings by using an online management service. Rather than accidentally double booking and not noticing that until it's too late, with a management system you will be alerted of this with a warning right from when you try to schedule the second, conflicting date. This can also help you out if you have an assistant. The assistant can make all your appointments in one place and know your schedule without asking you whether a certain date is okay. The managing software will easily tell them this.

Also, on the day of a meeting, you can be sent a reminder. Rather than having to check in your physical calendar for what time something is, you will be alerted the same way you would if an email were sent to you. You can also use **rules-based calendaring**. Rules-based calendaring is when a certain event takes place, such as a deposition or hearing, a number of calendar items are generated. For example if a deposition is being set, the rule may provide the following events be automatically calendared at the proper times, send deposition notice, serve subpoena, prepare deposition outline, notify court reporter, confirm appearance with deponent and adverse attorney, etc. This way, you know that you will be notified of that important event you need to attend.

You can also easily convert an appointment entry into a billing entry. Since it is all done from one site, you do not have to move back and forth from one folder to the next like you would with physical documents. With a simple click, you have converted your appointments into billing entries. This can be useful for **timekeeping**. You need to bill your clients, and you will want to make sure it is the right amount to keep your great reputation. Using calendar managing systems and time records can allow you to effortlessly track time for the purpose of billing clients.

Beyond being able to easily enter billing information, you also can track on the go. No more waiting to get back to the office or rushing to do work at the office so you can leave before rush hour. This makes it less likely that you will lose track of billable time, making everyone a lot happier.

You can also keep a strong time line of the case. All the facts of the case are logged with chronological listings of what has happened with the case, both old and new updates. This can help you see an overall picture of where the case was and where it is headed. You can also specifically mark any events in the case on your calendar. Any appointments, tasks, reminders, or things to do that are scheduled for specific dates can be logged and looked back on in your calendar. Overall, this helps you manage your deadlines better. Nothing can sneak up on you when you have a clear vision of what is in the past, present, and future of your work.

You can also more easily delegate your work to others. Delegating work can be a great way to free up your schedule and give those who want to learn from you a chance to complete work that may be on a higher level than what they are used to. With good software, you can list tasks by staff, category, and subject matter. This allows you to organize who does what in the most efficient way.

Finally, accounting is available on some systems to keep track of your books more seamlessly. This is an extra perk of the system. You can keep track of important information by keeping the records online. For example, a **check register** or book in which you keep records of checks, deposits, debit card transactions, and ATM withdrawals can be stored in the database and referenced when it comes time to do taxes. This makes it much easier on you and your accountant when it comes time.

Rules-Based Calendaring
When a certain event takes place, such as a deposition or hearing, a number of calendar items are generated.

Timekeeping
Tracking time for the purpose of billing clients.

Check Register
The book in which you keep records of checks, deposits, debit card transactions, and ATM withdrawals.

All journals you have of accounting records and transactions can be kept in a location that you know is secure and that will work for your firm. Calendaring and timekeeping services help you push your firm to the next level. We have all heard the phrase "time is money." Help your firm manage its time better and bring in more revenue by moving your processes online for a more efficient work flow.

Tech this Out!

Billseye.com

Billseye (Billseye.com) offers the first and only real-time mobile-call billing solution, allowing for the billing of client calls with the touch of a button on your cell phone. In the legal industry, attorneys lose millions of dollars annually from unbilled client calls. Some experts have estimated that approximately 40 percent of mobile calls with clients go unbilled. Mobile client calls are on the rise, making this an increasing problem. Billseye's slick user interface, integrated into your mobile phone, will allow you to bill mobile calls in real time with the touch of a single button. It is as easy as answering a phone call!

Conclusion

Case and practice management systems can help you level up your firm. While there are no hard-and-fast rules saying that you must have a management system, you are sure to succeed a whole lot more with one. The systems are not necessary for every attorney and/or law office to use, but they are necessary if you want your firm to operate the best. There is a reason that these systems are on the map.

Think about your previous (or current) system. In its old-fashioned way, the system relied on physical documents and the control of these papers. This means large file cabinets, messy desks, management of paper files, and communication through physical calendars. Beyond these burdensome material items, the old system also required a great deal of trust to be placed on the memory of your staff. There were no backups if the physical copy was lost, no way to have another form of checking whether the information logged was correct, and no reminders for when your scheduling might conflict with a prior engagement.

However, with case and practice management systems, all the information is stored in one place, giving you control and organization over all your cases. This is the future of the legal practice and will be a technology tool that is expected to be increasingly used for the benefit of your entire legal team. Start training your staff today and make the switch to a system that makes work easier on you and your firm.

Key Terms

Calendaring
Case Management System (CMS)
Check Register
Conflict Report Generator
Database Management System
 (DBMS)

Document Management System
 (DMS)
e-repositories
Integrated Database Systems
Matters
Optical Character Recognition (OCR)

Practice Management System (PMS)
Rules-Based Calendaring
Timekeeping

Discussion Questions

1. How have law practice and case management software impacted the practice of law?

2. What distinguishes practice management software from case management software? Explain similarities and differences with examples.

3. How vital are time records and calendaring in the practice of law? Make sure to provide examples.

4. Is it necessary that every attorney and/or law office use software programs to manage the law practice? Explain why or why not. Make sure to provide examples.

Additional Resources

The ins and outs of law practice management software
   By Nicole Black, January 11, 2019
   https://www.abajournal.com/news/article/the-ins-and-outs-of-law-practice-management-software

The latest on legal document management software
   By Nicole Black, April 27, 2020
   https://www.abajournal.com/web/article/the-latest-on-legal-document-management-software

Resolving Conflict: Another Case for Case Management
   By Deborah Tesser and Allan Mackenzie, January 12, 2018
   https://www.lawpracticetoday.org/article/resolving-conflict-case-management/

Law Practice Management Systems
   By Tom Caffey
   https://www.americanbar.org/groups/gpsolo/publications/gp_solo/2018/july-august
   /law-practice-management-systems/

Abacus Law-Management Systems (YouTube Video)
   Case Management
   https://www.youtube.com/watch?v=vDba-Vl4ZGw&t=1s

How to Start a New Case in Abacus Law Using Intake Forms
   https://www.youtube.com/watch?v=DV5H5BC_1eU&t=1s

Practice Management vs. Document Management Software—What's the Difference
   By Dennis Dimka
   https://lexworkplace.com/2019/07/20/practice-management-vs-document-management-for-law-firms/

2019 Practice Management
   TECHREPORT 2019
   By Alexander Paykin
   https://www.americanbar.org/groups/law_practice/publications/techreport/abatechreport2019
   /practicemgmt2019/
   November 6, 2019

Chapter 8

Document Management Systems and Document Automation

Learning Objectives

- Communicate the growing need for document management systems in the legal profession.
- Explain how law firms use document management systems to support their law practice.
- Evaluate and list the benefits of a cloud-based document management system.

NSLT Tasks Associated with This Chapter:

- Complete all learning modules and knowledge checks in the NSLT learning portal under iManage. Submit your completion certificate and software review.
- Complete all learning modules and knowledge checks in the NSLT learning portal under Worldox. Submit your completion certificate and software review.

The Growing Demand of a Document Management System in the Law Profession

Ever wondered what happened to that old filing cabinet? How about your mother's recipe book or the old family photo album? Well, say good-bye to the paper clutter. There is no need to stack up those papers and photos any longer—the age of digitalization is here. Welcome to our move into a paperless world!

Years ago, homes and businesses relied on paper-based principles to manage their records, but with the growing volume, velocity, and variety of information, they began to search for a more practical alternative to handling and storing large volumes of paper documents.

Document Management System (DMS)

A system used to receive, track, manage, and store digital documents. Most are capable of keeping a record of the various versions created by different users.

Today, a **Document Management System (DMS)** is the use of a computer system and software to store, manage, and track electronic documents. Images and information can be easily captured, stored, and retrieved in a simpler, faster, and more economical way, solving the problem of physical storage space and location. At the touch of a button, documents can be filed, duplicated, accessed, or shared at a greater speed, helping to bring them into one place quickly, easily, and securely.

How Firms Use a Document Management System

An effective document management system is a necessity to functionality in the legal profession. Law firms today use several different technologies to manage their practices and cases. They receive, produce, and process all kinds of data and information, including documents, video and audio files, emails, and notes. DMS offers law practices a simple way to use, save, access, and organize their documents without the extra expense of physical storage cabinets and additional employees while promoting efficiency in the workplace. They extract valuable data to improve business decisions and collaborate with clients, law partners, and other employees. Using a DMS enables firms to minimize costs, decrease risks, and grow their business, all while building a larger clientele.

An effective DMS allows your law office to do the following:

- Manage document and electronic file forms
- Increase efficiency within your organization
- Maintain multiple client accounts
- Retrieve files within seconds
- Collaborate and share documents
- Protect all confidential information
- Reduces your risk of noncompliance by retaining documents

Stop and Think!

Life in the Cloud

"Cloud based" is a term that refers to applications or files made available to users via the Internet from an Internet-connected provider's servers. Companies typically utilize cloud-based services to increase storage or computing capacity, enhance functionality, or easily access documents and information on demand from any location without having to commit to potentially expensive computer infrastructure. Cloud computing makes data backup, disaster recovery, and business continuity easier and less expensive. Data can be stored at multiple redundant sites on the cloud provider's network. Many cloud providers offer a broad set of policies, technologies, and controls that strengthen your firm's document security protocols, helping protect your data from potential threats, such as hackers, ransomware, or physical disaster. Do you know where your documents really are being stored? You did not really think they were physically on a cloud, did you?

How Can Document Management Software Save Law Firms Time?

The average law office worker spends 40 percent of one's time managing documents, 20 percent of one's time looking for documents, and most of that time failing to locate needed documents. Streamlining and automating this process by the conversion of paper documents, forms, and records to electronic files provides law firms with the ability to eliminate many of the obstacles related to misplaced originals and retrieving, duplicating, and archiving files. By simplifying work flows, firms can focus more on critical tasks.

A Cloud-Based DMS: How Can It Benefit Your Firm?

A competitive advantage for law firms is to use a cloud-based system. Linking and centralizing your information promotes a faster, more productive team. Cloud-based systems are economical, flexible, and scalable no matter your business size and provide the following benefits.

1. **Store all your case information in one centralized place.**

   All client documents and communication can be easily referenced and retrieved. Find any document, perform text-based searches, and locate what you are looking for online within seconds, increasing client satisfaction and improving relations.

2. **Access your files online from work or anywhere.**

   Work from home, the office, or while traveling. Synchronize your data from multiple devices, such as PC, smartphones, or a laptop, giving you more flexibility without the high costs of software programs.

3. **Efficiently increase work flow processes.**

   Save time by automating repetitive tasks. Time is money. Searching for and retrieving documents can be very time consuming. Using templates for documents, emails, invoices, and letters will save you from repetitive steps and actions. Documents can be digitized and archived on entry into the system, making them easier to locate and retrieve using cross-indexing.

4. **Collaborate on cases with colleagues at the same time.**

   Track your firm's interactions with clients from email, phone, or in-person meetings. Manage and track changes made by other coworkers, assign tasks between lawyers, and know when they are completed.

5. **Improve collection billing and rates.**

   Proficiently bill your time and invoices while you work. Streamlining your billing allows you to create professional, accurate invoices, making it smooth and effective for your firm and clients so that you can put more time back into practicing law.

6. **Safely share documents with colleagues.**

   Law firms need improved security from cyber-attacks or cyber-criminals. Safeguard client information by keeping sensitive data protected. A cloud-based DMS provides better control over sensitive documents at the folder level for various groups or individuals, thus reducing risks and liabilities. Cloud-based DMS can also leave an audit trail showing who has viewed, accessed, or modified any document. Tags can be added to managed documents to provide you with automated alerts.

7. **Be protected from disasters.**

   Using digital archiving ensures the protection of backup documents from flood, fire, or other disasters. Documents will no longer need to be replaced since they can be tracked and traced online. Central storage prevents lost documents, thus leaving your firm with peace of mind.

With the speed and pace of information growing every day, a DMS can change your work flow capabilities and help you automate your operations. Document Management Systems can meet the changing needs of any enterprise, bringing your law business into the paperless world.

Document Automation

A desk with a mountain of papers on it and shelves that are about to burst from the number of documents that are on them—haven't we all seen this scene at least once? For many years, this was one of the main problems for all firms that wanted to have better organization and better productivity by their employees. The work in this environment would always feel stressed, time consuming, and unmotivating. But with the development and progress of society, we could say that we are finally seeing the end—and the solution is document automation.

What Is Document Automation?

Document Automation (Document Assembly)
The design of systems and work flows that assist in the creation of electronic documents.

Document automation (document assembly) is the design of systems and work flows that assist in the creation of electronic documents. The main aspect of this technology is to create a more efficient process and to boost the work flow and productivity of all employees in the firm. Document automation entails arranging input data in the form of a questionnaire to facilitate document drafting. Law firms are gradually using this method to put together legal documents, contracts, and letters. Most document automation systems can also gather information from client databases and populate it where it goes in the legal documents. The system pulls information such as client name, matter number, case number, judge, and court information.

Benefits of Document Automation

There are numerous pros to utilizing this technology. Law firms may use automation systems to reduce data entry time, proofreading time, and the risks caused by human mistakes. For example, an employee in a law firm had a bunch of documents that she had to see each day. Each person had the designated physical document. Often, it would take the employees a lot of time to find a certain person's file, and if they would find the right document, they would need to make a new one with all information, just like they did before. The same situation would arise if they put someone's document in the wrong place. The control of the files would get difficult, and it would last for a long time. That is why document automation is so useful. It leads to a faster access to records, the sorting of documents, and time savings.

Another huge benefit is the management of the documents. In the past, employees would have to find certain files by hand, often through hour-long searches. Today, thanks to document automation, everything is available with a few clicks. Since all the records are digital, they can be grouped by transferring them from one place to another. Everything is standardized, so sorting is easy.

When a company uses document automation, it eliminates the need for employees to manually enter data, file full records, or archive them. Employees must fill in the details only once by using document automation. Data entry is as easy as filling out a survey. Employees have more flexibility to participate in other productive tasks because of the decrease in time spent manually drafting documents from scratch. Thus, employees will devote themselves to other jobs for which they would probably not have time. Since there is no time wastage, the organization's productivity steadily improves. High production equates to increased productivity. The law firm and its employees benefit from the decrease

Exhibit 8–1

Case management program document assembly/ generation

CASE MANAGEMENT DATABASE

Client Name:	First National Bank
Contact Person– First Name:	Sam
Contact Person– Last Name:	Johnson
Client Address:	P.O. Box 1000
Client City:	Philadelphia
Client State:	Pennsylvania
Client Zip:	98934
Client Phone:	555/233-9983
Case Number:	2012-9353
Court:	Philadelphia Superior Court—District 13, Philadelphia, Pennsylvania
Debtor Name:	Philip Jones
Debtor Address:	3242 Wilson Ave. SW
Debtor City:	Philadelphia
Debtor State:	Pennsylvania
Debtor Zip:	98984
Amount Owed to Client:	$225,234
Type of Debt:	Mortgage
Type of Asset:	House at 3242 Wilson Ave SW, Philadelphia, Pennsylvania

Merge function

MERGED DOCUMENT—Complaint

In the Philadelphia Superior Court – District 13, Philadelphia, Pennsylvania

First National Bank

Plaintiff

Case No. 2012-9353

Philip Jones
3242 Wilson Ave. SW
Philadelphia, Pennsylvania 98984

Defendant.

COMPLAINT

Comes now plaintiff, First National Bank, and states that the defendant, Philip Jones, is indebted to the plaintiff in the amount of $225,234 on a mortgage regarding a house at 3242 Wilson Ave SW, Philadelphia, Pennsylvania. Attached to this complaint as Appendix "A" is a fully executed copy of the mortgage above referenced.

DOCUMENT TEMPLATE 1—Complaint

In the {Court}
{Client Name}
Plaintiff
Case No. {Case Number}

{Debtor Name}
{Debtor Address}
{Debtor City} {Debtor State} {Debtor Zip}

Defendant.

COMPLAINT

Comes now plaintiff, {Client Name}, and states that defendant, {Debtor Name}, is indebted to plaintiff in the amount of {Amount Owed to Client} on a {Type of Debt} regarding a {Type of Asset}. Attached to this complaint as Appendix "A" is a fully executed copy of the mortgage above referenced.

in working hours on each project. This increase allows small firms to take on more challenging cases that require more time to properly manage.

Document Management Software Improves Document Security

Law firms have the ethical duty to maintain client confidentiality and privacy. This means protecting the client's files and the information contained in them. Firms are frequently dealing with the issue of someone looking at a client's data without permission. That was always a problem for firms because everything about clients should be kept private and viewed only by employees who work on that case. Security features vary from program to program, but all offer different features for securing sensitive documentation. The most popular way of protecting sensitive data is by requiring a password or code when accessing certain documents. Document management software makes sure that only employees who are authorized to see the document have the ability to do so.

Document Version Control

With the automation of today's business processes, problems can easily arise. Have you ever sent your colleague or work partner some documents and then continued working on that document until it became a whole different version? That can happen because of different work environments and work locations. But with document management, you can better prevent things like this from happening. All case documents are in the cloud and stored in one work flow for document management, allowing for document version control. No more files existing on different drives or lost in emails.

Tech this Out!

Automation with LegalMation

A relatively new player on the scene, LegalMation (legalmation.com), promises "a day's work in about two minutes." The appeal of this product—saving time—is not hard to see. You simply drag the complaint or discovery request as a PDF file and drop it into LegalMation's website. Select the applicable practice area and watch as LegalMation performs a detailed analysis of your complaint or discovery request in seconds. Within about two minutes, LegalMation even produces a first-draft response by generating discovery response shells and suggested target objections. To be clear, LegalMation is not just copy and paste from a prior pleading—it is helping you prepare your first response where you or your colleagues would previously have spent hours or more creating that initial draft. LegalMation is next generation in document automation using artificial intelligence. What ethical issues could you see arising from the use of this type of software?

Law Firms Are Going Paperless

There is no longer any need for paper, large workplaces, and everything else that comes with the traditional way of working. Document automation can help the planet be a better place. When a company wants to have a lot of employees, it will also need a larger space and more resources. That means that the cost of electricity, gas, paper, ink, and office supplies would be much higher. By adopting document management software, most of these costs are reduced or avoided altogether. That is a huge plus for the business of any organization.

Conclusion

There are almost no cons to this new way of working. The benefits that a single company can have from implementing document management software and document automation are huge. That is why you should immediately try this yourself and see that it could be a miracle in the business of your firm.

Key Terms

Document Automation (Document Assembly)

document management system (DMS)

Discussion Questions

1. What are the benefits of document management software? Provide an example to support your viewpoint.

2. What are some examples of document management systems?

3. Why is a Document Management System important? Provide an example to support your viewpoint.

Additional Resources

The Ultimate Guide to Document Management Systems
   https://blog.bit.ai/document-management

What Is Document Management?
   https://www.aiim.org/What-Is-Document-Imaging#:~:text=Document%20management%2C%20often%20referred%20to%20as%20Document%20Management,captured%20through%20the%20use%20of%20a%20document%20scanner.

What Is a Document Management System?
   https://theecmconsultant.com/document-management-system

Chapter 9

Electronic Filing Process in the Courts

Learning Objectives

- Explain the development and future of the electronic filing systems.
- Distinguish between PACER and CM/ECF.
- Properly prepare electronic filings using CM/ECF.

NSLT Tasks Associated with This Chapter

- Complete all learning modules and knowledge checks in the NSLT learning portal under Adobe. Submit your completion certificate and software review.

Introduction

The notion of the local courthouse as a place to which legal professionals must mail documents or where they must hand-file documents and access court records and court files using manual methods is rapidly disappearing. In many jurisdictions, legal professionals can now instantly file motions, briefs, and other documents electronically, and instantly access court dockets and court records using the Internet. In this chapter, we will cover the historical background behind the creation of electronic court filing systems. Additionally, we will review the process and procedures for filing as well as reviewing electronic court records, and the efforts of state courts to move toward a totally electronic filing system.

The Development of Electronic Filing Systems

Electronically Stored Information (ESI)

Information created, manipulated, communicated, stored, and best utilized in digital form, requiring use of computer hardware and software.

The federal court system was completely electronic by 2006. As such, the Federal Rules of Civil Procedures were modified to address **electronically stored information (ESI),** and every aspect of filing, reviewing, and preserving electronic documents. The court developed a management system to organize the records as well as procedures for submitting and filing those records using the Internet. But transitioning from traditional mail-in or hand-delivered filing methods to electronic filings, referred to as e-file, was done cautiously.

Early Stages of Electronic Court Filing: Pilot Program

During the 1980s, personal computer sales by consumers grew exponentially. And, while the World Wide Web was still being developed, many users had discovered the email system. As for the court systems, documents were, and in most state courts continue to be maintained in paper form. Reviewing and filing court documents was accomplished by physically going to the clerk's office. By the late 1980s, the federal courts authorized public access to court records using the Internet. This service was known as Public Access to Court Electronic Records (PACER). At first, PACER began as a pilot program in only a few courts and provided the public with basic case information. Users could access docket sheet information or case summaries on their computer screens via a telephone dial-up modem. This was extremely helpful to access case information given the increase of case filings in the federal court systems, particularly with complex multidistrict litigation and consumer bankruptcies. However, if you wanted to view the actual documents filed in the record, you still had to go to the court.

By the late 1990s, online access to the court records had dramatically changed. The federal courts developed a filing system known as Case Management /Electronic Case Filing (CM/ECF). Not only could you access records online through the computer, but you could also electronically file and update court records. The courts electronic case management system was no longer limited to internal uses. Again, this system was set up as a pilot program, and the bankruptcy courts were considered an invaluable testing ground given the large volume of cases filings throughout the country. The Texas bankruptcy courts were one of the earliest PACER and CM/ECF pilot programs. After several additional bankruptcy courts reported success within the systems, the Administrative Office of the United States Courts approved using PACER in all bankruptcy courts. By the early 2000s, all bankruptcy courts were using both PACER and CM/ECF. See Exhibit 9–1.

Federal Court Transition to Electronic Filings

With electronic filings, the courts accept electronic versions of legal documents via the Internet or other electronic means instead of requiring a hard copy of the document to be physically presented. The federal district and bankruptcy courts have been on the cutting edge of this technology for several years. After all the bankruptcy courts transitioned completely to the CM/ECF, the other federal district and appellate courts soon followed. Today, all federal courts use CM/ECF and PACER, providing access to hundreds of millions of online court documents. Millions of users, both legal professionals and the public, access or file documents over the Internet using these two systems daily. Additionally, the PACER Case Locator (PCL) allows the user to conduct nationwide searches, which is helpful in determining if a party is involved in federal litigation. The PCL is a one-stop location to search all federal courts for cases, which will generally appear within 24 hours.

e-File
The electronic filing of a document in the federal court using the Internet to transmit the record.

Public Access to Court Electronic Records (PACER)
Allows users to view, print, or download current and recently closed federal cases.

Modem
A device that converts signals produced by one type of device (such as a computer) to a form compatible with another (such as a telephone) to transmit and receive information.

Case Management/ Electronic Case Filing (CM/ECF)
Court management system used in the federal courts to access and file new cases and documents.

PACER Case Locator (PCL)
A national index for district, bankruptcy, and appellate courts.

Exhibit 9–1 PACER and CM/ECF

Source: Pacer

Today, one would be hard pressed to find a lawyer who dislikes the electronic filing systems. The stress over getting a pleading filed before the courthouse closes is significantly reduced when you know the document can be filed on the same day until midnight. And, filing electronically ensures the judge will receive the pleadings immediately, as will other parties registered with the court to receive notice through email.

State Court Transition to Electronic Filings

Although the federal court system has basically completed implementing electronic filings, state courts may take some years to catch up. Some states have completed the move to electronic systems, but many are still moving through the implementation stage. Traditional roadblocks to these types of systems include cost, standardization issues, security, and obtaining the hardware and software needed to support electronic filing. Much of this process depends on funding available to each county or parish within a state. For the most part, large metropolitan city area courthouses have made their case records and filing option available online but have fees associated with its access.

Electronic services such as Westlaw and LexisNexis also have access to some court dockets and can electronically track document filings in cases and access court records. Some of these services even automatically alert the legal professional (electronically) to new filings in cases at intervals, such as once or twice a week. Although a legal organization must pay the vendor for these services (as opposed to getting them free when states or courts implement the program), many legal organizations find it worth the cost.

Filing and Reviewing Electronic Records

Filing Records Online

Before documents can be filed electronically, an attorney must be admitted to practice in that court. It is important to check with each court to review the admission procedures as well as their guidelines for registering to file electronically. In some cases, parties of interest may be authorized or permitted to file certain documents, such as creditors filing proof of claim forms in bankruptcy cases. Nonetheless, those parties must register with the court to obtain filing access.

Filing documents using the electronic systems is easy. The user logs into a specific court's website with a court-issued password, enters some general information about the case, as well as the documents being filed, and then submits the document to be filed, most times, (and always with federal court), in **Portable Document Format (PDF)**. Once the file is received, a notice of receipt is automatically generated and sent through email to the parties listed and registered to receive electronic notice. The CM/ECF system also gives courts the option to make filed documents accessible to the public over the Internet.

Portable Document Format (PDF)
A format that allows a document to be read and viewed from any computer regardless of the original program that created the document.

Tech This Out!

Automated Data Compiling and Case Filing with MyCaseInfo

Software companies have created programs to simplify all aspects of the legal profession from office management to case management. BestCase bankruptcy software has created advanced features in its program that include MyCaseInfo. It allows clients to complete their questionnaire electronically and attach documents. Information collected using MyCaseInfo is then downloaded directly into the client's file on the BestCase program, automatically populating the data within the record to create the documents required to file in the bankruptcy court. The automated BestCase system connects directly with the appropriate courthouse, and with "one click of a button," the client's case is electronically filed with CM/ECF. These automated features save hours of time-consuming manual data entry of material.

Preparing Records to File Online

The documents being filed will likely exist in several formats. For example, a personal injury lawsuit will have a pleading, likely prepared in Word, with billing invoices from an accounting data program and electronic medical records. It may also have pictures (JPGs) or scanned records in text TXT format. To prepare a paper case filing that is hand-delivered to the courthouse, you would convert the different file formats into copies of a single format (photocopies). In the same fashion, an electronic document must also be properly prepared by converting documents into acceptable electronic format, such as PDF. With the Adobe Acrobat program, these files can be combined into a single record. Otherwise, each record must be separately filed on the website. This method is time consuming, but in some cases, the court will instruct parts of the pleading to be attached in a separate process.

Redact
To edit and remove information from documents filed in the court record, usually information that is confidential or private.

When preparing the documents to be submitted, you must **redact** privileged or personal information. A common redacted piece of information is the Social Security numbers; only the last four digits are viewable. Other examples would be children's names in juvenile cases. Once the files are converted into PDF format, Adobe has a redaction feature that will "mask," or cover up, the privileged material so that it cannot be seen. There are extra steps to take in Adobe that will review the file and make sure certain comments and other tracking features are additionally removed.

Adding Signatures to Electronic Records Filed Online

After the file has been reviewed to ensure that privileged material is removed, the document must be signed. In the early stages of electronic document filings, the process was accepted in the court using an "/s/" label with the attorney's name typed immediately below the label. Now, **digital signatures** are more commonly used. Adobe, along with other application software programs offer this feature. Most have signature features that include security. In other cases, the add-signature feature or draw feature works with touch screens using electronic pens to enter a signature in the same manner a paper document is signed.

Digital Signature
A means of electronically signing a document.

Searching Records Filed Online

Electronic filing or E-filing, has the advantage of creating documents with **Extensible Markup Language (XML)**. A document with XML contains codes that describe that data; this is helpful for **document tagging**. For example, the XML code can identify a name or description that will easily categorize information. When the documents are uploaded and filed, the XML codes will be recognized by the court's case management system to identify information for easier and quicker file searching. The XML codes within the file can be shared with programs having similar sets of standards for cross-referencing, giving outside vendors the opportunity to have records uploaded and then used by multiple parties. Consider the making of secure online payments of filing fees to a court. That information is entered into the court's website but transmitted and recognized by the specific credit card company used after being processed through another third party, such as PayPal. Some drawbacks to XML in documents include how the tags are applied and if the forms are truly efficient in applying codes. This is often resolved by creating intelligently tagged documents.

Extensible Markup Language (XML)
A way of writing data in a document for tagging and creating formats to identify and describe information.

Document Tagging
The general process of adding extra information to documents. With electronic documents, the extra information marks up the documents for further analysis or workflow.

Viewing Records Online

The PDF format allows a reader to view any filed document regardless of the program used to create the file. For example, the BestCase bankruptcy software is a program designed with special computer language and features to create the official bankruptcy forms required to file the case. If another party wanted to view the file created in BestCase, they would have to purchase the BestCase program to open the file and view it. This would be unfair and inequitable for parties. Adobe, which is the most popular PDF file maker program, converts files created with any program into a format that is portable, meaning it can be viewed. Adobe offers a free Reader program that is easily downloaded onto any computer or smart device so that PDF files can be viewed immediately when they are accessed.

Like the federal court system, many state courts have selected PDF as their standard for filing documents electronically. The Oklahoma State Courts Network (www.oscn.net) is a good example of state implementation of this technology. It allows users to access court dockets statewide, including the Oklahoma Supreme Court, the Court of Criminal Appeals, the Court of Civil Appeals, and 77 district courts. See Exhibit 9–2.

Education and Training for E-Filing

PACER provides a very detailed manual on how to access files using individual court websites as well as using the PCL to search the national database for case records. Additionally, there is a training manual for CM/ECF. These manuals are downloadable in PDF format, and the links are located under "Additional Resources" at the end of this chapter. In the early 2000s, the bankruptcy clerk's office offered in-person training and required the attorneys to attend before they were issued a login ID and password. Over the past 10 years, PACER offered training modules for CM/ECF that included step-by-step directions to practice opening a case file as well as filing motions and complaints. With the expansion of NextGen, PACER temporarily removed the training modules for CM/ECF but still has a module for PACER.

However, there are several district courts that maintain their own versions of CM/ECF training. For example, both the Middle District of Louisiana and the Middle District of North Carolina have excellent training for CM/ECF. These training modules are interactive and can be done repetitively for practice. The links are available under "Additional Resources" at the end of this chapter. It is highly recommended for lawyers and paralegals to reach out to their local federal and county or parish courts to determine if any on-site training is available. Additionally, many local and state bar associations as well as paralegal associations offer continuing legal education and seminars on electronic filing process and procedures.

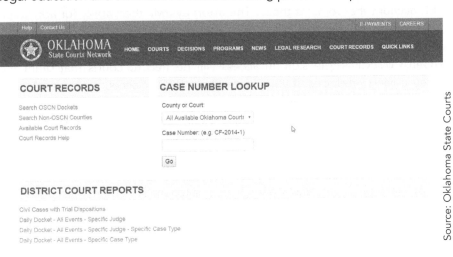

Exhibit 9–2 Internet access to the Oklahoma state courts network

Source: Oklahoma State Courts Network.

Stop and Think!

CM/ECF Court Filing: Have You Changed Your Password Recently?

In reality, nearly all documents filed electronically are done by paralegals or other staff members. This does not mean the attorney was not responsible for preparing and drafting the documents. However, the activities to prepare and submit documents to CM/ECF are viewed as an administrative task. Much like the task of court runners and couriers of the past when filing paper documents with court. But consider the fact that paralegals and staff may not remain in your office and will move on to other job opportunities. Attorneys must register with each court they practice in to receive access for electronic filings. The access includes a login name and unique password. Anything filed under that attorney's name is their responsibility. If the paralegal or staff members files documents in error, it is ethically the attorney's responsibility. Imagine the problems that exist with multiple nonattorney staff members having access to file legal pleadings in a court with electronically signed documents. When staff leave, how many attorneys remember to change their passwords to avoid unauthorized access? It might be surprising to know how often this simple task gets overlooked.

Future of Electronic Filing Systems

Updating PACER and CM/ECF

NextGen CM/ECF

The federal court filing system designed to access PACER and CM/ECF from a single sign-on to give access to both accounts from one sign-on.

Over the past several years, the Administrative Office of the United States Courts has begun updating features in both the PACER and the CM/ECF systems. **NextGen CM/ECF** was designed to have one account for PACER and CM/ECF, but not all federal courts have migrated to NextGen. For a long time, one of the biggest complaints has been maintaining a separate log-in for PACER and then multiple logins for each district court to electronically file cases and documents. A concern was access to filing records in courts where attorneys were not authorized to practice law. To overcome these concerns, attorneys were required to register with each district court for electronic access, and in turn that court would provide a username and password. This resulted in numerous logins for attorneys to maintain and update.

The benefits of NextGen offer attorneys the option to set up an individual PACER account that remains theirs. The attorneys will then apply for admission and register to file electronically from one central location. Attorneys are still bound by their specific state and federal court practice admissions, and the NextGen CM/ECF single sign-on access will be tied to courts that grant the attorney e-filing privileges. If you created your PACER account prior to August 2014, you need to upgrade your account.

PACER Administrative Accounts (PAA)

A consolidated billing and online account management process for groups such as law firms, financial organizations, and educational or research institutions.

In some cases, law firms and other groups, such as financial organizations, and educational and research institutions, may handle multiple PACER and CM/ECF accounts. **PACER Administrative Accounts (PAA)** allow groups to consolidate billing and manage all parties' online accounts. The administrator can add, remove, manage billing, and view invoices, account statements, and detailed transactions. It does not provide access to case information. PACER access charges are billed quarterly (January, April, July, and October), and the fee waiver amount was increased a few years ago from $15 to $30. It is worth noting that legislation has been proposed to make records obtained on PACER completely free, but to date, no laws for an entirely free PACER access have been passed by Congress. With NextGen CM/ECF, PAA accounts need to be upgraded to perform functions other than making payments. This is because all NextGen CM/ECF accounts are individually owned, so the administrator is unable to update, activate, or deactivate the individual accounts.

The Progress in State Court with Electronic Filing Systems

Although state courts must rely on their state and local governments for funding and resources to develop electronic filing systems, advances with Internet access continue to speed up the process of implementing electronic filings throughout all state courts, even in the most rural and remote areas. That said, all 50 states, as well as territories, have different rules for filing court documents. In most cases, each state supreme court will create general e-filing rules, but every jurisdiction may have unique situations that prevent state court electronic filings to have the same symmetry as the federals court PACER/CMECF systems. Because each court must contract with the software and hardware vendors, the cost will fluctuate, and in most cases require fees to the users. Unfortunately, it may be many years (if ever), before online access to all state courts will be free like PACER. And, even with free access to PACER, there is still a minimal charge to open a record online.

State courts are monitored by a national organization known as the National Center for State Courts (NCSC). This organization compiles a list of e-filing programs throughout the country and was updated with links in August 2019, excluding Oklahoma and American Samoa. The list includes hyperlinks to the e-filing Web pages at the state and county or parish levels. The website link can be found in the "Additional Resources" at the end of this chapter.

Conclusion

Electronic filings systems can be found in every federal court as well as many state courts throughout the country. Although many states courts are not entirely equipped to accept electronic filings, the technological advances with websites and the Internet are speeding up the process. In the very near future, you will likely see paper filings becoming as obsolete as they have become in the federal courts. That is not to say that no one will have the occasion to bring paper documents to the courthouse for filing. There are still individuals who file without attorneys, and do not have computer technology at the fingertips. Situations like these will certainly occur, and paper filings will not be refused in the interest of justice.

For those individuals and professionals preparing documents for electronic filings, it important to be familiar with the format type required for filing. Although some states courts have adopted the PDF format used in the federal system, this is not consistently done. This can be problematic with individuals accessing electronic records and not being able to read them on their computer systems. With time, however, given the ease and simplicity of PDF format, eventually all courts will likely require that filing method.

Key Terms

Case Management/Electronic Case Filing (CM/ECF)

Digital Signature

Document Tagging

e-File

Electronically Stored Information (ESI)

Extensible Markup Language (XML)

Modem

NextGen CM/ECF

PACER Administrative Accounts (PAA)

PACER Case Locator (PCL)

Portable Document Format (PDF)

Public Access to Court Electronic Records (PACER)

Redact

Discussion Questions

1. What distinguishes PACER from CM/ECF? Make sure to define/describe each one.

2. Briefly explain the process (method) for electronically filing cases.

3. Should all courts be required to provide the ability to file court documents electronically? Explain why or why not. Make sure to provide examples.

Additional Resources

How To Use PACER: https://pacer.uscourts.gov/help/pacer

PACER User Manual: https://pacer.uscourts.gov/help/pacer/pacer-user-manual

How To Use CM/ECF: https://pacer.uscourts.gov/help/cmecf

The following Court Website has several CM?ECF Training Videos:

(1) United States District Court - Central District of California CM/ECF training videos: Includes "How To Open a Civil Case;" and "How To E-File a Civil Complaint;"http://www.cacd.uscourts.gov/e-filing/electronic-case-opening

United States District Court - Western District of Missouri CM/ECF training videos: includes: "Filing a Document." https://www.mow.uscourts.gov/cmecf-online-training-videos

National Center For State Courts, 2019 State Court E-Filing Program Status List: https://courttechbulletin.blogspot.com/2019/08/2019-state-court-e-filing-program.html

Chapter 10

The Discovery Process and Litigation Technology

Learning Objectives

- Explain the various phases of the litigation process.
- Explain discovery basics and its purpose in litigation.

NSLT Tasks Associated with This Chapter

- Complete all learning modules and knowledge checks in the NSLT learning portal under CaseMap and submit your completion certificate and software review.
- Complete all learning modules and knowledge checks in the NSLT learning portal under TimeMap and submit your completion certificate and software review.

Introduction

Discovery is a fundamental part of the litigation process. When a dispute arises among parties and ultimately leads to a lawsuit filed in court, the evidence will be used to support each side's claims. Based on the evidence, a person will be innocent or guilty, liable, or not liable. So, how do the parties get the evidence? By discovery and review of evidence. Let us take moment and look at the complete litigation process to see exactly where discovery comes into play.

Step 1: The Complaint

All trials, whether criminal or civil, begin with a complaint. The plaintiff decides they have been wronged in some way and, as such, files a petition with the court to hold a formal trial so that amends can be made.

Complaint
A formal document that describes the transgressions that have been made against the plaintiff and why they believe reparations should be made.

Summons
Document used in civil cases to notify the defendant they are being sued and orders them to respond to the court.

Warrant
Document issued in criminal cases to give officers permission to seek out the defendant and arrest them pending trial.

Discovery
The formal process of exchanging information between the parties about the witnesses and evidence to present at trial.

Deposition
The process of giving sworn evidence.

Admissions
A set of statements sent from one litigant to an adversary for the purpose of having the adversary admit or deny the statements or allegations therein.

Request for Admission
A request for admission (sometimes also called a request to admit) is a set of statements sent from one litigant to an adversary, for the purpose of having the adversary admit or deny the statements or allegations therein.

A **complaint** is a formal document that describes the transgressions that have been made against the plaintiff and why they believe reparations should be made. Usually, these reparations are monetary relief (in civil cases) or jail time/community service (in criminal cases). A complaint can be filed against any person, corporation, or government entity.

In filing this complaint, the plaintiff is typically required to pay a fee (called a filing fee) to the courts. At this point, the court will issue a "summons" or a "warrant." The **summons** is used in civil cases to notify the defendant they are being sued and orders them to respond to the court, while the **warrant** is used in criminal cases to give officers permission to seek out the defendant and arrest them pending trial. The case cannot begin until the summons is delivered. The summons must then be served on the defendant by a process server or someone other than the plaintiff.

Step 2: The Discovery Process

Once the summons is delivered and the court proceedings have begun, both sides engage in discovery. **Discovery** is a formal process that involves both legal parties exchanging necessary information with each other. This can include items such as witnesses or documentation evidence. Failing to disclose anything you will present at trial to the other party can result in being unable to use said evidence at best and a mistrial at worst.

This process is designed to prevent "trial by ambush," which happens when one party fails to disclose their documents or witnesses before the trial and gives the opposing party no time to obtain counterevidence or prepare counterarguments.

Taking Depositions A very common method of discovery is to take depositions. A **deposition** is the process of giving sworn evidence. This can be used to obtain evidence from any person involved in the case and lying during a deposition is considered an act of perjury.

Depositions are important because they enable each party to know what a witness will say at trial, giving them the chance to prepare. Additionally, each party can compare the deposition taken pretrial to the witness's statement while they are on the stand for accuracy. Depositions are a useful tool to ensure a witness's story does not change as the case develops. If the witness's testimony at trial differs from the deposition testimony, a common thing a lawyer might say is, "Were you lying then, or are you lying now?" Depositions can also be used as testimony for a witness who will not be able to testify at trial.

Request for Admissions **Admissions** are another part of the discovery process. A **request for admission** (sometimes also called a request to admit) is a set of statements sent from one litigant to an adversary for the purpose of having the adversary admit or deny the statements or allegations therein so that those statements can then be considered absolute and will not need to be debated or proven during the trial. Partaking in requests for admission serves to determine precisely what areas of the trial are in question and limits the time it will take to examine evidence through creating trial boundaries. In short, it simplifies the trial and keeps the focus on only the parts of the case that are in dispute.

Stop and Think!

Depositions from a Distance

A deposition is a key part of litigation, allowing a party to ask questions and obtain sworn testimony from a witness prior to trial. Prior to the COVID-19 pandemic, most depositions occurred around a table in the law firm conference room, with the court reporter sitting at the head of the table and the lawyer asking the questions sitting directly across from the witness (known as the "deponent"). Most state laws required the court reporter to be present physically in the same space with the deponent, but states were quick to pass new regulations and alter this rule to allow for depositions via videoconference. While this new change in rules allows for more flexibility in schedules and far less travel, it also adds new complications caused by not being able to see what is happening off camera. With the camera solely focused on the deponent and not capturing the full room, it is challenging to know what is happening out of sight of the camera. Is the deponent reading from notes posted behind the camera? Are there other people in the room feeding the deponent answers or offering clues and advice? Who knows! These unanswered questions could cast serious doubt on the veracity of a deponent's testimony.

Request for Production of Documents A request for production is a discovery tool permitting parties to seek production or inspection of documents, electronically stored information, and tangible things deemed responsive to the issues involved in the litigation. The responding party must respond to this request by either delivering the documents or providing a written statement as to why the evidence cannot be delivered. Common reasons for not producing the documents might be that the information is privileged, destroyed, or no longer in their possession. However, failing to provide adequate reasoning for why requested information cannot be delivered can have serious consequences.

Request for Form Interrogatories Interrogatories are a common request in the discovery process of a lawsuit. A request for form interrogatories are judicially approved predefined sets of questions propounded upon the opposing party to help aid in the fact-finding process of the case. The opposing party must answer each question truthfully prior to the given response deadline (usually 30 days or so) or state why such question cannot be answered. Interrogatories allow the parties to ask who, what, when, where, and why questions, making them a good method for obtaining new information.

Request for Special Interrogatories Request for special interrogatories are much like form interrogatories in that they are sets of questions a lawyer will ask about the case during court proceedings. Special interrogatories, however, are written questions specific to the case at hand and cannot usually be applied generally to other cases the way form interrogatories can. Because of this, special interrogatories must usually be drafted by the legal team assigned to the case.

Request for Production
A discovery tool permitting parties to seek production or inspection of documents, electronically stored information, and tangible things deemed responsive to the issues involved in the litigation.

Interrogatories
A series of written questions for which written answers are prepared by a party to a lawsuit, usually with the assistance of the party's attorney and then signed under oath.

Request for Form Interrogatories
Judicially approved predefined sets of questions propounded upon the opposing party to help aid in the fact-finding process of the case.

Request for Special Interrogatories
Sets of questions propounded upon the opposing party to help aid in the fact-finding process of the case usually be drafted by the legal team assigned to the case.

Step 3: Pretrial

When a court case begins, it must be determined whether the trial will be a bench trial (judge decided) or a jury trial. During a bench trial, the judge serves as both the mediator to make sure court guidelines are followed and as the final decision maker who determines which party should win the case. In a jury trial, the judge serves only as the mediator, and the jury decide the outcome of the case.

Either party may make a request for a jury trial. Although a jury trial is most common, there are several reasons a bench trial might be preferable. If the case hinges on a very complex legal issue, it may be too complicated for a jury to understand the subtle nuances of the law being argued. That type of a case would be best decided by a bench trial. Bench trials are also much quicker in general and more cost effective.

Step 4: Opening Arguments

Opening arguments occur during the very beginning of a trial and are generally limited to known facts and statements that are not disputed. During this stage, each legal party has the opportunity to inform the jury or judge of the case at hand, set the scene, introduce the plaintiff and defendant, and give an overview of how the case is expected to go.

During this process, each party should also take the chance to introduce the jury to key witnesses and give a brief synopsis of what each witness is expected to say on the stand. This can be as simple as "Witness A will testify that she saw the defendant perform X action." The goal is to make your opening statement as persuasive as possible while also omitting any contentious arguments.

Motion to Dismiss A motion to dismiss can technically be filed at any point during a lawsuit, but it is usually filed by the defendant's lawyer at the beginning of the trial or after the opening arguments have been completed. Once a motion to dismiss is made, each party will present any information they have as to why the case should be dismissed (or not dismissed), and the judge will consider it in their decision.

Here are a few reasons a motion to dismiss might be filed:

1. The court presiding does not have the appropriate jurisdiction.
2. The trial is taking place at an improper venue.
3. Procedural errors were made by the plaintiff during the discovery or filing process.
4. Infallible evidence is presenting that the defendant could not have committed the acts of which they are being accused.
5. The law provides some provision that states that the defendant's actions are not technically courtworthy.

Step 5: Direct and Cross-Examination

Once the opening arguments have concluded, the trial proceeds to the direct and cross-examination stages. **Direct examination** is the process of presenting evidence by calling a witness to the stand and asking them questions. Direct examination is generally done by the party that called the witness to the stand, while cross-examination is done by the attorney for the opposing party.

Direct Examination
The process of presenting evidence by calling a witness to the stand and asking them questions.

This process can be used to present both direct facts and circumstantial evidence. In the case of expert witnesses, opinions may also be provided. For example, if your expert witness was a doctor, a question one might ask is, "In your expert opinion, would it have been physically possible for the defendant to commit this action given they had X ailment?"

A lawyer may not, however, ask leading questions to their own witness, as any information collected this way can be thrown out in court. A leading question is one that leads the witness to a specific conclusion. An example of this might be, "Isn't it true you saw the defendant exit his house at 8:00 that night?" Instead, this question would need to be rephrased to "What time would you say you saw the defendant leave his house that night?"

Some key indicators that a question might be a leading question are the following phrases:

- "Isn't it true . . ."
- "Wouldn't you say . . ."
- "Given this, is it fair we can assume . . . ?"
- "You were doing X, weren't you?"
- "You didn't do X, did you?"

In general, if the question elicits a simple yes or no response, there is a good possibility it is a leading question.

Once the direct examination is complete, the opposing party then has the opportunity to cross-examine the witness and ask their questions. Because cross-examination is usually limited to only information that was established during the direct examination, leading questions during this stage are generally allowed (though only if the information has already been established).

Tech This Out!

Jury Selection Software

Most trial lawyers love selecting their jury. During the selection process, each potential juror is questioned by each party's lawyer. Each side keeps separate notes on the potential juror's demographics (age, gender, occupation, etc.) and how they responded to the questions. Old-school attorneys use sticky notes, and arrange them according to where the juror is sitting in the jury box. If a juror is dismissed during voir dire, the sticky note can be easily removed, and the remaining notes rearranged accordingly. Tech-savvy legal teams will ditch the sticky notes and use a jury selection app, like Voltaire (Voltaireapp.com). With Voltaire, attorneys can enter basic information about the potential juror, and the app will automatically research and provide public, social, and behavioral records, eliminating hours of exhaustive human research time. With all this information rapidly at hand, attorneys can better discover hidden bias and spot potential issues before jurors cause problems at trial. Voltaire takes the uncovered information and converts it into a detailed report so the legal team can make a more informed decision. If this information were collected about you (as a potential juror), what would the personal and social media data say about you? How will the information garnered predict deliberation behavior?

This process usually goes back and forth. Each party calls their own witnesses, and the other party cross-examines them until both parties feel their case has been made or there is no more evidence that can be called upon or questioned. At that point, the case moves into closing arguments.

Step 6: Closing Arguments

The closing argument stage is reserved for both parties to make their final points and sum up the case for the jury. Since the information regarding the case has already been confirmed, gone over, and examined by both legal parties and the jurors, both the prosecution and defense can now make arguments regarding the evidence at hand and attempt to convince the jury of that evidence's significance (or lack thereof).

During this step, parties can also make hypothetical analogies or metaphors regarding the case or evidence involved, place doubt on a witness's credibility, or arrange the pieces of the case into a complete and compelling story the jury will believe. Generally, closing arguments involve the following sections:

- A summary of the evidence presented
- A plain statement on the inferences that can be drawn because of the evidence
- An attack on any holes the opposing party may have created in their arguments
- A summary of the laws in question for the jury and a reminder of how and why they should follow those laws
- A call to action or a plea to the jury to make a specific decision (acquittal, conviction, etc.)

Despite the free nature of closing arguments, there are some limitations. For example, the arguments must be based on evidence and cannot state something that is obviously factually incorrect, such as telling the jury a witness said something they clearly did not. Counsel can also not use closing arguments to introduce new evidence that was not gone over during the trial, as this evidence is not valid.

Additionally, the arguments cannot be confusing, irrelevant, or prejudicial. This is known as being inflammatory and is not permitted by the court. Name-calling is generally forbidden as well, and one may not ask the jury to "send a message" to other criminals, as the closing arguments must focus on the case at hand.

Step 7: The Verdict

Once closing arguments come to an end, the trial moves into the verdict stage. At the beginning of this stage, instructions are formally made to the jury on making a fair and nonpartial decision, and the jury moves into the jury room to begin deliberations. If the trial was a bench trial, the judge will render a decision at this point. If it is a jury trial, a foreperson is usually elected from among the jurors, and it is the foreperson's job to preside over jury discussion and votes. The foreperson usually delivers the verdict to the court. In the event a decision cannot be made by the end of the day, the jurors can be sequestered or put up in a hotel to be sheltered from all forms of media and contact. If they have reached their decision, however, they may now deliver it to the courtroom.

Most courts provide the jury with scripts to read for each possible verdict so that, once a decision is reached, the jury only must select that verdict and read it aloud. Therefore, you will usually hear jury verdicts delivered in much the same manner:

"We, the jury, find the defendant . . ."

What now? Just because the jury has proclaimed a decision does not mean the trial is over. There are a few motions that can be filed at this point.

Motion to Appeal An appeal can be made to reopen the case and escalate it to the appeals court if either party believes the judgment was made in error. However, the party filing must possess sufficient evidence in their favor to make this filing.

Motion of Arrest of Judgement This motion is designed to question the sufficiency of the judgment made if one party believes the punishment is cruel, is unusual, or does not fit the crime. In motioning this, the lawful party is asking the judgment not be enforced.

Motion for a New Trial This asks for a new trial to be granted to the motioning party due to some mistake they believe was committed by the judge, jury, or another legal entity involved in the case. In some states, a motion for a new trial must be filed before a motion to appeal can be made.

However, suppose that none of these motions (among others) are submitted. In that case, the case may not be reopened without new evidence coming to light (otherwise, it qualifies as double jeopardy, which is unlawful and not permitted). At this point, the case is considered closed.

Litigation Support Software

As you can see from the outline above, the litigation process can be quite complex and has many phases. Most court cases take three to five years from the date the complaint is filed to complete the litigation process and conclude the case. The average attorney works on 40 to 50 cases at a time, and with this long of a time span, it is essential for firms to use litigation support software to assist with keeping the documents and the case facts in order. **Analytical litigation support programs** help law firms analyze a case from several different perspectives and draw conclusions about cause-and-effect relationships between different facts and evidence in a case. See Exhibit 10–1.

Analytical Litigation Support Programs

Software programs that help law firms analyze a case from several different perspectives and draw conclusions about cause-and-effect relationships between different facts and evidence in a case.

CaseMap by LexisNexis

CaseMap (https://www.lexisnexis.com/en-us/products/casemap.page) is a litigation support and knowledge management tool made by software powerhouse LexisNexis (famous for their legal research software program). CaseMap helps you manage, organize, and connect case facts, legal issues, and essential witnesses. It assists with creating detailed chronologies of the facts and events in a case, charts the people involved, keeps a list of important facts and legal issues, lists important documents, and much more. CaseMap can link all this information together and allows you sort the information in various ways to get a better understanding of how the information relates to each other. CaseMap has a unique place in the litigation support market. It is not designed to be a full litigation support tool. Rather, it is designed to be a strategy/knowledge management tool that helps legal professionals think, prepare, and strategize about their cases. CaseMap is a relational database program but looks like a spreadsheet because it displays data

Exhibit 10–1

Litigation support tips

1. **Efficient and clean databases work best.** When you design and populate a litigation support database, keep it simple and straightforward, and enter only *relevant* information. Do not clutter your database with irrelevant information that will slow down the speed of the system or may retrieve unnecessary information during searches.

2. **Be an expert on the facts and legal issues in the case.** Before you can truly design a litigation support database that will meet your needs, you must fully understand the facts and legal issues of the case and understand the significance of the documents or information that you will be tracking.

3. **Legal documents are easier to search on than discovery documents.** You can search legal documents (depositions, pleadings, hearings, transcripts) more easily than discovery documents produced by parties.

4. **It is easier to search on documents that you produce rather than on documents the other party produces.** You can search your own documents more easily than documents you have never seen before.

5. **Searching on concepts is more difficult than searching on proper names or dates.** You can search for names and dates more easily than concepts. Concepts can be ambiguous and require you to be creative regarding what words might be used to describe them, whereas dates and names are usually straightforward and standard.

6. **Complex Boolean searches can be difficult to master.** It is sometimes difficult to construct complex Boolean searches that retrieve everything you need. It is sometimes easier to break down complex searches into smaller chunks.

7. **A quality team of legal staff who are educated on the specifics of the case and are using a well-thought-out database are more valuable than armies of untrained temporaries.** Computers cannot take the place of a good legal team. Armies of untrained office staff notwithstanding, often only an attorney or a paralegal is going to recognize the implications of a piece of evidence. Quality is more important than quantity.

8. **One piece of the pie is not enough.** Litigation support users truly need document abstract, full-text, and imaging capability for documents. The best approach is usually to standardize with one software package that can handle it all and search all of the modules at one time. Don't forget case management and analytical applications; they also add great value to litigation support.

9. **Don't build an inflexible litigation support database.** Design your database from the beginning for multiple purposes and multiple users. This way, if the players or the issues change, you will be prepared.

10. **Carefully number every page of every document.** Assign every document/page a Bates number, or use alternative technologies such as bar coding. To admit a document into evidence, you typically need a hard copy of the document. Thus, you must be able to lay your hands on the document. The only way this is possible is for your documents to be carefully numbered so that the needle can be found in the haystack under pressure and when it counts. If you will use imaging, you will need electronic Bates numbering as well.

11. **Make standardized rules.** Establish rules to govern the inputting of information and stick to them. Create and distribute a list of standardized rules for inputting data, and train all staff that are entering data on them. Data in the database must be consistent or problems will arise.

12. **Use the fewest amount of people possible to enter data.** The more people that are involved in entering information into the database, the more you have to train, the more you have to audit, and the harder it is to manage.

13. **Do quality audits and test as you go along.** Again, quality is more important than quantity. Don't wait until the end of the project to find out half the data was entered wrong. Do periodic quality audit checks as you go along, and test the data regularly to make sure the database is working properly. "Garbage in—garbage out" applies to databases.

14. **Input trial exhibit numbers for your opponents.** Input the opposing party's trial exhibit numbers into the database so that you will be able to quickly find your copy in the corresponding database folder when the opposing party offers the exhibit into evidence.

15. **Don't wait until trial to enter your documents.** Enter all documents in the database as they come into the case, if possible. Preparing for trial is hard enough without trying to do a big project like creating a litigation support database at the last minute.

16. **Update the database every day at trial.** Update the database after each day of trial with all exhibits, so at the end of trial you will have an up-to-date list of what was offered and admitted.

17. **Print hard copies of documents and make backups.** Print a paper copy of anything you could not live without a trial and make regular backup copies of your databases. Computer systems sometimes fail and usually do so at the worst possible moment.

in columns and rows. Using the program involves linking the various sources of evidence to facts that are relevant in the case and to the issues to be decided in the case.

TimeMap by LexisNexis

LexisNexis also makes a program for creating time maps and timeline visualizations. That program is called TimeMap (https://www.lexisnexis.com/en-us/products/Timemap.page) (see Exhibit 10–2). A time map or **timeline** is a visual representation of time, showing when events occurred and in what sequence. Timelines are extremely helpful in a litigation context because they allow a jury or fact finder to visualize how the events in the case occurred. Manual litigation support methods do not work well in the legal environment because they are not able to adapt fast enough to the fast-paced environment that modern court cases demand. Computerized litigation support programs can adapt to a changing environment due to the quick and efficient way they allow users to sort and arrange an unlimited amount of data in many ways.

Timeline
A visual representation of time, showing when events occurred and in what sequence.

Exhibit 10–2 CaseMap Suite

CaseMap® Suite is the end-to-end single resource for organizing case documents, crafting strategy and presenting a compelling case story.

Source: CaseMap Suite

Conclusion

In many cases, litigation support means the difference between winning and losing a case. This is particularly true for large complex cases. Whether the case is large or small, though, the law firm has the duty to present the case as well as it can. It includes being competent in using support software. If a litigation support system is not utilized correctly, then the client's entire case suffers. In most situations, the client is paying for staff time and expenses to set up and use the litigation support system. If the litigation support system fails, the client ends up being billed and paying for a system from which it did not get any benefit.

Key Terms

Admissions

Analytical Litigation Support
  Programs

Complaint

Deposition

Direct Examination

Discovery

Interrogatories

Request for Admission

Request for Form Interrogatories

Request for Production

Request for Special Interrogatories

Summons

Timeline

Warrant

Discussion Questions

1. Do you think technology will have a positive or negative impact on the litigation process? Provide examples to support your viewpoint.

2. Provide an example of how a case could benefit from using a time-mapping software program.

Additional Resources

How Courts Work
September 9, 2019
   https://www.americanbar.org/groups/public_education/resources/law_related_education_network/how_courts_work/discovery/

SCOTUS Overturns Attorney-Fee Sanction for Discovery Fraud
Robert J. Will, April 25, 2017
   https://www.americanbar.org/groups/litigation/committees/pretrial-practice-discovery/practice/2017/scotus-overturns-attorney-fee-sanction-for-discovery-fraud/

Chapter 11

eDiscovery and the Electronic Discovery Reference Model

Learning Objectives

- Explain the significance of electronically stored information and its impact on litigation.
- Identify the nine stages of the Electronic Discovery Reference Model.

NSLT Tasks Associated with This Chapter

- Complete all learning modules and knowledge checks in the NSLT learning portal under Cloudnine Concordance Desktop and submit your completion certificate and software review.

Introduction

Odds are that you are reading this sentence on a laptop, tablet, phone, or other electronic device. Our world is becoming more and more accessible digitally every day. We leave behind a digital paper trail every time we interact using the Internet. For legal professionals, this digital trail can be extremely important to building a case. We can no longer rely on only physical copies and records to defend our client. Now more than ever, the online world is more all-encompassing than any physical evidence a client would have on hand. Using eDiscovery is the way you can best defend your client and make the process easier on yourself as well. However, this process is not always easy or simple. That is why the **Electronic Discovery Reference Model (EDRM)** was created. The EDRM lays a basic format for you to best find and implement digital evidence into your client's defense.

Electronic Discovery Reference Model (EDRM)

A community of eDiscovery and legal professionals who develop practical resources to improve eDiscovery and information governance processes.

What Is eDiscovery?

Electronic discovery or eDiscovery is the process of identifying and delivering electronic information that can be used as evidence in legal cases. The word "eDiscovery" seems complex and foreign at first glance. However, when we dive into the meaning of the word, we find that it is rather simple and already commonly understood. eDiscovery could have easily fit under the definition of "discover." It is about finding evidence and information to build your client's case. The "e" is added to clarify that the information is obtained through electronic means. The eDiscovery evidence can then be used in legal proceedings to support a case.

It is a method of discovery just like any of the more outdated methods of discovery. The term is used largely to clarify the legality of obtaining and using electronic documents in state and federal courts. With this comes an obligation from the lawyer to obtain the digital records and evidence in a way that follows code and is carried out in a way that respects the legality of the eDiscovery process. Primarily, eDiscovery is used in litigation and other processes that require gathering factual evidence to back up claims and assertions.

Other Methods of Discovery

eDiscovery allows a broader range of information to be discovered and used toward a case. Still, other methods of obtaining evidence are largely important to litigation efforts. Despite the changing acceptance of eDiscovery methods, testimonies and recorded interrogations are still the most used forms of evidence used in court. This makes sense considering that it is coming straight from the witness's mouth. In eDiscovery, document authentication and fact checking are necessary to make sure that the information obtained is genuine and admissible.

The evidence that you find through eDiscovery is classified as **electronically stored information (ESI)** and is quickly becoming a primary method of discovering evidence and presenting a case. ESI is an umbrella term that various forms of digital evidence can fall under. ESI can include emails, social media records, cell phone data, digital audio or video recordings, global databases, apps, global positioning data, data stored in a household appliance, onboard computers in a car, and any other digital records that are produced by the thousands every day.[1]

Challenges of the eDiscovery Process

As we said earlier, the eDiscovery process is not a walk in the park per se. Like anything, eDiscovery has its own learning curve and challenges that come with it. However, just because you may encounter challenges when figuring out how to operate the eDiscovery process does not mean you should not use it to your advantage. We all have a personal digital trail we leave behind. If you opt out of using eDiscovery, you miss out on loads of evidence that can strongly help build up and support your client's case. In the digital world, we need to use new technology, such as data and digital records, to our advantage. eDiscovery allows you to do this.

---

[1]The Ultimate Guide to eDiscovery: The Basics | Logikcull.

The challenge with this process and the learning curve that first appears in EDRM is the cost of the initial use of the eDiscovery method and the confusion that occurs with the introduction of the new process in a firm. If we think back to how court cases use to be developed and brought to life, we will see that people only used physical evidence to build their case. Now, with eDiscovery documents, people must learn how to navigate from using only physical evidence to incorporating digital evidence into their casework. This can have a learning curve for new users at first.

As we start to incorporate this new method of finding digital evidence, the eDiscovery process will prove to be more cost effective and simpler than antiquated methods of discovery and review. Yes, physical copies were simpler and more straightforward. After all, this is how we operated for many years on end. Any new addition to this system is sure to come as a surprise and act as an added layer to your work. You had your client bring in what evidence you need, they knew where to get it, and you got to work.

With eDiscovery, it can be more difficult to know what information needs to be brought in, sifted through, and determined what is the best for the case. However, as you become more comfortable in eDiscovery, you will find that this process is more effective than using only physical documents to round out your case. You have a treasure trove of digital information out there, so use it. EDRM can help you understand this process with efficiency so that eDiscovery works for you, not against you.

Stop and Think!

Exponential Digital Growth

Electronically stored information has dramatically changed the way the world communicates and conducts business. Every day, 306.4 billion emails are sent, and 500 million tweets are made.[2] The number of daily emails is expected to grow to 361 billion by 2024. The pace of data growth is exponential. In 2020, more than 44 zettabytes of data were stored in off-site cloud-based storage locations. This trend showed that companies were digitizing most of their business for easy access by employees who were forced to work from home during the COVID-19 pandemic. This led to an increase in cybercrime and ransomware attacks. The most notorious case was in May 2020, when the cyber gang called "REvil" stole a terabyte of data from the New York City–based law firm of Grubman Shire Meiselas & Sacks. The gang demanded $21 million in ransom for return of the data. As proof of the data's legitimacy, the gang released 2 gigabytes of contracts and other documents relating to their celebrity client, Lady Gaga. After the gang discovered files in the stolen data that related to emails from President Trump, they doubled the ransom to $41 million.[3] It is now common for law firms to carry ransomware insurance, and protection on law firm data is a top priority. What steps do you take to keep your data secure?

---

[2]https://techjury.net/blog/how-much-data-is-created-every-day/.

[3]https://www.forbes.com/sites/forbestechcouncil/2021/03/12/ransomware-attackers-take-aim-at-law-firms/?sh=6c5ab973a13e.

What Is the EDRM?

Before we jump into the steps of EDRM, let's clarify what it is. EDRM is an abbreviation that means Electronic Discovery Reference Model. In the simplest terms, it is a model that outlines and explains the various stages of the eDiscovery process. This can help lawyers who are just beginning to incorporate eDiscovery into their practice know what eDiscovery looks like in an investigation and how to go about collecting and using the ESI. As we said earlier, this can help simplify an otherwise confusing process.

The digital landscape is new and largely untouched. Due to this, the EDRM process helps us navigate this terrain and use it to our advantage. The model was created in 2005 by George Socha and Tom Gelbmann. The pair wanted to create a method that lawyers could follow when engaging in eDiscovery. This makes the process a more digestible system that can be understood and followed by anyone. Eventually, the process of eDiscovery will become second nature, but learning a method to navigate this new terrain more easily is important for lawyers to keep in mind when first embarking on eDiscovery.

EDRM is also not a strict model. The way that you use it is largely up to you and up to each specific case. You can complete the steps of the model in various orders to fit your needs. The model is an iterative process. You can repeat steps, go back, skip forward, and customize the model to best fit the case you are working on. This can be helpful to note so that you are not trapped in a linear progression when using the model. As the case changes or new data come into view, you can circle back to an earlier step to make sure that you have the best approach to eDiscovery.

The method is useful for training lawyers to properly use eDiscovery to their advantage. It is also here to serve as a reference for discussion and analysis. There is no one way to go about using this method. Feel free to test out various approaches to eDiscovery and find what works best for you.

Exhibit 11–1 The nine stages of the EDRM

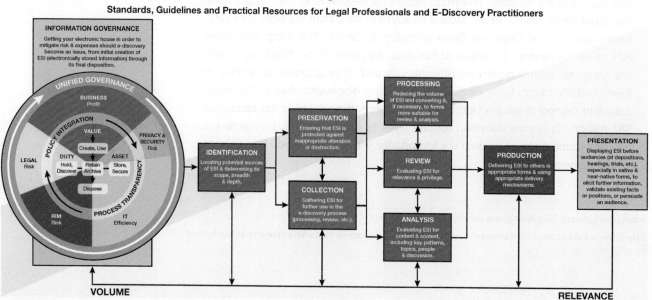

The founders of EDRM even said themselves that "the EDRM diagram represents a conceptual view of the ediscovery process, not a literal, linear, or waterfall model. One may engage in some but not all of the steps outlined in the diagram, or one may elect to carry out the steps in a different order than shown here."[4] With this, EDRM is a great process to reference and follow when you are stuck on what to do next with eDiscovery or when you want to make sure you are following the proper legalities associated with the collection and distribution of ESI. See Exhibit 11–1.

The EDRM has nine stages that lawyers should go through to build a case with compelling eDiscovery evidence. As we said earlier, these steps can be taken in any order and can be circled back to at any time. However, this is the general linear direction in which the EDRM process will be handled.

1. Information Governance

Information governance consists of getting everything in order. Your electronic devices should be safely approved to store your client's digital records and information and any other supporting evidence you gather in this process. This will help you minimize the risks you can encounter when storing digital files. If eDiscovery ever becomes an issue for your firm down the line, this step will keep you covered and your expenses related to eDiscovery low. This gives you protection over the entire process from initial creation of ESI all the way to your final deposition.

This step is so vital in the EDRM process that it even has its own model, separate from the larger EDRM stages. Managing information in this process is done through an understanding of legal risks, privacy and security risks, and rim risks. This is combined with knowing your business's potential for profit and the efficiency of information technology in this case. Information management should be used throughout the process, not just at the beginning. You can come back to this step as new data are added to the case and new risks pop up that are relevant and need to be addressed in your firm. Without information governance, you can easily run into many problems and fail to properly move through the model.

Information Governance
A systematic business process for managing information: classifying, storing, and deleting electronic and paper-based information so that it is retained only while it has significant business value and can be deleted before it becomes an operational or legal liability.

2. Identification

This next stage is all about locating where ESI is and the potential sources that you can gather this data from. This also involves determining the scope, breadth, and depth of the case and the documents you want to obtain. This includes case reviews, interviews with people associated, documents, and more.

This stage is best started with an identification strategy. You will need to identify not only key quantitative data but also key people who can help build your case. Next, build a team that can execute the identification plan. This can be comprised of information technology specialists, in-house legal counsel, outside counsel, records management personnel, human resources personnel, service providers, and more.

Once you have your team, you can identify relevant ESI sources for your case. After you have obtained the sources, verify that they are defensible and usable by the head of the eDiscovery team. This stage is all about identifying what you need for the case to move forward. Here we are not collecting the sources just yet. Instead, we are seeing what more is out there and how much we will need to discover and pull from. This is where you determine the scope and breadth of how much ESI sources the case must sift through.

---

[4]EDRM Model | EDRM.

Exhibit 11–2 Litigation hold letter

Dear Sir or Madam:

As critical evidence in this matter exists in the form of Electronically Stored Information ("ESI") contained in the computer systems of ABC Company, this is a notice and demand that such evidence identified below in paragraphs 2 through 5 be immediately preserved and retained by ABC Company until further written notice from the undersigned. This request is essential, as the printed contents of text and images contained in a computer file do not completely reflect all information contained within the electronic file. Additionally, the continued operation of the computer systems identified herein will likely result in the destruction or spoliation of relevant ESI due to the fact that electronic evidence can be easily altered, deleted, or otherwise modified. Failure to preserve and retain the ESI outlined in this notice will subject ABC Company to legal claims for damages and/or evidentiary and monetary sanctions.

1. For purposes of this notice, "Electronically Stored Information" shall include, but not be limited to, all text files, spreadsheets, email files and information concerning email (including logs of email history and usage, header information and any "deleted" files), Internet history files and preferences, graphical image files (including JPG, GIF, BMP, and TIFF files), databases, calendar and scheduling information, computer system activity logs, and all file fragments and backup files containing ESI.

2. Please preserve and retain all ESI generated or received by [insert appropriate date].

3. Please preserve and retain all ESI containing any information about [insert appropriate date].

4. Unless and until all potentially relevant ESI has been preserved, ABC Company must refrain from operating (or removing or altering fixed or external drives and media attached thereto) stand-alone personal computers, network workstations, notebook and/or laptop computers used by [insert names of appropriate persons].

5. ABC Company must retain and preserve all backup tapes or other storage media, whether on-line or off-line, and refrain from overwriting or deleting information contained thereon, which may contain ESI identified in paragraphs 2 through 4.

---

3. Preservation

An affirmative responsibility to preserve ESI is triggered when litigation is initiated or is reasonably anticipated. The intentional destruction or inadvertent loss of evidence in a case is called **spoliation**. Whether purposeful or not, spoliation can occur if this stage of preservation is not executed properly. The moment litigation is reasonably anticipated, a **data preservation plan** should be made, and a legal hold notice should be sent to all ESI custodians. A **legal hold** notice informs all relevant custodians to preserve the ESI and cease the destruction of documents that take place during the normal course of business. It is important to have procedures and programs in place to protect material from accidental destruction. See Exhibit 11–2.

Preservation of important documents can happen through the documents being collected and removed their current location or preserved and stored in place. This allows the data to be essentially frozen and preserved, as it is the moment that the legal hold goes into effect. The goal for this stage is to mitigate risks by protecting and isolating relevant data relevant to the case. The process for preservation involves developing a preservation strategy, suspending the destruction of files and evidence through legal holds, preparing the preservation plan, selecting the preservation method, and executing it through. Preservation is essential so that hiccups down the road do not occur.

Spoliation
The destruction or alteration of data that might be relevant to a legal matter.

Data Preservation Plan
A detailed plan made by the legal team outlining the course of action for how preservation of documents and other pieces of digital evidence relevant to the case will be preserved from destruction.

Legal Hold
A communication requesting the preservation and the resulting preservation of information that is potentially relevant to current or a reasonably anticipated legal matter.

4. Collection

This stage is all about gathering ESI. You have already identified what sources you have out there, but now it is time to gather what you have available to you. You will have to collect in an authentic manner that can be recognized by the court. Developing a collection strategy, preparing your collection, selecting the collection method, and executing the collection plan is the guide you will want to follow for this step of collecting evidence. Make sure that the ESI you collect is legally defensible, efficient, auditable, proportionate, and targeted. Throughout eDiscovery, making sure that your actions are clear, well documented, and transparent is key to having the evidence survive in the long run.

5. Processing

In the collection stage, you will end up with a large pile of evidence to sift from if done correctly. However, it is impossible to build an effective case with every single ESI you find. This next stage of processing is vital in narrowing down what you want to include in the case. This means reducing the amount of ESI at this stage and converting any ESI if necessary. During this stage, you make ESI more aligned and ready for the later steps of review and analysis.

This is your chance to clean up files ahead of the attorney review stage. In processing, you will delete irrelevant data from your collection, convert any incompatible files, and gather all your evidence into a single software platform. The goal here is to narrow down the ESI that will be needed for the next step, the review stage.

Many people use eDiscovery software platforms for this step to execute this stage easier and reduce human error. Start this stage by assessing your data and plan. Then prepare your data and select and normalize the data relevant to the case. Next, validate your output and handle exceptions. All this will cumulate with exporting the file of ESI that you have now processed for production to the opposing counsel or for presentation at trial.

6. Review

This next step of the process of eDiscovery is often the costliest stage and the stage that can take the longest. Luckily, **artificial intelligence (AI)** has helped to ease the time and financial burden of this step.

The **review stage** involves going back over your curated data and reviewing how each piece relates to your overall case. Here you evaluate ESI in terms of its relevance and privilege. Through this stage, you organize the evidence into subgroups that will better be used when building your case around these ESI documents. Start this stage by developing a review strategy, then set up a review training for those working on the case. Next, perform a data analysis and conduct your work flow. This will then lead you to conducting the review and eventually evaluating your plan and wrapping up the review stage. This can be a costly stage, so it is best to go about it in the smartest and most productive way that saves you time and money.

Artificial Intelligence (AI)
The capability of a machine or computer to imitate human behavior. Also known as machine learning.

Review Stage
The document review phase of the EDRM is where the lawyers are able to view, tag, manage, download, and notate every document and other pieces of digital evidence related to the case.

7. Analysis

This stage of analysis is not exclusive to this position in the EDRM steps. You should be employing analysis throughout your process of eDiscovery. This is why it does not appear before review. While this is the final analysis, it is not the only analysis that lawyers should follow when using EDRM. This stage is all about evaluating ESI in terms of its content and context. You will identify patterns in the data, topic, people, and discussions that are at the forefront of what you have found.

This stage consists of both content analysis and process analysis. In the content analysis phase, you will look at whether your ESI has been approved as fact, whether it can be enhanced through a search, and whether further review is necessary. Analyze whether your ESI is at the level it could be. If not, go back to a previous step and see what you may have omitted. Also, check that your process is serving you. Do you feel comfortable with the position of the process you are in? If you feel you have neglected a stage, go back and take care of your initial stages so that the later ones can thrive in their own regard. This final analysis stage is where you will fix any blunders you have made and make final changes to the content you want to use in your case.

8. Production

At this stage, you will have all your ESI content ready. You have put in the work of selecting the most vital parts of evidence and making sure it applies to the case and is an effective piece of ESI. Now the production stage consists of the preparation for your presentation. Move on to the production stage only after you have all your ducks in a row with the former stages.

The production stage consists of delivering the ESI you have collected in appropriate formats and through correct delivery mechanisms. This involves asking yourself the question of how you will present the digital information you have gathered in a way that is authentic and defensible. Start by confirming all your forms of production to ensure that the authenticity of your evidence is clear.

Next, begin data analysis. There are a few forms of data. Make sure you familiarize yourself with each type so that you can produce your evidence accordingly. Native data are files that are in their native format. If your ESI is native, it may include load files, extracted metadata, and searchable text. Near-native files are the same files as native ones, but they are extracted or converted into a different format. Often this is done to make the file more searchable.

There are also near-paper or image files. These are files that are converted into images. These are typically the PDF and TIF files. Finally, ESI can be a paper format. This step of analyzing which data piece goes into what subgroup is important for the final step. After data analysis, identify the production requirements for your specific case. What form of file will be best utilized for your case? Then prepare the files that you will be using in your presentation and copy the files to a media format.

9. Presentation

You have made it to the final step of the eDiscovery process! The presentation process can be broken down into its own form of a model with how important it is for the success of a case. Your presentation is made up of various parts that can either make or break your case. Knowing how to display ESI in the best manner before your audience is important to keep in mind at depositions, hearings, trials, and more. Keep in mind that native and near-native forms are the best way to go to elicit further information, validate existing facts, and persuade a jury. See Exhibit 11–3.

The joy of presentation now is that it has switched from being executed in only a paper format. Now digital presentations are expected. These digital presentations can help show off your client better and help enhance your case by

No.	E-Discovery Production Steps
1.	Legal team issues letter to client advising them to preserve data related to litigation.
2.	Legal team meets with client to discuss strategies and problems related to ESI early on in case, including cataloging the ESI and discussing any special problems (unique or uncommon file formats, location of files/access, dates of files that may be requested, and any problems such as backup issues, etc.).
3.	If litigation is imminent, client and legal team decide whether production will be handled by a third-party vendor or the client's internal information technology (IT) team.
4.	If a third party will be used, a request for proposal may be issued, bids received, and a vendor selected.
5.	Parties to the lawsuit have a meet and confer conference to disclose ESI information and try to reach an understanding/resolution on ESI issues, including format of requested ESI.
6.	Document request is received. Legal team analyzes the request and decides if a protective order should be sought.
7.	Legal team meets with client and third-party vendor/client's IT team regarding production strategy, timelines, and any problems.
8.	Third-party vendor/client's IT team harvests ESI, processes the data into a common file format, and creates a database.
9.	Legal team reviews the ESI gathered. Sufficient time is allowed so that relevance and privilege issues are considered. If a third-party vendor is used, it is usually done at their site or remotely using the Internet and proprietary custom software. Such review includes the ability to search the database.
10.	ESI is produced and delivered to the opposing party.

Exhibit 11–3 Steps in ediscovery production process

keeping the jury engaged. To best show off your ESI evidence, develop a strong presentation strategy. Go about this by selecting the exhibits that you think will best represent your case. You have probably found a ton of exhibits through your eDiscovery process, but sometimes it is best to keep the quality high and present only a few strong exhibits.

Next, prepare these chosen exhibits and test them out before you present in court. Come prepared. Following your trial run, you will present these exhibits you have worked on and then move to storing your exhibits. It is important to continue to keep a database of your cases, even after they are finished.

Technology Assisted Review

Remember when we said that the review stage can be the costliest of all the steps in the EDRM format? It can take up unnecessary time and money that you do not have to be wasting. In fact, according to a study,[5] 73 percent of the costs involved in the eDiscovery process comes from the review stage alone. Luckily, thanks to AI, technology assisted review (TAR) is here to help you get through the review stage with a bit more ease than before. TAR reduces the cost and time that is eaten up by the review process. This is done by using AI to analyze data sets that are found together, identify those data sets, and then tag documents that may potentially be helpful in the case you are building. Beyond this process of saving time and money, it also saves you from human error.

Technology Assisted Review (TAR)

An approach within the document review phase of eDiscovery that leverages computer algorithms to identify and tag potentially responsive documents based on keywords and other metadata.

Tech This Out!

Social Media Searcher

So much of our lives are being documented through what we post on social media on Facebook, Twitter, Instagram, and LinkedIn. We check in online to various businesses we visit and post about who we were hanging out with or what we ordered to eat. Such data are potentially relevant to a growing number of lawsuits each day. The challenge the legal industry faces is how to collect and review the volumes of data we generate, especially as the prior year's software programs are not equipped to deal with the various new media that are popping up as technology advances. Several companies have started building software to address this ever-increasing issue. TransUnion (tlo.com) is one of those companies. TransUnion's TLOxp solution offers search and report functionality for access to publicly facing (does not search private sites) social media to support and enhance your investigations, research, and due diligence. TLOxp helps you gather information from a broad variety of social media sites to help you more effectively assess risk and gather information about your clients, opposing party, or witnesses. Is there anything in your social media posts that would make a potential employer change his or her opinion of you?

Benefits of TAR

Many benefits can come through using TAR alongside what you already know from going through the EDRM yourself. TAR is not here to replace human efforts but instead to enhance how well your work is done and how efficiently it is created. TAR finds relevant documents to what you need and tags them for you. This is a great way to ensure that all the documents needed for your case are found in one review rather than multiple reviews.

This benefit of TAR was proven in a study[6] by Anne Kershaw in 2005. The study looked at a TAR system next to a group of humans. The goal of the study was to see which was the more efficient way to complete the review stage of the EDRM process. Through the study, the TAR software identified 95 percent of the relevant documents. This was a great accomplishment, especially stacked up next to the group of humans, who found only 51 percent of the relevant documents available. The TAR system is programmed by humans but operates more efficiently through the review stage than its human counterparts.

TAR can also help your firm avoid sanctions and fines, both of which can be bad for business and your reputation. Sanctions and fines are given when a legal team fails to produce electronic data in a timely or appropriate manner. With TAR, everything is completed in a timely and accurate manner.

TAR has also helped increase access to courts for those who did not have the time or the money beforehand. This has allowed the justice system to operate more effectively and has helped the courts keep up with how they are expected to function as a system. Also, early case resolutions become more frequent when

---

[5]Where the Money Goes: Understanding Litigant Expenditures for Producing Electronic Discovery | RAND.

[6]www.knowledgestrategysolutions.com/anne-kershaw/.

the review process is sped up, allowing for a swifter justice turnaround. The last benefit we will include is the ability for the TAR system to update regularly. This allows new information to consistently be located and introduced into the collection of ESI.

Cons of TAR

While there are many benefits to TAR, we must acknowledge where TAR is lacking. The main problem that TAR technology faces is its inability to analyze and locate files that are not text based. TAR can find PDFs and Word documents, but it falls short with images, spreadsheets, and other documents that are not text rich. The software is currently built to identify only words alone. Humans still need to have insight into ESI. Other AI programs have bridged the gap that TAR has left. For example, the program Pagefreezer (pagefreezer.com) works in conjunction with TAR to overcome the previous limitations. However, the best way to have a TAR system work to its full capacity is by having a human reviewer involved in the process as well.

Steps to Take in the TAR Process

The TAR process has a few steps that should be followed to best implement the system into a firm and have it succeed through training and real-life practice among the legal team. While much of TAR is done through AI, the human is still in charge of programming and reviewing.

1. **Set Goals.** Start by setting goals for your TAR process. Ask yourself what you want from the process and how it can improve your working day. Some goals to consider are how TAR can help you prioritize the necessary documents first, reduce and discard the nonrelevant documents, and act to double-check quality. Yes, human employees can make sure the evidence found is up to a quality standard, but AI can do this before humans can so that they do not have as heavy of a load to deal with. Let technology work for you.

2. **Set a Protocol.** When your firm begins to use TAR, do not go into it blindly. Still have human coding rules and the same regulations you had when AI was not involved. Now, those same protocols can be combined with the introduction of TAR. Set up the coding using a method that makes sense for you. This should happen early in the TAR training process. This way, staff can test out what coding patterns and categories work best with your current case issues.

   Coding
   Refers to the process of reviewing documents and summarizing key elements in a structured format.

3. **Educate Reviewer.** The entire TAR process should take place alongside the person who is heading the review stage. Both happen in conjunction. The reviewer must be fully informed of how the new TAR process will function.

4. **Code Documents.** Coding documents can help the TAR system better understand what to look for. You can use example documents that fit a certain category. With this, the TAR system will recognize documents that are alike and add them to your review collection or remove them.

5. **Predict Results.** Next, the TAR system will take over and begin to collect and label documents based on the coding you set up. The TAR system knows what you want it to look out for.

Sampling
The process of testing a search query by searching a limited number of records against to total volume to determine an accurate search response.

6. **Test Results.** There's still room for error with the TAR program. To avoid error, test the results of the TAR. Have the reviewer look over the results while using a validation process. A good way to validate for accuracy is by using statistical **sampling**.

7. **Evaluate Results.** After you know that the results are accurate to what you programmed, ask yourself if the TAR system performed as you expected. Go back to the goals you set and see if they were achieved.

8. **Achieve Goals.** If the goals you set at the beginning were not achieved, then go back and see what you can correct in the review process. Once your goals of the review process are achieved, move on with the rest of the EDRM eDiscovery process.

Conclusion

Often, a sense of mysticism surrounds new technology. This can make it confusing to understand, difficult to use, and a drag to implement. However, models like EDRM help us scrape away the illusion of new technology and get to the core of technology's productivity factor. eDiscovery can be a confusing beast to tackle when it is left to person-to-person interpretation. However, when it is broken down by the EDRM model, you cannot go wrong. When used used right, you can successfully manage the discovery process of electronically stored information (ESI).

Key Terms

Artificial Intelligence (AI)
Coding
Data Preservation Plan
Electronic Discovery or eDiscovery
Electronic Discovery Reference
   Model (EDRM)

Electronically Stored Information
   (ESI)
Information Governance
Legal Hold
Review Stage

Sampling
Spoliation
Technology Assisted Review (TAR)

Discussion Questions

1. Has electronically stored information had a positive or negative impact on discovery process and analysis? Provide an example to support your viewpoint.

2. Why do you think the EDRM stages would not always follow in the order they are presented on the diagram? Provide an example to support your viewpoint.

3. How can artificial intelligence help to efficiently process and analyze eDiscovery? Make sure to explain, not just list the reasons.

4. Should the volume of electronically stored information impact the parties' ability to discover information? Explain why or why not. Provide an example to support your viewpoint.

Additional Resources

Document Review in the Digital Age
Julia Voss and David Simmons, April 30, 2018
https://www.americanbar.org/groups/litigation/publications/litigation-news/technology/document-review-the-digital-age/

A Brief History of Technology Assisted Review
Thomas C. Gricks III and Robert J. Ambrogi, November 17, 2015
https://www.lawtechnologytoday.org/2015/11/history-technology-assisted-review/

Chapter 12

Using Technology to Make Legal Presentations

Learning Objectives

- Identify and explain different types of presentation software and their uses in litigation.
- Identify and explain best practice tips for presenting an effective presentation using technology.
- Identify and explain the types of equipment that is utilized with presentations.

NSLT Tasks Associated with This Chapter

- Complete all learning modules and knowledge checks in the NSLT learning portal under PowerPoint and submit your completion certificate and software review.

Introduction

Presentations for any professional are a part of life and a part of doing the job well. That is no exception for lawyers. Whether you must present information to your client, teach a seminar, or host a meeting, knowing how to make an effective and engaging presentation is essential to conveying your information in the best way possible. Legal presentations help you advocate for your client more effectively, explain information better in legal meetings, and help involve your coworkers during presentations. A good presentation will do all of this to help your cause and more, while a bad presentation will only deter from your central idea. Think of this book as a guide to making the most effective legal presentations out there for any scenario you may come across.

Why Are Legal Presentations Helpful?

We know how trial presentations can be used in court to help persuade a jury and fully educate them of their case. However, in today's age, legal presentations are growing outside of the courtroom as well. Back when technology was first booming, the cost for technology was too expensive to be used outside of the courtroom. Budgeting for rental equipment and software was reserved only for the courtroom, where it mattered the most for lawyers to persuade the jury. However, with the abundance of technology in today's digital world, presentations can easily be held outside of the courtroom to inform your client, coworkers, and external people about the case at hand.

Legal presentations can be a great persuasive tool to get the audience you are speaking to engaged in the matter you are discussing. They are a great tool to relate with your audience and hold their attention for the entirety of your notes. Also, they are time effective and clear. Presentations deliver your message in a clear and concise way that saves you time and energy in the long run. The same goes with your audience: They can digest the information, know what to take notes on, and know what to sit back on and listen to throughout the entirety of your presentation.

Technology with legal presentations does not have to exclude traditional methods, either. Technology is here to help you and add to the presentation methods you are already used to. It does not have to take away from what you know and love in presenting but instead should accompany and expand your traditional methods of presentation. For example, paper products can now be replaced by screen display. This allows a bigger audience to see the same information that would have formerly been on an 8½-by-11-inch sheet of paper. However, if you still prefer this traditional method, you can use it in conjunction with screen display. Pass out paper copies to your audience and then bring up the same document on the screen where you can highlight, annotate, and so on along with your audience.

The same goes for the traditional use of trial boards. These can be replaced by **PowerPoint** or used in conjunction with it to highlight a specific piece of evidence you want your audience to notice. The physical nature of the trial board can help emphasize the point you want to make along with the ease of using PowerPoint. Another example is read into record. This can now be replaced by video playback for a more expansive and thorough viewing of what happened outside of simple document transcription.

As we go through the various ways in which a legal presentation can help emphasize the point of your speech, keep in mind that technology is here to aid you. If your traditional methods work well for you and your clients, then continue with them and add technology to enhance these methods. Even the least tech-savvy person can benefit from a bit of technology presentation tactics.

PowerPoint
A Microsoft Office application program that allows you to create professional-looking multimedia presentations.

What You Need for a Good Legal Presentation

A good legal presentation revolves around three things: software, equipment, and people. If you have all three of these concepts perfectly laid out, then your presentation will be solid and persuasive to your audience.

Software

The software you choose will be used to display the content you are delivering. In this chapter, we will discuss a variety of software systems that are extremely beneficial for delivering your point in the best manner possible. Selecting the software that you wish to use is ultimately a style choice for you and what you think will best appeal to the public you are presenting to.

An emphasis must be placed on dynamic versus nondynamic software. Dynamic software consists of programs (e.g., PowerPoint), effects (e.g., **animation**), and graphics (e.g., time lines). These are all demonstrative and clarify your point in a way that is interactive with the audience and mailable in the prep stages. You can interact with PowerPoint, create the animations and time lines, and fully prep what goes where and how you want the flow of information to be received by the audience.

Nondynamic software is used only for display purposes. This can be things like PDFs put on-screen for display, transcripts of interviews or videos, audio and video files, and multimedia file exhibits. These nondynamic software options are important to combine with dynamic choices to really enhance your legal presentation. Multimedia file exhibits can be particularly effective in legal presentations. This can easily help you lay out your case or presentation in a way that delivers everything you need on one **slide** at a time. See Exhibit 12–1.

This nondynamic software is best used with trial **presentation software**, such as **TrialDirector** or Sanction. These examples and others can help you bring your nondynamic material to life much better than desktop software. Trial presentation software has many tools that can highlight what you want to explore. For example, zoom and callout tools can be arranged on the trial presentation page. This can help you point out important information and lead the audience's attention to exactly where you want it.

Along with zoom, annotation tools, such as highlight, arrows, and underlines, can help draw the audience toward the vital information that you want them to take away from the presentation and alert them of the information they should be taking notes on. Side-by-side displays can also be created to display exhibits from one to the next. This can be a side-by-side of a deposition video and an exhibit currently being discussed. This feature brings your nondynamic content to life and explains your point better to an audience. Clip creation and editing specifically designed for video depositions are available for trial presentation

Animation
Movement of text, graphics, or other objects within a slide.

Slide
A single page of a presentation.

Presentation Software
Programs used to create graphic presentations with visual aids, handouts, slides, and so on or for creating text with graphics, audio, and/or video.

Trial Director
A software program used at trial to organize, annotate, and customize exhibits for cases.

Exhibit 12–1
PowerPoint slide

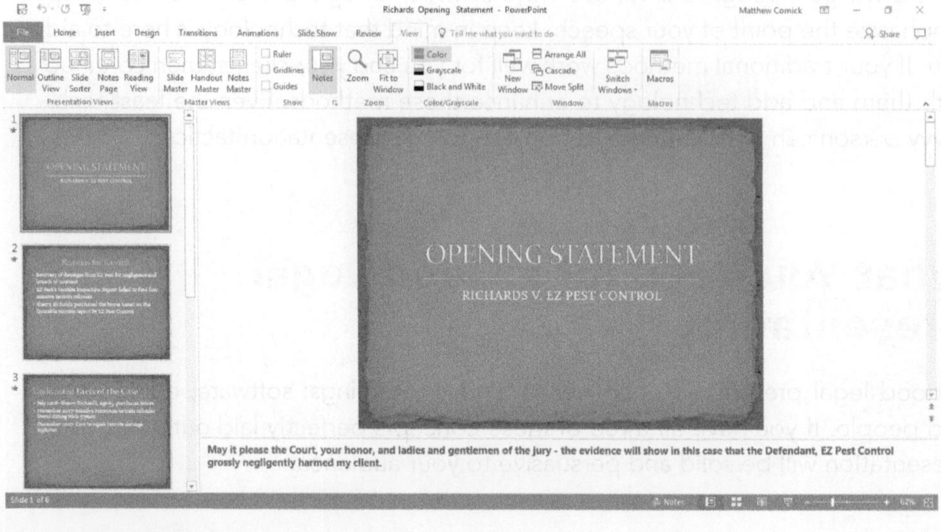

Source: Microsoft.

software. Additionally, there are programs that allow you to create design templates to develop professional-looking drawings to insert directly into the slide. SmartDraw is a very popular program for flowcharts and system documentation.

The benefits of trial presentation software are expansive when it comes to legal-specific presentations. However, traditional desktop software can and should also be used in conjunction for presenting dynamic content that interacts naturally with your audience on its own.

SmartDraw
Software used to create flowcharts and other forms of systems documentation.

Equipment

Once you have your software options chosen, you also must prioritize selecting equipment that will aid you in your presentation. Equipment will include computers, screens, cables, and anything else you will need to get the software up and running for display. With the increase use of videoconferences and hearings, it is also important to consider the options that include Internet telephone communications or Voice Over Internet Protocol (VoIP). A popular cloud-based program is RingCentral, a webinar platform that is great for any telecommunication calls. Particularly when hosting webinars, this platform can act as an easy meeting point for various parties. Beyond video chats, messages, faxes, and more can be sent through the software. It is an easy interface to understand and can act as an excellent collaboration tool for when you need to begin prepping your presentation with your team. RingCentral can be a pricey option, and with its auto-renew feature, you must stay on top of canceling to avoid additional costs.

Voice Over Internet Protocol (VoIP)
A technology that allows you to make voice calls using a broadband Internet connection instead of a regular (or analogue) phone line.

To determine your software needs, start with determining the environment you are presenting in. You may already be familiar with that environment. If not, you will need to clarify the environment before it comes time to present. Begin with evaluating the equipment you will have available for your presentation. Will you have a large single-screen projector that you will use to talk to a large group? Will you be using only a monitor to talk one-on-one with a client? Or will you be using a hybrid of both methods? Find out both what is available at the site of your presentation and what equipment would specifically work best to convey the message you are trying to deliver. To find this out, decide if your space is adequate and conducive to your audience. From there, determine if you will need one large projector or if small monitors are enough to make the point you want to make come across naturally.

Also, if the space you are presenting in does not have the equipment you need, consider a rental service. There is no need to go out and buy a completely new set of equipment for one presentation. However, rental services nearby can help fulfill your technology needs with ease. Make sure you have a variety of cables and converters so that your equipment can attach to whatever screen is available at the venue you present at. When considering this option, establish a budget. This is vital to make sure you get all your technological needs met without breaking the bank.

People

The final step for a fantastic legal presentation is having the right people to carry out your operation. You will need to gather a presentation team to help you out along the way. These are people trained in how to use the software and equipment you will use to execute your project. In this team, you will want people on hand to prep the presentation, create and deliver the presentation, take down the equipment at the end, and help troubleshoot any technical glitches along the way. All these bases should be covered by your presentation team.

Of course, you do not need a single person for every job. One person can easily fulfill multiple roles. You can even have only one person operate the entire presentation from beginning to end. However, if you find that you are lacking the ability to do one of these roles, there is no shame in asking for help. Do not overwhelm yourself with too many moving parts in the presentation. The best way to go about the presentation is to stick to doing what you are good at and then find people to fill in the gaps in your team along the way. If you know you are a great presenter but awful at technical errors, find a person to help you troubleshoot along the way. A good presentation relies on a good presentation team—the technology cannot do it all for you.

Stop and Think!

How Much Is Too Much?

An old cliché, "A picture is worth a thousand words," is certain to be appropriate when preparing slides for any presentation. Everyone can relate to sitting through a lecture or seminar that includes slides with nothing but words. No one wants to listen to a presenter give a presentation as you read the words being spoken. A picture will convey the speaker's words much more effectively. One picture can tell a story—the presenter's story. Along with pictures, there are other features, such as graphics and illustrations, that will keep the audience engaged as the presenter speaks. The visual aspect gets the audience to think about the words being spoken, which creates a more memorable experience. Slide presentation should be balanced between words and visuals to effectively capture the entire audience. So how much is too much when it comes to writing slide content on a PowerPoint or slide presentation program?

Pros and Cons of Different Presentation Software

When you are choosing a presentation software to display dynamic content, there are many options out there to choose from—so many that, at times, it can be overwhelming to know what to pick. Here is a breakdown of the pros and cons of various presentation software options you can use for legal presentations that are sure to shine.

PowerPoint

This is a classic, go-to option in presentation software for a reason. This is the blueprint for all other slide presentation software. The benefits to PowerPoint are many. To start, you have time on your side. PowerPoint has been around since 1987. Since then, updates and changes have been made time and time again to ensure that the best final product is given in return. PowerPoint is reliable in this aspect. Also, this software works on almost any system. Whether you have a Mac or a Windows computer, your PowerPoint can easily be created and displayed on either. Since PowerPoint is recognizable on systems other than your own, you can rely on any venue you go into having the ability to showcase your presentation. This takes the guesswork out of what technology will be compatible with your system when you show up to a presentation room you have not been in before.

There are downsides to PowerPoint, however. To start, if the creator of the slides is not careful, a PowerPoint slide can easily become crowded with unnecessary information and clutter. From **transitions** to sounds, PowerPoint has it all, but that does not mean you need to use it all. Another downside to PowerPoint is the recurring cost. Since the plans are not a one-time fee for the software but instead a monthly or annual cost, the bill can rack up in the long run. However, it is trustworthy and reliable software, so if you can get past these bumps, it is worth a try using PowerPoint. See Exhibit 12–2.

Keynote

The next presentation software we must discuss is the Apple version of Power-Point. Since Keynote is a Mac app, it is ideal if you are not a Windows user. The app allows you to move your presentation easily from iPad to computer to phone through the cloud. It also has many of the same features as PowerPoint but is stored under different names. If you are an avid Mac user, Keynote will be a breeze to use on your computer. Many presenters also prefer to start crafting on Keynote but then export to PowerPoint when it comes time to present. Keynote projects transfer over well to PowerPoint and can then be easily brought up on any computer.

Another addition to Keynote is the chalkboard feature. This is an excellent example of traditional technology melding with current updated tech. If you know your audience is made up of lawyers who are not very tech savvy, a chalkboard may be a more comfortable format for them to see and understand your presentation better. The major drawback for Keynote is that it can be accessed only on Mac computers. This is an automatic reason for most of the legal world to not use Keynote as their primary presentation software. However, if you have a Mac, this software can offer some incredible features to really bring your project to life.

Transition
Effects that move one slide off the screen and the next slide on during a slide show.

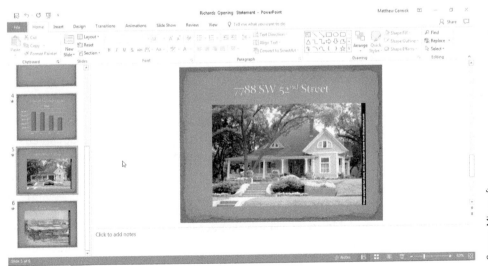

Exhibit 12–2 Photographs in PowerPoint

Source: Microsoft.

Prezi

Prezi is another presentation software that branches off PowerPoint in a creative way. Rather than slides, Prezi makes more of an informational Web that you can circulate between. When used correctly, the dynamic nature of Prezi can make for a persuasive and illuminating presentation. It can keep the audience's mind and eyes engaged fully on the presentation. Prezi has a ton of moving parts, so the audience must continually paying attention in order to not miss any vital information.

Prezi has its own set of unique flaws. Some have experienced nausea when watching a Prezi presentation. The moving parts and swirling nature of a Prezi leave a sense of vertigo in some viewers. This can be distracting and not a very pleasant feeling. Be cautious of this when choosing Prezi as your software. Know your audience and their preference for presentation software. If you do not know your audience well, Prezi may be too big a gamble for your first presentation with that audience. Another downside is how long it takes to make a Prezi presentation. With so many effects to use, it can feel overwhelming to create the presentation and can leave some users giving up and moving to a more standardized slide software, such as PowerPoint.

Google Slides

Sticking with slide presentation software, Google Slides is another option that you can use. One of the major advantages to Google Slides is that it is free. This is great in comparison with PowerPoint. Another large benefit for Google Slides is its collaboration tool. Many users can be added to the same presentation and work on the project at the same time. This leads to great collaboration and ease of access between parties. Changes are made in real time, so users know what not to duplicate. This has made Google Slides a popular option for presentation teams. Your legal team could benefit from this software. Also, Google Slides is a Web-based platform, so no downloading of software is needed. This also means you can pull it up on just about any computer with Internet.

Google Slides is great if you prepare and present from it. However, it does not transfer presentations from other software over to yours well. Another disadvantage is that you need a Google account to use Google Slides. This is free and easy to make but may still be a deterrent for some. Finally, Google Slides does rely on the Internet since it is Web based. Make sure the place you are presenting in has reliable Wi-Fi or keep reading to find out a hack for how to get stronger Wi-Fi with just your phone.

Snagit

This software is not a complete presentation software but instead a tool to add to the previously discussed slide methods. This is a capture software that can easily allow you to screen shot or screen record the information you will need to use in your presentation. You can then add this information in one of the presentation software options of your choice above. Snagit is important because pulling up data from the Internet during your presentation immediately distracts from the presentation at hand. Not only will this distract from your amazing presentation, it will likely cause a delay in your presentation. Remember, we want to keep these presentations effective and time sensitive. Also, you do not want to risk switching from the Internet and back to your presentation which may result in technology disruptions that you will then have to spend time fixing.

Evernote

This is another software that is good for prep work. When creating your presentation, keep any note you think of throughout the day on Evernote. Then you can translate these notes effortlessly over to your PowerPoint or other presentation software. Rather than taking notes in a traditional physical notebook, Evernote allows you to quickly search for the key word you are looking for and jump to the notes you had related to the topic you were developing. However, this application is only for preparing all your notes, audios, visuals, and other clippings beforehand. Think of this as the messy steps you must take before you lay it all out nicely in your final presentation software.

Tips for Presentations

Once you pick out your software and decide how you want to proceed with your presentation, you have already made some great first steps. Here are a few tips to help you swiftly go through your presentation and get the most out of it.

Be Intentional

Start by incorporating the presentation technology of your choice into your practice from the beginning of developing your presentation. Do not make a PowerPoint at the last minute; use the tech as a tool to help you out rather than weigh you down. If you leave the PowerPoint as a last-minute creation, you are using it not to help you but rather because you think it is essential but are not sure why. The software can help you with outlining your content, creating the presentation, and following through on execution. The same goes for adding videos, pictures, and other graphic tools. Add them to enhance what you are discussing, not just because you can. You want them not to distract but to help your content.

Tech This Out!

Follow Me!

Follow Me technology allows the presenter to move about the room while the camera "pivots" and "turns" to track all movements. When planning for a presentation, a big factor is where to place the camera. The audience is more attentive when the person presenting does not stand still, but getting the camera positioned correctly to capture those movements is difficult. "Pivot" Follow Me is a wearable tracker that automatically captures the presenter's movement on any camera or smartphone. "Pivot" is simple to use—just attach the device to the mount, wear the tracker, and then record to activate. The wearable tracker will be synced with the "Pivot" patented tracking technology, which then allows the presenter's movements to automatically be tracked. It has a long-range wireless communication that tracks distances up to 600 feet and can track anywhere in the world. "Pivot" is small enough to fit into a backpack or briefcase but strong enough to move cameras that weigh up to 1.2 pounds. What privacy concerns exist when recording devices are used with an audience?

Operate within a Budget

Make sure to operate within your budget. Money can be a huge source of stress. There is most likely a way for you to get the exact presentation you want at the cost you can afford. Do not buy cheap equipment, and also do not spend above your means. A great way to budget is to use rental equipment, ask around about what your coworkers prefer to use, and take time with your research before committing to one presentation program. Do not be afraid to ask for help and suggestions from your presentation team. They are there to work just like you are. Let them help and learn from what they say.

Test Your Tech

Our next tip is to test your technology before the presentation. We cannot stress this tip enough. Test both your software and equipment the day of your presentation. Make sure that no glitches are occurring. Also make sure everything looks good on-screen. Different screen sizes and equipment will make each presentation show up differently on each screen. Be cognizant of this fact and check before the presentation that your slides still look as they should before you start your presentation. Now is the time to check for all these mistakes and fix them with your tech-savvy team members. Also, if you are presenting in a large room, test your microphone. Have someone stand in the back and make sure you can be heard clearly. Remember that you are trying to appeal to everyone in the room.

This last tip will also ensure that you do not have any delays. Try to minimize delays whenever possible in your presentation, as they distract from the topic at hand. Keep your presentation at a generous pace so you do not distract too much from the topic at hand or delay the presentation severely. If a technical error happens, roll with it and keep the presentation moving. See Exhibit 12–3.

Exhibit 12–3

Trial presentation software can manage both video and documentary material

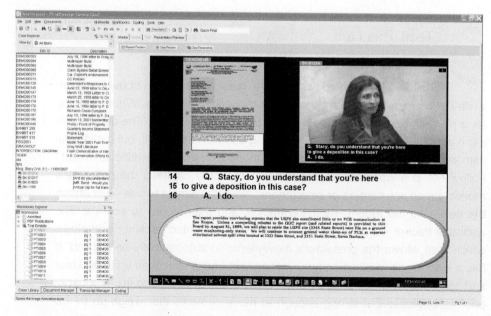

Source: Ipro Tech, LLC

Backups Are Essential

Next, have a backup copy on a flash drive and even a hard copy of your slides just in case a technical error happens that you have no chance of fixing. This is the worst feeling, but having a backup will at least allow you to present your information, which is better than nothing. It is even a good idea to have a hard copy of your slides so you can glance down at them rather than turning your back to the audience to glance at the screen.

Keep It Simple

A key to any presentation is simplicity. You may have a ton of information you want to talk about, but do not let the slides express that. The slides are there as a visual guide for you and the audience. The in-depth discussion of the topic should come from you. Having larger fonts and more white space is pleasing to the eye and allows the audience to jot down only the most important information and follow along with your voice rather than be distracted by reading what is on the slide.

You can even feel free to include slides that are only pictures. This can be a nice break for your audience and can allow them to switch from reading the information on each slide to analyzing and observing the picture you have provided. Clip art is an option to use and comes with nearly Microsoft programs as well as Google and other proprietary programs. If you want to incorporate a few words, use a placeholder on the slide to add text that can be positioned at any spot of the slide and may include animation. Often a design template is useful for creating a theme for the presentation that aids in the overall visual presentation.

Clip Art
A predefined graphic.

Placeholder
A boxed outline on a slide that can be used to insert text or an object when clicked.

Design Template
A predesigned presentation background and format that you apply to all the slides.

Get Internet Anywhere

Remember earlier when we discussed how Google Slides is a Web-based platform that requires Internet? If the venue you are at does not have Internet, use your hot spot on your phone for a strong Wi-Fi connection. This will use your cellular data but will allow you to operate through your presentation without a technical glitch (hopefully).

Connect with Your Audience

A good presentation is more than just fancy slides and who has the best effects and animations. As we said, a presentation is nothing without the right people. You must learn to appeal to your audience. Be charismatic and get them interested and involved in the process. Try to interact with your audience every 10 to 15 minutes to keep them engaged. You can do this by asking questions. You do not have to save all your questions for the end. Ask if anyone has any questions and take one or two every couple of slides. You do not want someone to forget a great question they had later in the presentation.

Also, you can incorporate polling questions. Ask the audience to give you a show of hands if they have done something relevant to what you are talking about. This audience poll can also happen at the beginning of your presentation to learn more about your audience. You can then cater your presentation around their interests and who you discover they are from this simple initial question.

This is especially important if you were unable to gather any information about your audience before this presentation.

Another way to connect with your audience is to weave a story throughout the presentation. People forget random facts, but they remember stories. Even the dullest information can be converted into an interesting metaphorical story that will stay in the listeners' minds. You can also use props if they are relevant to the case. Focusing on something physical amidst the 2-D presentation can add a level of interest that was lacking before.

To stay personable, make eye contact around the room as you present. This will make your audience feel like you are talking directly to them and their concerns, which, at the end of the day, you are, even if it is approached through a group setting. Also, use gestures and vary your tone. No one wants to listen to a dull, monotone presenter, so show excitement and enthusiasm. You worked hard on this, so present it with pride.

Cue Your Audience

You and your presentation team know the information on the slides better than anyone else. Let your audience know important information when it comes up. Tell them, "You'll want to write that down" when an important topic comes up. Do not leave it to them to guess everything. The easier you make it on your viewers, the more of a success the presentation will be.

Admit What You Do Not Know

Our last tip is one of personal acceptance. One of the scariest parts of presenting is the end, when you are asked questions. If you do not know the answer, say that. Fumbling through an answer that you are not confident in will look worse than admitting that you do not know.

Keep these tips in mind during and before your presentation. This all will come very naturally to you if you do the right amount of prep work, but how can you effectively do this?

Prep Work for Presentations

Before you use any of the above tips during your presentation, you must prep for the actual day. Prep work can ensure that you can smoothly run through your presentation, know all the information, and be able to relay what you know with ease. The unprepared will fail with their legal presentations, but a little prep work will help you succeed immensely.

Timing Matters

You will want to make sure you have your timing correct in your presentation. Know your information well enough that you can speed up and slow down without missing a beat. Run through the presentation a couple times beforehand and time your presentation. Try to see how you can increase or decrease the length of your presentation depending on the circumstances of your presentation day. This way, you know what slides take more or less time and how to mix and match your rhythm to accommodate the overall timing.

Review Your Slides

In the review stage, look for a good flow of information. The benefit of all the presentation software we discussed is that it is not set in stone. Do you think you can make a more persuasive argument if you move a slide from the middle to the front? Do it. This review stage is experimental for you. Like a puzzle, try to see where the pieces fit the best to achieve the goals you have in mind.

View from the Back

Become an audience member for your own presentation and see how the information looks from the crowd's perspective. Stand in the far back, the front, and to the side. See where you can best position yourself and a podium (if you have one) to ensure that no blind spots occur for the viewer. You are not appealing to only one person, unless it is a one-on-one presentation to a client or coworker, so make sure everyone is satisfied with the presentation they are seeing.

Prep for the Unknown

Try to find out who your audience is so you can anticipate questions they may ask. Sometimes your audience will be obvious, and other times it will not. Try to prep as much as you can for the audience. Still, know that you cannot fully prepare for every event. However, prepping extra material is important in case you receive no questions and must fill that awkward dead silence in between or at the end. Your audience may still be interested in what you have to say but unsure of what questions to ask. Prompt them with questions or discuss parts of the presentation you left out to save time. Now is the time to pull out these extra pieces of information that you did not think you would have time for.

Also, come prepared with your technology. Bring different adapters and devices. You never know what will work with the venue's system unless you have already used their equipment before. Even then, still bring this extra tech. You never know what may have changed from the last time you were there.

Collaboration Is Key

Make sure that your entire presentation team and you are on the same page for the presentation. Collaboration and communication from start to finish will ensure that you deliver the best presentation. After all, if your team is not on the same page, how do you expect the audience to be?

Prep work is essential to knowing your presentation and being confident in delivering it on the day of the presentation. Prepare as much as you can and be ready to roll with the uncertainties as they come up.

Conclusion

Lawyers require persuasive attitudes in all that they do. To win over the jury, help the client, and even present information at legal meetings, a lawyer must be clued in to how they can use tools of persuasion and explanation. Presentation technology is the greatest aid of persuasion a lawyer has (aside from their own smarts and charisma). Try out various presentation software until you find one that is right for you. Work with your team and be confident in what you have created when you present. This is your chance to state your case and have the audience listen without hesitation.

Key Terms

Animation
Clip Art
Design Template
Placeholder

PowerPoint
Presentation Software
Slide
SmartDraw

Transition
Trial Director
Voice Over Internet Protocol (VoIP)

Discussion Questions

1. Has trial presentation software had a positive or a negative impact on the practice of law?

2. How do attorneys use PowerPoint and/or other proprietary presentation programs to create electronic presentations for the electronic courtroom? Make sure to provide examples.

3. Do electronic presentation programs provide a better option to demonstrate a court case or settlement? Explain why or why not. Make sure to provide examples.

Additional Resources

How to Create a Prezi Presentation in PowerPoint
https://youtu.be/AlvWXa_uiZo

Basics of Presentation Technology for Legal Advocacy—Part I
https://www.jdsupra.com/legalnews/basics-of-presentation-technology-for-22072/
March 10, 2020

Making the Most of Presentation Technology: Software, Equipment, People—Part II
https://www.jdsupra.com/legalnews/making-the-most-of-presentation-93887/
April 22, 2020

3 Common Mistakes with Presentation Technology and How to Avoid Them—Part III
https://www.jdsupra.com/legalnews/3-common-mistakes-with-presentation-77066/
The ACEDS eDiscovery Voice Community Blog, May 12, 2020

Trial Technology: What Has & Hasn't Changed in Nearly Two Decades
https://www.litigationinsights.com/trial-technology-changes/
Adam Bloomberg, November 5, 2018

New Media's Impact on Jurors (and How Your Trial Graphics Should Respond)
https://www.litigationinsights.com/new-medias-impact-jurors-then-now/
Adam Bloomberg, June 12, 2017

New Media's Impact, Part II: Trial Graphic Foundations
https://www.litigationinsights.com/new-medias-impact-jurors-graphics-foundation/
Adam Bloomberg, June 15, 2017

New Media's Impact, Part III: Tweaking Your Graphics for the Modern Juror
https://www.litigationinsights.com/new-medias-impact-tweaking-graphics-modern-juror/
Adam Bloomberg, June 28, 2017

The Art of the Presentation
https://www.lawtechnologytoday.org/2016/10/the-art-of-the-presentation/
Law Technology Today, October 31, 2016

Switching from PowerPoint to Prezi for Trial Presentation
https://abovethelaw.com/2014/07/switching-from-powerpoint-to-prezi-for-trial-presentation/
Jeff Bennion, July 1, 2014

Chapter 13

Courtroom Technology in Action

Learning Objectives

- Identify equipment used in most electronic courtrooms.
- Identify and explain policies and procedures with outside electronic equipment, including backup plans without electronics.
- Identify and explain different presentation tools that can be utilized in the courtroom.
- Identify and explain skills with trial presentation software to integrate with electronic equipment in the courtroom.

NSLT Tasks Associated with This Chapter

- Complete all learning modules and knowledge checks in the NSLT learning portal under TrialDirector and submit your completion certificate and software review.

Introduction

The day starts out like any other as you head to court for a case you are defending. However, when you get there, you notice that the courtroom has none of the technical features you were looking to present with. You shuffle through your physical documents and try to find the right documents you were planning on using as evidence. Meanwhile, the judge is checking the clock, and the jury is half asleep. This is the doomed fate you risk being subjected to if you do not have all your ducks in a row technology-wise. In our digital world, it is important that lawyers use these technological tools to their advantage in a courtroom. That is why we are here to walk you through the most needed courtroom technology and top tips to help you expect the unexpected when presenting with technology to the court.

The Ban on Cell Phones

Before we discuss all the various technology that is on your side in a courtroom, we must discuss a piece of technology you typically cannot have on you. In many states, you cannot bring a cell phone into the courtroom. Different states and counties have different laws on how strict they are about cell phone usage. Some courts allow you to have your phone, but you cannot broadcast from it, take pictures, and show documents from it for evidence. Other courts ban cell phones from even being brought into court in the first place. This is a piece of technology you should plan on avoiding in the courtroom. When traveling to new courthouses, you never know the rules unless you call ahead. Stay safe by not relying on your cell phone as a courtroom technology tool.

This ban exists for various reasons. For one, it eliminates distractions. If every jury member could have their phone on them, there is a constant distraction from the case at their fingertips. In addition, random calls, text and other notification alerts can create multitude distractions for the speaker on both sides.

The ban also exists to protect witnesses from photographic evidence. Witness protection is a safety measure that needs to stay firmly in place. However, not allowing cell phones in the courtroom does prove to inconvenience the lawyer, client, and jury members. This conflict with the justice system can be seen when clients and jury members arrive and then find out they cannot bring their cell phone into the courtroom. This creates a panic about where they should store their phone. Many courtrooms have lockers and safe protection for phones, but this ban can affect the ability for people to show up on time and be ready for their court appearance.

The executive director of the Massachusetts Appleseed Center for Law and Justice in Boston, Deborah Silva, said that the cell phone ban is "a real barrier to access to justice." She made this statement to point out how bans like this affect those who are representing themselves without a lawyer. However, as lawyers, we have the luxury of being prepared for court with proper courtroom technology. We need to familiarize ourselves with the ins and outs of technology to stay ahead of these bans that make display of evidence more difficult.

As lawyers, we must be prepared to adjust our technology around the courtroom's needs and rules. Rather than expecting the courtroom to operate around us, we must operate in accordance with them. This means using technology that works in the setting we are presenting in. We need to strike a balance between justice and safety and security when it comes to courtroom technology.

Importance of Courtroom Technology

Why is technology important in the courtroom? For years, physical evidence, in-person testimonials, and other evidence were the basis in court. However, we live in a digital world, so why not incorporate technology from it into our justice system?

Go anywhere, and you will see people pressed to their screens. Whether this is for entertainment or business, people love staring at the little screens in their hands. Technology has become more engaging and can be seen and used in many different areas of work. Formal presentations are given using technology, plans and scheduling are laid out with technology, and the career world runs on the same platform as the digital age advances. Lawyers would be greatly missing out if they did not take advantage of this technology in the courtroom.

Courtroom technology can help you better convey your message. Let technology be a guide for how you structure your work. It is here not to replace your work as a lawyer but rather to enhance it. Using audio, visual, and physical displays in the courtroom can help you convey your message with more clarity to the judge or the jury. Although most courthouses are old and historic in nature, most courtrooms have been upgraded to be **electronic courtrooms**.

Speaking of the jury, your displays with technology can help keep the attention of an impatient jury. Jury members are people just like you. That means they are just as easily distracted and ruled by the technology they use every day. Help them better synthesize and engage with information through delivering the evidence in a visual, audio, and physical capacity. This can also help jurors remember information that you lay out. Our minds have become quick to learn and promptly forget thanks to technology. This means that having a bit of a visual cue can help evidence stay in the minds of the jury for longer than traditional forms of evidence.

Standing out and appealing to the jury and judge the best way that you can is easy with technology. Technology is here to help and serve you—it is not a crutch. Start thinking of courtroom technology not as a replacement for your work but as an enhancement of the case you are working on.

What Is Courtroom Technology?

The benefits of courtroom technology are truly outstanding. However, what is classified as courtroom technology? We know that in many courtrooms, cell phones are banned. With this, what technology can we bring into the courtroom to help enhance our case? Keep in mind that not every courtroom will have these technological tools available. You may have to supply your own or switch up which tools you want to use to make your case.

Stop and Think!

Law & Order in the Court

Although many people have never stepped foot into an actual courtroom, most people have seen court hearings played out on TV in some fashion, either drama shows like *Law & Order* or *Court TV* with real litigants. With the onset of *Court TV* in the 1990s, we saw live trials that went on for weeks, captivating American audiences that otherwise likely would have never known how court was conducted. And recently, with the advances in technology, live hearings are conducted remotely through virtual conference platforms like Zoom, Skype, and WebEx. Still, jurors expect to be dazzled by technology in the courtroom. They expect to see those 3-D renderings and CGI crime-scene re-creations like they saw on *Law & Order*. Far too many cases are lost not on facts but on the inability to present the case properly to the jury. How has *Court TV* impacted the public view and expectations of how trials function? Do you feel that public broadcasting of a trial would affect the outcome?

The presentation controls are usually set up to be run from the counsel table. Each counsel table is equipped with a laptop port so that display presentations can be facilitated from the counsel's personal laptop. Visual display devices are positioned so that the witness can see the display while providing testimony to the court. The witness box usually contains an annotation monitor so that witnesses can make on-screen annotations when appropriate. See Exhibit 13–1.

Other display units are positioned at the opposing counsel table, judge's bench, and jury box. The judge's bench contains a kill switch so that the judge can control what is displayed to the jury and cut the display if it is ruled to be inappropriate information to show the jury. It is important that the judge be able to control the flow of information to protect the jury from being influenced by inappropriate material that could possibly cause a mistrial.

PowerPoint This classic technology tool can be used in presentations of all kinds. From business to school presentations, this program seems to be the go-to for all your explanatory needs. This makes it a great tool to use in the courtroom. PowerPoints are especially powerful during open and closing statements. This visual cue that goes along with the PowerPoint can help with memorability in your jury's mind. Remember that the jury will not recall everything you say, so making a lasting impression matters. Your PowerPoint slides can also help you explain advanced terms to your jury. If you have more complex terms in your trial, your jury may grow tired, bored, or confused. Keep them in the know with explanations about each complex term you discuss.

Effective PowerPoints are not about the length of information but rather about the power of information. You should strive to have only a few bullet points on each slide. A good rule of thumb is five bullet points on each slide and no more than five words for each bullet point. This will keep your information brief, memorable, and understandable. Your PowerPoint should lead you along your case and help the jury better understand what you are saying. Leave the crazy graphics and transitions at the door when it comes to PowerPoints. Keep it simple and use a color scheme that is pleasing to the eye and not distracting from your work. Ask other people how they like your PowerPoint before you use it in court to make sure everything looks good.

Laptop Port
A connection into which a laptop may be plugged.

Visual Display Device
A device that produces pictures or images, either still or live. Common visual devices include screens, monitors, and projectors.

Annotation Monitor
A monitor that allows a witness to easily make on-screen annotations with the touch of a finger.

Kill Switch
A control at the bench allowing the judge to turn off monitors until a particular piece of evidence is admitted or in an instance where the judge determines that certain images should not be shown to the jury.

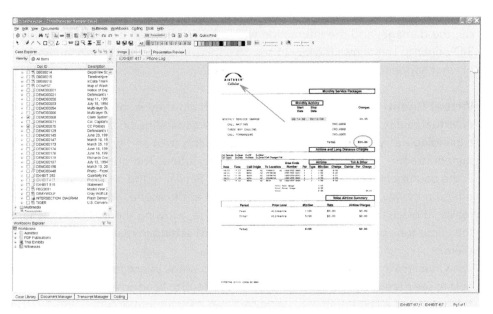

Exhibit 13–1
Annotations on a TrialDirector Slide

Overhead Projector
A visual aid used to project transparencies (often charts and graphs) onto a blank wall or screen.

Evidence Camera
A very small video camera that captures high-quality images of documents, photos, or objects placed within the camera's field of vision. Successor to the overhead projector.

Import
Method to bring documents and images into the program.

Visual Presentation Cart
Media center located in the courtroom.

Elmo This is an old-school technology tool but a trustworthy one. We are not talking about the furry red monster here but instead an **overhead projector** that can display your physical documents onto a big screen for the jury, judge, and everyone in the courtroom to see. An Elmo is a type of **evidence camera**. This lets the jury see the documents you are discussing firsthand. In the digital age, there are of course ways to easily **import** files digitally. However, Elmo is a trustworthy tool that can help you if something happens with your other forms of technology. If your digital files are lost for any reason, if you have Elmo and a physical copy of your documents, you can still easily show them to the court. You can also rely more on Elmos being in more courtrooms, even if the courthouses are not new and improved with their technology usage. There is also something special about seeing the paper copy of a document. Not that this physicality proves the legitimacy of your argument, but it does help you make your evidence clear and direct. The Elmo device is usually mounted onto a **visual presentation cart** that can be moved and relocated around the room to accommodate any need.

3-D Printing 3-D printing tools are huge in science, architecture, and many other fields. Such tools can also be easily used to help enhance your side in court. A 3-D printer works by pushing out molten plastic through a small nozzle. From there, the machine layers the plastic and molds it into the shape programmed into the computer. This makes for great physical demonstrative evidence in court. Having evidence that's not only visual and audio but also physical is great for diversifying your case and how you appeal to the jury. Remember, you want to be memorable, so give them something to remember.

This can help in cases of personal injury, assault and battery, car accident cases, or any case where an injury occurred. Instead of showing only 2-D pictures of the injury, you can deliver your message clearer with a model 3-D printing. These cases rely on the type of injury and the severity of it to issue a decision and ruling. You could show aftermath pictures and have witnesses and victims tell their stories, but the true power comes in being able to show the jury something tangible that they can see, hold, and pass around.

A good way to use 3-D printing is to mimic the injuries that a client sustained. This can give the jury an idea of how the injury truly looks and feels in full dimension. The same can be said for vandalism charges or car accidents. Models of the car, the damage, and the interaction with other parties can be laid out through 3-D printing. This allows the jury to see an unbiased and full-dimensional product of what happened in the accident or crime.

Virtual Reality It sometimes feels like we have only scratched the surface of virtual reality. Artificial intelligence and the capabilities of virtual reality are expanding every day. We can certainly hop on this train and use virtual reality in our courtrooms, either now or in the expanding future. The goal of virtual reality in the courtroom would be to stage the scene. Similar to the 3-D model, this can offer a new way of seeing what truly occurred at the scene. You can use virtual reality to place the courtroom at the crime scene, allowing the jury to see where the crime took place and view the evidence and setting in real time surrounding them.

Virtual reality is only beginning to expand its wings to accomplish a courtroom able to see a scene setting at the same time. We need to keep an eye on virtual reality technology as a courtroom tool because it can offer a more accurate visualization of what happened at the scene. Words and pictures can say only so much. Taking the jury to the scene of the crime transforms the narrative into a relatable piece of evidence.

Video Chat With the COVID-19 pandemic in 2020, we saw a rise of videoconference meetings and conference calls held over video chat. We even saw this structure weave its way into litigation. Video chat is a huge piece of courtroom technology that is now, luckily, starting to be explored. This can be used for videoconference court appearances. If witnesses or otherwise cannot come to court physically, they can call in. The legitimacy of their testimony still stands entirely, the only difference being that they are not present physically in court. This could cut down on travel time and allow more accessibility to coming and going into the court. This could allow more people to testify on a case.

Make sure to check with the courthouse that video chats are allowed in court. Also, ask if you can set up and test the videoconference equipment before jumping right into it. This will make sure that there are no technical errors from the call. Nothing is worse than an image freezing up or becoming blurry or sound and movement lagging on the call. Avoid all these mistakes prior to asking any questions. You want technology to work as a tool for you, not be a distraction.

Videoconference Equipment
Equipment that facilitates a two-way real-time transmission of audio and video signals between specialized devices or computers at two more locations.

Electronic Court Filing Electronic court filing has been adopted by many courtrooms—and for good reason. This started out as an effort to go paperless. This is a great help not only to the environment but also to the clients and lawyers who operate in a courtroom setting. For clients, an electronic court filing system means convenience for the clients. This means that clients will not have to stop by court to file a claim but can instead do so from the comfort of their homes electronically.

For lawyers, you can easily see a time line of when everything for court was submitted. Rather than sorting through a ton of documents to locate a piece of evidence, you can pull up your time line of the case and easily locate different documents for reference. This beats searching through a stack of files for that one document you may have never given to court. This also gives you more time to focus on your case strategy rather than on the mundane details. This is a safe and easy way to ensure that all files are accounted for and kept in a space you can easily refer to.

Blockchain Technology Blockchain technology is used a lot in the business world and now can be incorporated into the law world. Blockchain technology is a "cutting-edge digital ledger that creates decentralized records of peer-to-peer transactions."[1] This is what allows you to make immediate payments and transfers without being connected to a financial institution. Blockchain technology is extremely difficult to hack into, change, and destroy information associated under it. This is precisely why it is a great courtroom tool.

With safety and security at the core of technological advancement in law, blockchain technology checks all the boxes. Blockchain technology can be helpful for signing and creating smart contracts. These contracts can be protected and secured under blockchain technology. Also, automated terms and conditions can be made and dealt with through blockchain technology. Another benefit of blockchain technology is that it can serve to record long events. This can help

---

[1]What the Future Holds for Technology in the Courtroom.pdf.
https://www.law.com/legaltechnews/2020/01/23/what-the-future-holds-for-technology-in-the-courtroom/

in criminal charges and intellectual property claims. Blockchain technology keeps your information and classified data safe and secure from hackers that could sneak into less secure systems.

Cloud Computing "It got sent to the cloud" is a popular phrase you may have heard tossed around the past couple of years. That is because of the evolving and expanding amount of cloud computing systems. Broken down, cloud computing is the storage or hosting of your documents and files. This can be either on your actual computer or on a server that is run through a paid network. An example of this cloud computing software would be Dropbox or Microsoft SharePoint. There are a lot of other cloud options out there, so you should be able to find one that is right for you.

Once you have all your files and documents onto the cloud, you can synchronize them to all your computers and mobile devices. This means you do not have to lug your laptop with you to the courtroom. Since everything is in the cloud, you can pull up documents from anywhere. These cloud services are safe and secure, so you will not have a problem losing documents like you would with a traditional physical file organizer. This can be a great way to easily sort through your documents and find the files you need for the case easily and from one source. Cloud computing means more efficient organization and thus more efficient presentation.

All about Trial Presentation Software

Trial presentation software allows you to organize evidence, keep it in one place, and display it for the jury. It is a great method to layer text over video and picture, compare documents side by side, and truly customize your case presentation. Trial presentation software systems are like PowerPoint slides that are geared toward helping lawyers in the best possible way. They help with storage, management, retrieval, and display of documents, photos, images, and anything else you want to showcase to the jury.

Trial presentation software is especially important when dealing with complex concepts. Like we said earlier with the PowerPoints being a source of reference and explanation for large concepts and definitions, the same applies to trial presentation software and its capabilities. There are many different trial presentation software systems out there, but three particularly stand out from the crowd: Sanction, TrialPad, and TrialDirector.

Each software tool will have different benefits to them. Therefore, it is important that you pick one that matches your needs for your trial and allows you to effectively get the trial prepped so that mistakes do not happen later. First, think of how many exhibits you have. If there are fewer than 50 and no videos to your presentation, the free option of TrialDirector is perfect for you. If you have fewer than 200 exhibits, you may want to try out TrialPad. The system costs $130 but is better for handling larger cases. Both tools are tablet based. However, if you have more than 200 exhibits, you will need a more powerful system that can hold more. Systems you control through your laptop are best for these extra-large cases. See Exhibit 13–2.

Trial presentation software can help you show multiple documents at a time for comparison. It can also allow you to show impeachment videos without scrolling through text. You can split your screen with videos and exhibits. You can also have live callouts and make annotations while the presentation occurs. One of the

Exhibit 13–2 TrialDirector screen

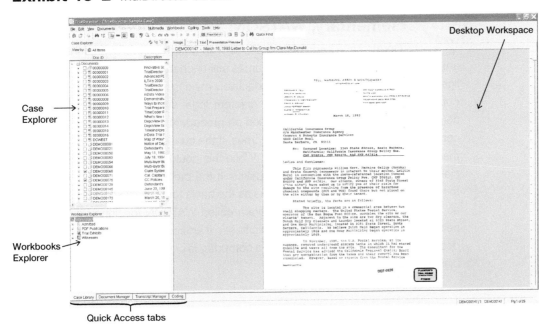

best things about trial presentation software is that it brings up evidence quickly and efficiently. No one wants to waste time on a lawyer who is sifting through his documents rather than asking questions and explaining his case.

Trial presentation software is great for comparing images, documents, and so on because you can put up every document and file you need at once. This can offer a great visual aid to the jury that will better help them understand the case at hand. Make sure that the courtroom you are going into allows such presentations and can host the display technology you need.

The main difference that comes with PowerPoints versus trial presentation software is that trial presentation software offers relief and compensates for what PowerPoint lacks. PowerPoint is great for simple presentations and trials, but trial presentation software allows you to fully incorporate everything you need for your trial through a law perspective. This tool is optimized to meet the needs of lawyers (rather than laypeople) who need to give a presentation. Consider getting free or low-cost trial presentation software to make putting together and delivering your case much easier and more efficient.

Tips for Courtroom Technology

You now have a clear idea of what courtroom technology is at your disposal and the importance of it. However, there are still some things to watch out for when beginning to use technology in the courtroom.

Anticipate Auditory Needs If your case involves parties or witnesses who are nonnative English language speakers, the court may require the use of an interpreter so that court proceedings can be properly understood without any language barrier issues. The interpreter speaks into a microphone, and the listener receives the interpretation through an **audio output device**, such as **infrared headphones**. An **interpreter box** will control where the audio feed is sent and is usually controlled by the judge or an employee from the courthouse.

Audio Output Device
A device that produces music, speech, or other sounds, such as beeps. Common output devices include speakers and headsets.

Infrared Headphones
Headphones used for listening that are cordless; used for the hearing-impaired during court proceedings. Most infrared headphones have a 30-foot range.

Interpreter Box
Routes audio channels of language translations for simultaneous interpretation to the witness/defendant's headphone or the courtroom's Internet system.

Tech This Out!

Elementary, WATSON!

Courts have been historically slow to adopt technology, so the role of artificial intelligence in the court system is still uncharted territory. Artificial intelligence could play a role in judicial decision making, where algorithms predict outcomes resulting from the use of different legal strategies. This change will come from the theory that law is based on precedent and therefore it is easy to compare current facts with prior outcomes. If the current case is like a prior case, then the results should be the same. While this could create much-needed efficiencies, it could also perpetuate injustice. If the precedent cases were biased, the cases dependent on that outcome as the basis for its decision will be biased as well. An artificial intelligence program called WATSON (designed by IBM) is being tested by a juvenile court in Ohio to see if artificial intelligence can properly decide case outcomes. Do you think a computer is capable of eliminating human bias to render an impartial decision?

Have a Backup Plan To start, always have a backup plan. This is a good rule for life and especially in the courtroom. Like we have been saying, things happen. Technology breaks down, certain cords do not line up, or the courthouse does not have the technology that you need available. Have a backup plan for what you are going to do if technology fails you. You never know what will happen, so it is good to be prepared. An Elmo machine is a great backup plan if your trial presentation software falls through.

Find replacements like this that you can have readily available if something happens. You may have to ditch your new technology for physical documents if something happens and your technology crashes. Be aware that this could happen at any time. Do not let this premise wear you down and scare you from using new technology. Instead, just make sure you are extra prepared for your trial.

How Technologically Advanced Are the Courtrooms? Find out ahead of time how technologically advanced the courtroom you are presenting in will be. This goes along with the theme of preparing beforehand. You do not want to show up day of the trial wondering if you will be able to use all your technical tools. Instead, call prior and see how you can efficiently set up your technology in accordance with what the courtroom has.

Take Your Time Remember in school when the teacher would put up a slide for you to take notes on and right when you were on the last sentence, the slide would change? It gives you a sense of being incomplete and not fully knowing all the information. Do not put the documents up too quickly and do not move too quickly from one slide or document to the next. Leave them up for a bit so the jurors can really soak in the information. Feel out the room, and you will know when the jurors have digested all the information and are ready to move on to the next topic. Rushing through your trial only takes away from the power that the technological tools give you to fully express your case.

Most Important Documents Use only the most important documents in your presentation. Yes, you can throw up a million and one bits of evidence and documents. However, like we said earlier, people are forgetful. Leave people on a note of wanting more rather than feeling like they have been overwhelmed with information to the point where none of it matters. Sift through and find the most important bits of evidence and information to talk about. People can digest only so much information at a time. Just because you have access to all of these documents doesn't mean you have to use every single one.

Have Someone Else Operate the Computer   This is not always possible, but if you can, have someone else operate the technology you have set up while you present your case. You may think you can multitask, but you will do much better on your own not focusing on two or more tasks. You can also connect with the jury more when you are not asking questions and operating the computer at the same time. You can set up your own assistant to help with this or call the courtroom ahead of time to see if they will have someone to assist you with your technology.

Labeling Matters   When it comes to your documents, labeling them simply and efficiently matters. Do not give your files a complex name. You do not want to waste the judge's or jury's time by locating the documents too slowly. Keep the labels simple and in a way that makes sense to you. Trial presentation software can also help you out with having all the documents in one place. Do not go with the automatic label that the computer gives you when saving your document. You want to make labels relevant to your case and easy to find. Physical evidence is often given a bar code sticker that is placed on the item. The sticker can be read using a **bar code reader**, and a digital copy of the item can then be imported into your computer for easy display.

Bar Code Reader
An input device that uses laser beams to read a group of characters (bar code). When activated, the bar code reader translates information from bar codes into commands to software, usually to locate an exhibit.

Practice with Technology Ahead of Time   Finally, it is vital to practice beforehand with the technology you are going to use. This goes back to always being prepared. Have a practice session before. You do not have to fully run through your trial presentation, but make sure all your technology works properly. Do not rely on simply trusting that it will work.

Conclusion

The importance of technology in the courtroom and adapting to the new digital world will only rise in the years to come. Make sure you are technically competent and compliant with the courtroom technology. Technology tools are here to assist the lawyers, and their legal team in making a better court presentation. These tools are not a replacement for the legal work performed but rather a way to enhance the brilliant job already done. Consider adding in trial presentation software to the next case presented in court instead of going old school with the Elmo projector. Let these tools serve you.

Key Terms

Annotation Monitor	Infrared Headphones	Videoconference Equipment
Audio Output Device	Interpreter Box	Visual Display Device
Bar Code Reader	Kill Switch	Visual Presentation Cart
Evidence Camera	Laptop Port	
Import	Overhead Projector	

Discussion Questions

1. Has courtroom technology had a positive or a negative impact on the practice of law? Provide examples to support your viewpoint.

2. Has courtroom technology affected the methods by which attorneys conduct trials and hearings? Provide examples to support your viewpoint. Consider both personal technology and courtroom equipment issues.

3. Should all attorneys be trained to use technology in the courtroom? Explain why or why not. Provide examples to support your viewpoint.

Additional Resources

Courtroom Technology System—Introduction and Why Training Matters
https://youtu.be/morg0AbGbDo

LexisNexis Sanction—Recreating Trial History Using the Latest Technology
Lexis Sanction: Timothy McVeigh Oklahoma Federal Building Bombing
https://youtu.be/MRUIZcPeSrl

Lawyer Breaks Down 30 Courtroom Scenes from Film & TV
https://youtu.be/we6qm0zXMYU

What the Future Holds for Technology in the Courtroom
By Leon Hilliard "Hill" Hughes, Morrison & Hughes January 23, 2020
https://www.law.com/legaltechnews/2020/01/23/what-the-future-holds-for-technology-in-the-courtroom/

Technology and the Courts: A Futurist View
By Judge Herbert B. Dixon Jr., July 1, 2013
https://www.americanbar.org/groups/judicial/publications/judges_journal/2013/summer/technology_and_the_courts_a_futurist_view/

The Basics of a Technology-Enhanced Courtroom
By Judge Herbert B. Dixon Jr., November 1, 2017
https://www.americanbar.org/groups/judicial/publications/judges_journal/2017/fall/basics-technologyenhanced-courtroom/

Do Court Bans on Electronic Devices Impede Access to Justice?
By Kate Silver, April 1, 2019
https://www.abajournal.com/magazine/article/court-bans-electronic-devices-a2j

Courtroom Effective Technology
Matt Lalande, August 14, 2019
https://www.lawtechnologytoday.org/2019/08/courtroom-effective-technology/

Chapter 14

Legal Apps and the Access to Justice Movement

Learning Objectives

- Explain access to justice, how it affects the average person, and why it is important.
- Identify and explain how technology can assist and expand the justice system.
- Identify and explain multiple apps that assist in accessing the legal system in order to help achieve access to justice.

NSLT Tasks Associated with This Chapter

- Having completed all the prior chapter tasks, the requirements for earning the NSLT Legal Technology Certificate should be met. Complete any prior unfinished task and submit the request for your certificate.

Introduction

The legal system, like every other system on Earth, is not without faults. Often the less fortunate, undereducated, and even small businesses are left behind in the wake of legal teams and structures. However, in the digital age we live in, a new promise for the future awaits us. Technology can expand access to the justice system and level the playing field when it comes to accessibility for the less fortunate. It is time to let technology stand hand in hand with lawyers in the fight for justice. We will cover why access to justice can be accomplished through technology, the apps we can use to expand this, and overall how technology will not only improve but also expand the legal system.

Justice
Just behavior or treatment.

What Does Access to Justice Entail?

The legal system still has a way to go when it comes to access and accessibility in the market. Technology can ultimately tackle this by reducing cost, freeing up lawyers, and giving customers greater control over their legal problems. This is mainly in commercial law practice and intended for small-business owners and individuals who have cases they need to discuss or expand on. With this being said, what does access to justice entail?

In a broad definition that means better access to lawyers and the courts. This can come through the ability for the layperson to understand what the legal system entails at every step of the process. This means that consumers know their legal rights, can exercise their rights, and achieve a just outcome according to their case. Often, a gap between lawyers and their clients occurs because the legal jargon used is not accessible and understandable to the layperson. Technology can give access to more user-friendly services. This can avoid problems coming up at court and instead having the problems be discovered before the arrival at court and dealt with from the jump. This speeds up the legal system and makes everything run more smoothly.

Benefits of Tech for Clients

Beyond how tech can make the legal process understandable for clients, it also serves many other purposes. For one, technology can link every step of the legal process together in a way that allows a simplistic route from start to finish to happen. This allows the client to have more trust that the system will care for their needs and accomplish their goals. This will make a system that can reach a conclusion to the case in the most efficient and smooth manner. With technology, cases are organized better, structures are set up for success from the start, and a fair outcome is always maintained in the quickest fashion.

Also, with the amount of technology out there aiding the justice system, there is a solution for any problem the client may face along the way, be it large or small. This can range from automated tools for smaller and urgent needs around the clock, additional assistance even when clients are representing themselves, and overall advice at every step of the process.

This is all achieved through tech's ability to make complex answers simple. When both the client and the lawyer know what is happening in the legal process, both can spot solutions. The client can also begin to better understand what problems constitute legal action. Before a case even begins, a person can know what one's legal rights are and what actions one can take alongside a lawyer. Overall, technology can be used to guide clients toward the proper support they need for their case. Every legal case is different, so guidance for those who are unaware of where to go for support is necessary to make a legal system that is just for all.

Technology can also help with affordability. If clients cannot afford their own private lawyer, they can at least be empowered by technology to understand the legal system and the journey they are about the embark on. Barriers between understanding the legal system are stripped away when everyone has access to technology that clarifies the case they are in. The entire legal process becomes less aloof and mystic when transparency, through technology, is offered to the layperson. In addition, client and lawyer communication can be limited. With technology, the client can have access to a plethora of information at any time. Transactions and response times can be minimized between clients and their legal team.

Benefits of Tech for Providers

Technology in the legal system has benefits for not only the client but also the legal provider. Technology is here to serve lawyers and ease them from busywork so that they have more time to focus on case strategy and other important details of the client's case. Technology can make a provider's workflow more productive. Time is spent on more important tasks, while the client gets more tedious and unofficial work and questions answered by legal tech. Productivity is at the head of legal technology.

The issue of fees and keeping tabs on the work that has been done can also be streamlined and automated. Fees can be restructured and automated through technology's help. Along with this, data from the case can be better organized with technology compared to using only physical documents for cases. Data and client information can also be stored more securely through legal technology, a luxury that is not possible without the introduction of tech in the justice system.

It is currently estimated that the United States spends around $1.5 billion on legal tech every year. Globally, the estimate is at about $15.9 billion spent on tech. The need for technology in the justice system and improvements every year is quite clear.

Access to justice in the United Kingdom and Wales is not working for individuals and small businesses. This is mainly because the costs of legal services are too high. Along with this, citizens are not able to easily compare providers and make an informed decision for who they want to represent them. According to one study,[1] over half of the adults in the United Kingdom and Wales have a problem that would best be handled through legal action. However, only one in three people will seek out legal assistance. The others will deal with the problem on their own or not at all.

Stop and Think!

Justice for All!

That phrase is tossed around frequently, but what does it really mean? Across the United States, there are many vulnerable and underserved communities in need of social justice. There should be a fairness within our society that applies equally to everyone regardless of race, gender, or socioeconomic conditions. No one should be without the essentials (food and shelter), and everyone should have access to basic needs, such as medical and legal services. Although there are legal aid programs throughout the country, budget constraints limit these services, and therein lies the problem with "access" to the justice system. It is our most vulnerable members of society that face the inability to pay legal fees when they often need the most protection. To have "justice for all," the government, local communities, and the private sector will need to partner together in providing resources to give everyone equal protection under the law. What could be done to ensure that everyone has access to justice?

Make sure to check out the American Bar Association's article on access to justice at https://www.americanprogress.org/issues/courts/news/2021/04/08/497950/justice-requires-access-justice.

---

[1]Legal Access Challenge, "The Use of Technology to Widen Access to Justice," https://legalaccesschallenge.org/insights/the-use-of-technology-to-widen-access-to-justice/.

Without legal technology, people do not feel empowered to have a say and ask for help from the legal system. Most do not even know whether a problem is warranted for taking legal action because of the gatekeeping that is being done by the legal community. This lack of awareness creates a lack of trust in consumers. People begin to think that lawyers do not have their best interest at heart whenever education through technology is not available as a resource. With legal technology, we tear down the barriers between client and provider, thereby enacting a more fair and just legal system.

Tech That Can Expand the Justice System

The uses for tech in the legal system are expansive. To better achieve an equal status between providers and clients, tech must be mixed in. This means that specific technology must be used in the fight toward a more just system. What tech can we use in the legal area to expand and create the environment we want and need? Let us see.

Guided Pathways

Guided Pathways
A movement that seeks to streamline a student's journey through college by providing structured choice, revamped support, and clear learning outcomes—ultimately helping more students achieve their college completion goals.

Creating **guided pathways** can help streamline clients toward success with their case. This is a method popular in colleges to inform students of how they should navigate their college experience and in what ways administration can help along the way. Why don't we do the same in our legal system?

A good place to start is to make questionnaires for clients. Questions that are simple to understand can help the client efficiently answer and give all information a lawyer would need for their case from the start. A questionnaire is also a simple method that most people considering legal action would not shy away from. Going back to our case study from the United Kingdom and Wales, possibly more people would seek legal action if a standard questionnaire were available for them to understand their possible options and know the next steps to take.

The technology could automatically set the client's case on one of a few different paths, based on their answers, that is best suited to their needs. This also means pairing the client with the best provider for the case without much effort being made by the client or provider in establishing the connection. Technology gets the initial work done so that providers and clients can focus on what really matters.

Automated Document Assembly

Document automation can allow legal teams to create documents online and send them to their clients through their computers. This reduces the back and forth that comes with the exchange and processing of legal information. This is a part of the acceleration of the legal process with the help of technology. Legal documents are automated, and the creation and completion of court forms can happen without the client and provider having to meet up and get the information signed and approved in person. Less back and forth means less time wasted on menial tasks.

Online Dispute Resolution

One of the more advanced ways the legal system can accelerate the process with technology is through online dispute resolution. Not every case has to be taken to court. If the client and lawyer agree that going to court is the next best step, then great. However, many disputes can be solved outside of court and even online. Online tools that we will talk about later allow the client's case to be solved through means separate from going to court. This can involve negotiation, mediation, and arbitration. All of this can be achieved more effortlessly with the help of technology on the side of the client and provider.

Originally, this technology was made to help consumers and sellers manage and resolve their problems in a cordial way. Now, courts are beginning to see how this system can actually help the justice system expedite and make the process much simpler for all parties. This type of resolution happens through email, video chat, and other online means. If a problem cannot be sorted out this way, the case can come to court. This is a system that can save time for everyone and allow the legal system to run as smoothly as possible.

Artificial Intelligence

In the past couple of years, the advance of technology and Artificial Intelligence (AI) in the public and private spheres has occurred, and the possibilities of expanding AI have circulated. The law field can surely benefit from the help of AI. In the legal sphere, AI can help with problem solving and application where the human mind would not be able to. This can prove beneficial for data extraction, decision making, and operational planning.

It could take a lawyer far too many hours and days to extrapolate data that would relate to the client's case and organize that data to speak to the case at hand in a way that makes sense. Technology can sift through and store data in a more eloquent and efficient manner so that lawyers can focus on using their critical thinking skills and talents for the case.

AI systems have many different tools that make the legal process smoother. One AI system that can be used in law is expert systems. These expert AI systems will use rule-based or knowledge-based approaches to sift through the expansive amount of information on the Web for exactly what the lawyer or client needs. This way, the user can easily find expert information on a subject, saving time and effort that can be better utilized elsewhere on the case.

The next AI application that can be used in law practice is natural language processing (NLP). This includes speech recognition and text-to-speech programs. These NLP programs can help computers analyze and understand human language. In the same way, NLP programs can learn to respond to the client's question when brought to the technology's attention. This can also help break down language into understandable terms for the average person no matter their education level.

Chatbots can help customers as well when lawyers are not available. The more sophisticated the NLP system, the more a chatbot can understand and discuss with the client. This stretches the lawyer's hours past the classic 9 to 5 without their having to be there in person with the client. The extraction of relevant information can be processed and organized thanks to AI. All these features that are brought to the stage could have been accomplished by people without AI, but the addition of technology eases the burden of these sometimes menial tasks. See Exhibit 14–1.

Online Dispute Resolution

A branch of dispute resolution that uses technology to facilitate the resolution of disputes between parties. It primarily involves negotiation, mediation arbitration or a combination of all three.

Mediation

Intervention in a dispute to resolve it.

Artificial Intelligence (AI)

The capability of a machine or computer to imitate human behavior. Also known as machine learning.

Data Extraction

The process of retrieving data out of data sources for further data processing or data storage.

Extrapolate

Extend the application of (a method or conclusion, especially one based on statistics) to an unknown situation by assuming that existing trends will continue or similar methods will be applicable.

Natural Language Processing (NLP)

A branch of artificial intelligence that deals with the interaction between computers and human language.

Chatbots

A software application used to conduct an online chat conversation via text or text to speech in lieu of providing direct contact with a live human agent. A chatbot is a type of software that can automate conversations and interact with people through messaging platforms.

Exhibit 14–1 Chatbot photo

mohamed hassan/Pxhere

What Apps Can Help?

Several apps are available for the general public and lawyers alike. These apps make access to the legal system easy, affordable, and quick. Many of these apps use the principles of AI to help clients and lawyers. The vision that AI can be used for good, progressive measures has been adopted by Microsoft. The company now has a mission to use AI for human rights. This is documented in their AI for Human Rights Action of 2018 and involves some legal apps as a part of the fight for equality and justice through AI.

TrialWatch

One of the apps under Microsoft's Human Rights Act is TrialWatch. This app focuses its attention on injustice happening around the world. They particularly keep a close eye on those who are affected the most negatively in courts, such as minorities. TrialWatch monitors trials and advocates for the rights of those who are being unfairly tried. TrialWatch has people attend every hearing that they want to report on. From there, the monitor will report any injustices happening, and those on the app can take steps to correct the wrongs.

This app is opening the closed door of the courtroom. Often, we are told everything before a case but not shown the case as it occurs in court. TrialWatch provides transparency about what happens at every step of the hearing. TrialWatch notes an important comparison of technology in voting and how it should also apply to legal trials, stating,[2] "International election monitoring allows us to know if an election was free and fair; TrialWatch provides the same capability for trials."

TrialWatch also offers a text-to-speech function so that those who do not speak the language in which the trial is taking place can still see what is being said and add their input to the case. This is one of the many AI tools that is helping to expand justice through these apps.

---

[2] Clooney Foundation for Justice, "Justice for Victims of Unfair Trials," https://cfj.org/project/trialwatch/.

Teams and Zoom

Teams, Zoom, and other video call apps are other essential technological tools to have in the legal world. One of the barriers that keeps people from obtaining justice is the time and distance it can take people to meet up with a lawyer. For those without a reliable mode of transportation or with a demanding schedule, seeing a lawyer is simply not feasible. With video call apps like these, people can begin to reach out to a lawyer for help anywhere. It is a good idea for any lawyer to consider offering videoconferences as a way for clients to meet up and discuss a case with them. Understanding law can be complex, and no barriers should exist for civilians being able to reach out to a professional for help.

Cloud-Based Software

Some legal apps and teams collaborate with their clients through the cloud. An example of this is with the A2J Project that helps people that do not have legal representation put together their case through online means. This keeps the work manageable in one place and accessible to the client and lawyer at all times and allows easy communication without the burden of travel. This project takes place in the United States, but we are seeing similar programs evolve around the world. For example, in the United Kingdom, a service called CourtNav helps people put together their divorce petitions specifically.

Uthority

This is a German technology app that has users scan in their case and have it "translated" into standard English. The key points are given, and the large legal jargon words are broken down into everyday language. This bridges the gap between lawyers and the clients they serve to make sure everyone is on the same playing field. Users simply take a picture of a legal letter or court document they have, and the app takes over from there with its smart technology and AI system.

Civil Resolution Tribunal

Remember when we talked about resolving issues without the interference of a court? Well, this app does just that. The app Civil Resolution Tribunal acts to referee small claims, mainly motor vehicle injury cases and housing disputes. The app works by having both plaintiffs file an application online. Then a mediation occurs between both parties and the AI system. The goal is to solve the problem mutually and avoid going to court. If no agreement can be reached, legal action can be placed. This is a great way to solve small claims that do not necessarily have to go straight to court.

Ask a Lawyer App

Ask a Lawyer is an app that gives free **consultation** advice from attorneys. This app is beneficial for both client and lawyer. Clients get a basic understanding of the process that lies ahead and whether the lawyer with whom they talk is a good match. They can do all of this from the comfort of their home. Lawyers have the ability to find new potential clients. If the preliminary consultation goes well, the lawyer may have a new case to work on.

Consultation
The action or process of formally consulting or discussing.

> ## Tech This Out!
> ### Do Not Pay!
> Chatbot apps that allow you to state your claim and find the solution through the help of an AI computer are expanding on the work of cloud-based software. We see this in the app Do Not Pay. This is an app that helps people appeal parking tickets in the United Kingdom and in parts of the United States. This service does not even require lawyers to be on the other end since smart AI technology takes care of it all from start to finish. This type of software could expand to cover small-claims and civil cases.

CitizenshipWorks

This app makes the naturalization process for immigrants easier and more digestible. People can see if they are eligible to become a U.S. citizen, what documents they need to have in order to start the process, see what free or low-cost legal help can accompany them along their journey, and even study for the tests that are required during the naturalization process. This app makes citizenship more accessible to those who are not sure where to begin. For a process that is rather long and confusing, CitizenshipWorks breaks down the process into manageable steps.

Disastr

You often cannot avoid a natural disaster wreaking havoc on your community. However, you can get help to rebuild your life after the disaster happens. With the Disastr app, users can have direct access to disaster relief, news regarding the natural disaster, and advice for legal action to take to rebuild their lives. After a tragedy strikes, it can feel like there is nothing you can do to return to normal. However, apps like these make the process of transitioning into your new life a bit easier and can help you make the best of your situation.

LawZam

This is another free advice app from lawyers to clients. Here, clients can ask a lawyer questions and receive free consultations about their legal problem. With these types of apps, neither party is locked in. Clients can decide to not follow through with their case or choose a different lawyer to represent them. The same is true for lawyers: they do not have to pick up the client's case after the initial free consultation. These free advice apps get clients in the door and them asking questions they want answers to but aren't exactly sure where to find them. See Exhibit 14–2.

Legal Aid News

Remember what we said about empowering the layperson to be curious about the legal system and take steps toward seeking out answers? Well, this app does just that. Up-to-date legal articles circulate through this site so that everyone can keep up with legal aid news. This can be general legal aid information, particular to a subject you are curious about, or a piece of legal news that's specific to the

Source: Lawzam

Exhibit 14–2 LawZam website

state you live in. Also, this app contains information on national legal aid centers for low-income clients who otherwise may not reach out for legal help.

Phone View

This app will cost you about $30, but it is worth it for clients to have if their particular case depends on this function. In Phone View, all your messages, call logs, and voice mails are transferred swiftly to the cloud, where you can access them on your computer. This makes it easier for the process of scrolling, making screenshots, or however else you would transfer data from one type of technology to another. In addition, cell phones are not allowed in many courtrooms. With this app, you will not need your cell phone to display the evidence that you have on it.

Shake

This app allows you to come up with your own legally binding agreements and send them to whomever you need to sign on. This app has templates that you can choose from that are created by attorneys—for you. The documents can be signed from your phone, making the entire process easier. This ensures that you are protected in whatever agreement you go into without having to jump through hoops to make it all happen. The terms and conditions are also in everyday English, so there is no need to do an Internet search for certain definition meanings.

My Attorney

Having constant contact with your attorney is not feasible unless an AI system steps in to help. However, you can download this app so that making contact with your attorney is a bit easier. The My Attorney app allows you to text and chat with your attorney rather than through email or in person. Again, this allows clients to have a preference for how they reach their attorney beyond the standard method of contact. Also, attorneys can upload past verdicts and cases to their profile on the app. This way, clients can look over the information and determine if they want to use the attorney again in the future for a different case.

Many other apps exist to make the process of finding information, deciphering that information, and knowing what the next steps are to take in a legal action. We already see technology in the legal field growing and can expect this trend to continue in the future as we become more well versed in the current technology and the technical possibilities for the future.

The Future of Technology and Law

We are already seeing the future of technology evolve and change with time. We can expect that these innovations in legal technology will expand and compound as well. Let us take a look at what we may see in terms of legal tech 5, 10, and 15 years from now.

Remote Legal Advice

We discussed some examples of how much legal work can be done through a screen. Whether this is through a video call, an AI server analyzing a document, or a chatbot giving you real-time feedback, the remote way of working and living is no longer just a theory. The COVID-19 pandemic showed the world that remote work could be accomplished successfully. We can expect that this trend of less travel and fewer unnecessary commutes will continue, and that the technology to support this remote lifestyle will grow.

Video Communication and Rules around It

Along with remote legal advice, we may see an expansion of court cases taking place through video communications. This means that we also will see regulations around what qualifies as a case that should be taken up in person and what does not. When video communication courses are done out of necessity, such as during the pandemic, fewer rules are established because it is such a new scenario. However, if we want to keep this way of communicating in the legal field, rules for what works and what does not will need to be expanded on.

Opening the Courts to the Public

We are sure to see the courts becoming less mystified in the future. Young people are interested in trials that they feel are unjust. With today's technology, an expansion of apps like TrialWatch will allow people who never went to law school to ask questions, be curious, and take note of injustices they see the system perpetrating. From live video feeds to monitored trials, we will see an opening of previously closed legal doors. People will begin to be self-empowered to understand their rights, take note of when injustice is happening, and pivot their approach to react to injustice.

Rise in Digital Competency

We are sure to see a rise across all businesses and fields in educating employees on digital competency and how to be technically adept. Lawyers will have to also jump on this train of technological competency. We can already see all the terrific and new ways that the legal realm is changing. For lawyers to stay on top

COVID-19

An acute respiratory illness in humans caused by a coronavirus, capable of producing severe symptoms and in some cases death, especially in older people and those with underlying health conditions. It was originally identified in China in 2019 and became a pandemic in 2020.

Technological Competency

The ability to create and use a particular field of technology effectively.

of all the changes, they must learn to adapt. Digital competency courses may begin to be offered for jobs, classes may be added to the school curriculum, and, overall, more changes to incorporate digital competency into the workplace will occur.

How the Pandemic Has Pushed Change

As mentioned previously, the future of legal technology is sure to expand as a response to the changes that have occurred with the recent pandemic. Remote work has been proven to be a method that can work in society, as shown by the COVID-19 pandemic's push for employees to work from home. The pandemic also pushed people to accept change and the technology that comes with it.

Before the pandemic hit, the American Bar Association was already beginning to develop a way to go virtual. Some of the reasons were long commutes, high office costs, traffic impeding on the legal process, and a desire to better serve clients in their practice. All these reasons were valid but not immediate causes for concern. The push for a virtual law system could have been put off for several years. However, the pandemic hurried this process and pumped the change out in an efficient manner because we had to.

This allows us to now see that decisions can be made rather quickly and still work to our advantage. Many law firms had already begun to enforce new rules before the pandemic and then were quickly led to enforce them. While all decisions should be made with thought, the pandemic showed us that we can make decisions and changes with the same amount of thought but with less time spent. The positive response of legal technology that came out of the pandemic can only be expected to stay and evolve as time goes on.

Conclusion

The future is digital. That includes the legal world. Lawyers should be excited about the prospect of more efficient workflows, more help with their cases, and the empowerment of the people to seek justice in the courts. Technology cannot stop injustices from happening, but it can transform the outcome that comes from that injustice. Legal technology and the apps that make it easily spread to the public allow the legal system to no longer be untouchable to the public. We will soon see how this evolves our justice system in the future.

Key Terms

Artificial Intelligence (AI)
Chatbots
Consultation
COVID-19
Data Extraction

Extrapolate
Guided Pathways
Justice
Mediation
Natural Language Processing (NLP)

Online Dispute Resolution
Technological Competency

Discussion Questions

1. How has the use of legal apps impacted the practice of law?

2. How is the access to justice better accomplished using technology?

3. How does the use of technology benefit the client? How does it benefit law firms? Provide examples to support your viewpoint.

4. Does using AI impact the justice system? Provide examples to support your viewpoint.

5. How do you see mobile applications impacting the future of legal practice?

6. What was the impact of the COVID-19 pandemic in relation to legal practice? Do you foresee these changes continuing? Why or why not? Provide examples to support your viewpoint.

Additional Resources

Department of Justice-Access To Justice Publication.
https://www.justice.gov/archives/atj/publications

THE LEGACY OF GIDEON V. WAINWRIGHT
https://www.justice.gov/archives/atj/legacy-gideon-v-wainwright

Human Rights and Access to Justice
https://www.americanbar.org/advocacy/rule_of_law/what-we-do/human-rights-access-to-justice/

Glossary

A

Admissions   A set of statements sent from one litigant to an adversary for the purpose of having the adversary admit or deny the statements or allegations therein.

Analytical Litigation Support Programs   Software programs that help law firms analyze a case from several different perspectives and draw conclusions about cause-and-effect relationships between different facts and evidence in a case.

Animation   Movement of text, graphics, or other objects within a slide.

Annotation Monitor   A monitor that allows a witness to easily make on-screen annotations with the touch of a finger.

Artificial Intelligence (AI)   The capability of a machine or computer to imitate human behavior. Also known as machine learning.

Attorney–Client Privilege   A rule of evidence requiring that communications between a client and their attorney be kept confidential unless the client consents to disclosure.

Audio Output Device   A device that produces music, speech, or other sounds, such as beeps. Common output devices include speakers and headsets.

Auto Text   Entries that are inserted automatically when you type a specific set of characters.

B

Backup   A copy of a user's hard disk or other storage device that can be restored if the hard disk is damaged or lost. Backup utility programs allow users to schedule times to ensure reoccurring backups to protect the data.

Bar Code Reader   An input device that uses laser beams to read a group of characters (bar code). When activated, the bar code reader translates information from bar codes into commands to software, usually to locate an exhibit.

blockchain technology   A type of database (collection of information) that is structured into chunks of information that are "chained" together, creating an irreversible timeline of data that are added to the database.

Boilerplate   A document using standard language and/or fill-in-the-blanks to create a form.

C

Calendaring   A term used to describe the function of recording appointments for any type of business.

case management system (CMS)   Central repository to manage all client documents maintained by the lawyer or law firm.

Case Management/ Electronic Case Filing (CM/ECF)   Court management system used in the federal courts to access and file new cases and documents.

cell   A box formed by the intersection of a row and column in a worksheet or a table in which you enter information.

cell address   The row and column location of a cell, usually expressed with column identifier first and row identifier second.

Central Processing Unit (CPU)   Also known as the microprocessor; the brains of the computer.

Chatbots   A software application used to conduct an online chat conversation via text or text to speech in lieu of providing direct contact with a live human agent. A chatbot is a type of software that can automate conversations and interact with people through messaging platforms.

check register   The book in which you keep records of checks, deposits, debit card transactions, and ATM withdrawals.

Clip Art   A predefined graphic.

Coding   Refers to the process of reviewing documents and summarizing key elements in a structured format.

column   A vertical series of cells in a table.

Compatibility   In technology, the ability of the computer hardware to effectively operate the application software and communicate with software updates.

Competence   Rule 1.1: A lawyer shall provide competent representation to a client. Competent representation requires the legal knowledge, skill, thoroughness, and preparation reasonably necessary for the representation.

Complaint   A formal document that describes the transgressions that have been made against the plaintiff and why they believe reparations should be made.

Computer   An electronic device that receives, processes, outputs, and stores data or information.

Confidentiality   Rule 1.6: A lawyer shall not reveal information relating to the representation of a client unless the client gives informed consent, or the disclosure is impliedly authorized in order to carry out the representation or otherwise permitted by rules.

Conflict of Interest   In law, representing one client that will directly and/or adversely affect the client's interest, the attorney, or another third party that is not a client.

conflict report generator   A program for sorting names of parties and clients to identify similar names or cases.

Consultation   The action or process of formally consulting or discussing.

COVID-19   An acute respiratory illness in humans caused by a coronavirus, capable of producing severe symptoms and in some cases death, especially in older people and those with underlying health conditions. It was originally identified in China in 2019 and became a pandemic in 2020.

D

data   As it relates to computers, these are facts, figures, or information that may be in the form of text documents, images, audio, software programs, and so on that are stored in or used by a computer.

Data Extraction   The process of retrieving data out of data sources for further data processing or data storage.

Data Preservation Plan   A detailed plan made by the legal team outlining the course of action for how preservation of documents and other pieces of digital evidence relevant to the case will be preserved from destruction.

database   A collection of organized data, generally collected in tables, that allows access, retrieval, and use of data.

Database Management System (DBMS)   A software program that handles the storage, retrieval, and updating of data in a computer system.

Decoding Key   A password or a data file that allows a message or document to be decrypted.

Deposition   The process of giving sworn evidence.

Design Template   A predesigned presentation background and format that you apply to all the slides.

Desktop (Computer)   A device designed for regular use at a single or stationary location, often with all components that fit on top or near a desk due to its size or power requirements.

Digital Signature   A means of electronically signing a document.

Direct Examination   The process of presenting evidence by calling a witness to the stand and asking them questions.

Discovery   The formal process of exchanging information between the parties about the witnesses and evidence to present at trial.

Docketing   Entries that track a list of court proceedings and hearings that must be attended.

Document Automation (also known as document assembly)   The design of systems and work flows that assist in the creation of electronic documents.

Document Management System (DMS)   A system used to receive, track, manage, and store digital documents. Most are capable of keeping a record of the various versions created by different users.

Document Tagging   The general process of adding extra information to documents. With electronic documents, the extra information marks up the documents for further analysis or workflow.

Drivers   A group of files that enable one or more hardware devices to communicate with the computer's operating system. Drivers allow the computer to send and receive data correctly to the hardware devices.

E

E-File   The electronic filing of a document in the federal court using the Internet to transmit the record.

Electronic Discovery or eDiscovery   The process of identifying and delivering electronic information that can be used as evidence in legal cases.

Electronic Discovery Reference Model (EDRM)   A community of eDiscovery and legal professionals who develop practical resources to improve eDiscovery and information governance processes.

electronic spreadsheet   A program used to perform numeric calculations as well as to analyze and present numeric data using formulas created within the program.

Electronically Stored Information (ESI)   Information created, manipulated, communicated, stored, and best utilized in digital form, requiring use of computer hardware and software.

Email   Messages distributed by electronic means from one computer user to one or more recipients via a network.

Encryption   The process of converting readable data into unreadable characters to prevent unauthorized access.

Encryption Key   A binary input to the encryption algorithm—typically a long string of bits used to scramble the file or message to render it unreadable.

Endnotes   Notes at the end of a document acknowledging sources and providing additional references or information.

End-User License Agreement   A license agreement between the software creator and the software user.

e-repositories   Web- or cloud-based services that store electronic information.

Ethics or Legal Ethics   The minimum standards of conduct required by an attorney in practicing law.

Evidence Camera   A very small video camera that captures high-quality images of documents, photos, or objects placed within the camera's field of vision. Successor to the overhead projector.

Extensible Markup Language (XML)   A way of writing data in a document for tagging and creating formats to identify and describe information.

Extrapolate   Extend the application of (a method or conclusion, especially one based on statistics) to an unknown situation by assuming that existing trends will continue or similar methods will be applicable.

F

Facsimile (Fax)   Technology that transfers images electronically using telephone lines.

field   A single characteristic of data that appears in a table as a column.

filter   To display only the rows in a list that satisfy the conditions you specify. You use the AutoFilter command to display rows that match one or more specific values, calculated values, or conditions.

Firewall   A computer security system (hardware and software) designed to block unauthorized access.

Footer   The area consisting of the bottom margin of the page.

Footnotes   Material that is printed at the bottom of a page; marked in text by a numbered referent.

Formula   A sequence of values, cell references, names, functions, or operators in a cell that together produce a new value. A formula always begins with an equal sign (=).

formulas Bar   A bar located between the ribbon and the worksheet in which users can edit the contents of a cell.

function command   A predefined calculation used in a spreadsheet program to speed up the process of entering complex formulas.

G

gridlines   The lines in a table that form the rows and columns.

Guided Pathways   A movement that seeks to streamline a student's journey through college by providing structured choice, revamped support, and clear learning outcomes—ultimately helping more students achieve their college completion goals.

H

hard-copy   a printed version on paper of data or documents that are also electronically held in a computer.

Hardware (Computer) The physical components of a computer system.

Header The area consisting of the top margin of the page.

Hot Spot A place where a wireless Internet connection is available.

HTML (Hypertext Markup Language) The predominant language used to create Web pages.

I

Import Method to bring documents and images into the program.

Information Governance A systematic business process for managing information: classifying, storing, and deleting electronic and paper-based information so that it is retained only while it has significant business value and can be deleted before it becomes an operational or legal liability.

Information Technology The technology details involved with the development, maintenance, and use of computer systems, software, and network uses for processing and distributing data.

Infrared Headphones Headphones used for listening that are cordless; used for the hearing-impaired during court proceedings. Most infrared headphones have a 30-foot range.

integrated database systems The sharing of different functions within multiple databases.

Interpreter Box Routes audio channels of language translations for simultaneous interpretation to the witness/ defendant's headphone or the courtroom's Internet system.

Interrogatories A series of written questions for which written answers are prepared by a party to a lawsuit, usually with the assistance of the party's attorney and then signed under oath.

J

Justice Just behavior or treatment.

K

Kill Switch A control at the bench allowing the judge to turn off monitors until a particular piece of evidence is admitted or in an instance where the judge determines that certain images should not be shown to the jury.

L

label(s) Refers to text that is typed into the cells of a spreadsheet; it has no numeric value and cannot be used in a formula or function.

Laptop (Computer) A portable, personal computer, also known as a notebook. It carries out the same functions as a desktop.

Laptop Port A connection into which a laptop may be plugged.

Legal Hold A communication requesting the preservation and the resulting preservation of information that is potentially relevant to current or a reasonably anticipated legal matter.

Limited Licensed Professional Legal permission to engage in a regulated activity on a limited basis.

Local Area Network (LAN) A computer network that interconnects computers within a limited area such as a residence, school, laboratory, university campus or office building.

M

Macro (Macroinstruction) A sequence of input instructions or keystrokes performed by a command.

Mail Merge A feature that helps create a batch of documents personalized for each recipient, such as a form letter or notice sent to multiple recipients. A data source, like a list, spreadsheet, or database, is associated with the document.

matters Any item, case, file, or project that you need to track.

Mediation Intervention in a dispute to resolve it.

Model Rules of Professional Conduct The rules developed by the American Bar Association to govern the conduct of lawyers in practicing law.

Modem A device that converts signals produced by one type of device (such as a computer) to a form compatible with another (such as a telephone) to transmit and receive information.

N

native format A file structure created in a specified application.

Natural Language Processing (NLP) A branch of artificial intelligence that deals with the interaction between computers and human language.

Network Server A powerful, central computer with special software and equipment that enable it to function as the primary computer in the network.

NextGen CM/ECF The federal court filing system designed to access PACER and CM/ECF from a single sign-on to give access to both accounts from one sign-on.

Nonlawyer Assistant Responsibility Rule 5.3: A requirement that lawyers having direct supervisory authority over nonlawyers make reasonable efforts to ensure that the person's conduct is compatible with the professional obligations of the lawyer.

O

Online Collaboration Using the Internet to conduct meetings and share documents.

Online Dispute Resolution A branch of dispute resolution that uses technology to facilitate the resolution of disputes between parties. It primarily involves negotiation, mediation arbitration or a combination of all three.

Operating System Software used to control the computer and its peripheral equipment.

Optical Character Recognition (OCR) Technology that can translate a scanned document image into text that can be edited and formatted.

Outsourcing A decision to have independent outside parties handle the business's workload and production responsibilities.

Overhead Projector A visual aid used to project transparencies (often charts and graphs) onto a blank wall or screen.

P

PACER Administrative Accounts (PAA) A consolidated billing and online account management process for groups such as law firms, financial organizations, and educational or research institutions.

PACER Case Locator (PCL) A national index for district, bankruptcy, and appellate courts.

Page Break A feature used to create a layout where a page ends, and a new page begins.

Password Protection A security process that prevents access to information via computers and requires authorization codes for reveal.

Personal Information Management A system and software program utilized to acquire, organize, maintain, retrieve, and use information.

Phishing An attack that sends an email or displays a Web announcement that falsely claims to be from a legitimate enterprise in an attempt to trick the user into surrendering private information.

PivotTable An interactive, cross-tabulated Excel report that summarizes and analyzes data, such as database records, from various sources, including ones external to Excel.

Placeholder A boxed outline on a slide that can be used to insert text or an object when clicked.

portable document format (PDF) A format that allows a document to be read and viewed from any computer regardless of the original program that created the document.

PowerPoint A Microsoft Office application program that allows you to create professional-looking multimedia presentations.

practice management system (PMS) Central repository to manage case files and the business side of the law practice.

Presentation Software Programs used to create graphic presentations with visual aids, handouts, slides, and so on or for creating text with graphics, audio, and/or video.

Professionalism or Legal Professionalism The proper morals and behavior one should exhibit in the representation of clients and the law profession.

Proofreading An editing feature in Word that checks spelling and grammar as a document is typed.

Public Access to Court Electronic Records (PACER) Allows users to view, print, or download current and recently closed federal cases.

Q

Quick Part Building block you create from frequently used text, such as a name, address, or slogan, and then save so that you can easily access them.

R

RAM (Random Access Memory) The area on the computer's workspace that stores the information and data for processing by the computer's CPU.

Read Only A setting that allows a file to be read or copied but not changed or saved.

record A collection of fields that appear as a row in a database or table.

Record Retention Policies General principles determining the length of time that records, in which data is stored, must be maintained in accordance with policies and law.

Redact To edit and remove information from documents filed in the court record, usually information that is confidential or private.

redaction The removal of confidential information from a "protected" document.

Remote Collaboration A process in which two or more parties work together on common documents and other resources regardless of their location.

Request for Admission A request for admission (sometimes also called a request to admit) is a set of statements sent from one litigant to an adversary, for the purpose of having the adversary admit or deny the statements or allegations therein.

Request for Form Interrogatories Judicially approved predefined sets of questions propounded upon the opposing party to help aid in the fact-finding process of the case.

Request for Production A discovery tool permitting parties to seek production or inspection of documents, electronically stored information, and tangible things deemed responsive to the issues involved in the litigation.

Request for Special Interrogatories Sets of questions propounded upon the opposing party to help aid in the fact-finding process of the case usually be drafted by the legal team assigned to the case.

Review Stage The document review phase of the EDRM is where the lawyers are able to view, tag, manage, download, and notate every document and other pieces of digital evidence related to the case.

Ribbon A Microsoft user interface that consists of tabs, each with specific groups of related commands, providing quick access to commonly used commands needed to complete tasks.

row The horizontal placement of cells in a table or worksheet.

rules-based calendaring When a certain event takes place, such as a deposition or hearing, a number of calendar items are generated.

S

Sampling The process of testing a search query by searching a limited number of records against total volume to determine an accurate search response.

scanning Paper documents converted to electronic format.

Section Break A feature used to create layout or formatting changes in a portion of a document.

Server A computer or computer program that manages access to a centralized resource or service in a network.

Slide A single page of a presentation.

Smart Device An electronic gadget that can connect, share, and interact with its user; despite its size, it typically has enormous computing power (gigabytes).

SmartDraw Software used to create flowcharts and other forms of systems documentation.

Software A list of instructions for the computer to follow that is stored in the computer's memory.

Spam Unsolicited email.

Sparkline A tiny chart embedded in a cell that provides a visual representation of data.

Spoliation The destruction or alteration of data that might be relevant to a legal matter.

Summons   Document used in civil cases to notify the defendant they are being sued and orders them to respond to the court.

System Administrator   A person in charge of managing and maintaining computer systems within a business or institution.

T

Table   An arrangement of data made up of horizontal rows and vertical columns.

Table of authorities   Used in legal documents and pleadings to index cases, statutes, and legal authorities contained within the material.

Table of Contents   A snapshot of the headings and page numbers in a document that can be updated as changes are made.

Technological Competency   The ability to create and use a particular field of technology effectively.

Technology Assisted Review (TAR)   An approach within the document review phase of eDiscovery that leverages computer algorithms to identify and tag potentially responsive documents based on keywords and other metadata.

Template   A pre-designed document.

text   Descriptive data, such as headings and titles, used for reference purposes in a spreadsheet; cannot be used in making calculations.

Thin Client   A computer terminal that resembles a desktop but has limited capabilities and relies on a network for resources to operate programs.

timekeeping   Tracking time for the purpose of billing clients.

Timeline   A visual representation of time, showing when events occurred and in what sequence.

Track Changes   A feature that keeps a record of the modifications made to a document.

Transition   Effects that move one slide off the screen and the next slide on during a slide show.

Trial Director   A software program used at trial to organize, annotate, and customize exhibits for cases.

U

Unauthorized Practice of Law (UPL)   Rule 5.5: The practice of law by a person, typically a nonlawyer, not licensed or admitted to practice law in a given jurisdiction. This also applies to lawyers not admitted to practice in a particular jurisdiction as well as a disbarred or suspended lawyer.

Uninterruptible Power Supply (UPS)   A device that provides backup power when the electrical power fails or drops to an unacceptable voltage level.

utility Software   Programs that help analyze, configure, optimize, or maintain computer systems and their performance. The programs usually focus the computer's infrastructure (hardware, operating system, data storage, and application software).

V

values   Numbers that are entered into a spreadsheet program for the purpose of making calculations.

Videoconference   A virtual meeting using a network or the Internet to connect two or more people in different geographic locations and share data by electronic means.

Videoconference Equipment   Equipment that facilitates a two-way real-time transmission of audio and video signals between specialized devices or computers at two more locations.

Virus   A destructive program that harms data, hard drives, operating systems, and computer programs.

Visual Display Device   A device that produces pictures or images, either still or live. Common visual devices include screens, monitors, and projectors.

Visual Presentation Cart   Media center located in the courtroom.

Voice Over Internet Protocol (VoIP)   A technology that allows you to make voice calls using a broadband Internet connection instead of a regular (or analogue) phone line.

Voice Recognition   The use of software to convert spoken words to text.

W

Warrant   Document issued in criminal cases to give officers permission to seek out the defendant and arrest them pending trial.

Wide Area Network (WAN)   A network that covers a large geographic area and includes other networks; a "network of networks."

Wireless Network   A network where users can access the Internet without the use of fixed cables.

workbook   An Excel file with one or more worksheets.

Workflow   Includes the tasks, activities, and responsibilities required to execute each step in a business process.

Worksheet   A "page" within an Excel workbook that contains columns, rows, and cells.

Workstation   A computer that runs a desktop operating system and connects to a network.

wrap text   A feature that allows text to be included with pictures, shapes, or tables without covering or hiding under the image, giving the user control over how the text is positioned.

Index